PENGUI

LA

THE LATE WRITI

COUNT LEO TOLSTOY was born in 1828. He took part in the Crimean War, and married Sofya Andreyevna Behrs in 1862. Over the next fifteen years they had thirteen children and Tolstoy managed his vast estates in the Volga Steppes, continued his educational projects, cared for his peasants and wrote *War and Peace* (1869) and *Anna Karenina* (1877). *A Confession* (1882) marked a spiritual crisis in his life; he became an extreme moralist and in a series of pamphlets after 1880 expressed his rejection of State and Church, indictment of the weaknesses of the flesh and denunciation of private property. In 1901 he was excommunicated by the Russian Holy Synod. He died in 1910, in the course of a dramatic flight from home, at the small railway station of Astapovo.

JAY PARINI, a poet and novelist, is Axinn Professor of English at Middlebury College in Vermont. His books include *The Art of Subtraction: New and Selected Poems* (2005) and *The Last Station* (1990), a novel of Tolstoy's last year. He has also written biographies of John Steinbeck, Robert Frost and William Faulkner.

LEO TOLSTOY

Last Steps

The Late Writings of Leo Tolstoy

Edited with an Introduction by JAY PARINI
Translations by R. F. CHRISTIAN, CONSTANCE GARNETT, MICHAEL R. KATZ, JANE KENTISH, AYLMER MAUDE, JAY PARINI *and* LEO WIENER

PENGUIN BOOKS

PENGUIN CLASSICS

Published by the Penguin Group
Penguin Books Ltd, 80 Strand, London WC2R ORL, England
Penguin Group (USA) Inc., 375 Hudson Street, New York, New York 10014, USA
Penguin Group (Canada), 90 Eglinton Avenue East, Suite 700, Toronto, Ontario, Canada M4P 2Y3
(a division of Pearson Penguin Canada Inc.)
Penguin Ireland, 25 St Stephen's Green, Dublin 2, Ireland
(a division of Penguin Books Ltd)
Penguin Group (Australia), 250 Camberwell Road, Camberwell, Victoria 3124, Australia
(a division of Pearson Australia Group Pty Ltd)
Penguin Books India Pvt Ltd, 11 Community Centre, Panchsheel Park, New Delhi – 110 017, India
Penguin Group (NZ), 67 Apollo Drive, Rosedale, North Shore 0632, New Zealand
(a division of Pearson New Zealand Ltd)
Penguin Books (South Africa) (Pty) Ltd, 24 Sturdee Avenue, Rosebank, Johannesburg 2196, South Africa

Penguin Books Ltd, Registered Offices: 80 Strand, London WC2R ORL, England

www.penguin.com

This selection first published in Penguin Classics 2009
1

Set in 10.25/12.25pt PostScript Adobe Sabon
Typeset by Rowland Phototypesetting Ltd, Bury St Edmunds, Suffolk
Printed in England by Clays Ltd, St Ives plc

ISBN: 978-0-141-19119-5

www.greenpenguin.co.uk

Contents

Chronology

1724 Pyotr Tolstoy (great-great-great-grandfather) given hereditary title of Count by Tsar Peter the Great

1821 Death of Prince Nikolay Volkonsky, Tolstoy's grandfather, at Yasnaya Polyana, Tula Province, 130 miles southwest of Moscow

1822 Marriage of Count Nikolay Tolstoy and Princess Marya Volkonskaya

1828 28 August (Old Style). Birth of fourth son, Leo Nikolayevich Tolstoy, at Yasnaya Polyana

1830 Death of mother

1832 The eldest, Nikolay, informs his brothers that the secret of earthly happiness is inscribed on a green stick, buried at Yasnaya Polyana (Tolstoy later buried there)

1836 Nikolay Gogol's *The Government Inspector*

1837 Death of Alexander Pushkin in duel
Death of father

1840 Mikhail Lermontov's *A Hero of Our Time*

1841 Death of Lermontov in duel
Death of first guardian Alexandra Osten-Saken, an aunt. The Tolstoy children move to Kazan to live with another aunt, Pelageya Yushkova

1842 Gogol's *Dead Souls*

1844 Enters Kazan University, reads Oriental languages

1845 Transfers to Law after failing examinations. Dissolute lifestyle: drinking, visits to prostitutes

1846 Fyodor Dostoyevsky's 'Poor Folk'

1847 Inherits estate of Yasnaya Polyana. Recovering from gonorrhoea, draws up scheme for self-perfection. Leaves university without completing studies 'on grounds of ill health and domestic circumstances'

1848–50 In Moscow and St Petersburg, debauchery and gambling, large debts. Studies music

1850 Ivan Turgenev's *A Month in the Country*

1851 Travels to the Caucasus with Nikolay, who is serving in the army there. Reads Laurence Sterne: starts translating his *Sentimental Journey* (not completed). Writes 'A History of Yesterday' (unfinished, first evidence of his powers of psychological analysis). Begins writing *Childhood*

1852 Death of Gogol. Turgenev's *Sketches from a Hunter's Album*

Enters the army as a cadet (*Junker*); based mainly in the Cossack station of Starogladkovskaya. Sees action against the Chechens, and narrowly escapes capture

Childhood

1853 Turkey declares war on Russia

'The Raid'

1854 France and England declare war on Russia. Crimean War starts

Commissioned, serves on Danube front. November: transferred at own request to Sevastopol, then under siege by allied forces

Boyhood

1855 Death of Nicholas I; accession of Alexander II

In action until the fall of Sevastopol in August. Gains celebrity with 'Sevastopol in December' and further sketches, 'Sevastopol in May', 'Sevastopol in August 1855' (1856), 'Memoirs of a Billiard Marker', 'The Woodfelling'

1856 Peace signed between Russia, Turkey, France and England

Turgenev's *Rudin*

In St Petersburg, moves in literary circles; associates with Turgenev, Ivan Goncharov, Nikolay Nekrasov, Afanasy Fet and others. Leaves the army. Death of brother Dmitry

'The Snowstorm', 'Two Hussars', 'A Landowner's Morning'

1857 February–August. First trip abroad, to Paris (lasting impression of witnessing an execution by guillotine), Geneva and Baden-Baden

Youth, 'Lucerne'

1858 Long-term relationship with peasant woman on estate, Aksinya Bazykina, begins

'Albert'

1859 Goncharov's *Oblomov*; Turgenev's *The Home of the Gentry*

Founds primary school at Yasnaya Polyana

'Three Deaths', *Family Happiness*

1860 Death of his brother Nikolay from tuberculosis

Dostoyevsky's *Notes from the House of the Dead* (1860–61). Turgenev's *On the Eve*

1860–61 Emancipation of serfs (1861). Other reforms follow: Elective District Councils (*zemstvos*) set up (1864); judicial reform (1865). Formation of revolutionary Land and Liberty movement. Commencement of intensive industrialization; spread of railways

Serves as Arbiter of the Peace, dealing with post-Emancipation land settlements. Quarrels with Turgenev and challenges him (no duel). Travels in France, Germany, Italy and England. Loses great deal of money through gambling. Meets Proudhon in Brussels

1862 Turgenev's *Fathers and Sons*

Starts a magazine at Yasnaya Polyana on education for the peasants; abandoned after less than a year. Police raid on Yasnaya Polyana. Considers emigrating to England and writes protest to the Tsar. Marries Sofya Andreyevna Behrs (b. 1844)

1863 Polish rebellion

Birth of first child, Sergey (Tolstoy and his wife were to have thirteen children – nine boys and four girls – of whom five died in childhood). Begins work on a novel 'The Decembrists', which was later abandoned, but developed into *War and Peace*

'Polikushka', *The Cossacks*

1865 Nikolay Leskov's 'Lady Macbeth of Mtsensk'

First part of *War and Peace* (titled *1805*)

1866 Attempted assassination of Tsar Alexander II

Dostoyevsky's *Crime and Punishment*

1867 Turgenev's *Smoke*
Visits Borodino in search of material for battle scene in *War and Peace*
1868 Dostoyevsky's *The Idiot*
1869 Publication of *War and Peace* completed
1870–71 Franco-Prussian War. Municipal Government reform
Dostoyevsky's *Devils*
Studies ancient Greek. Illness; convalesces in Samara (Bashkiriya). Begins work on primer for children. First mention of *Anna Karenina*. Reads Arthur Schopenhauer and other philosophers. Starts work on novel about Peter the Great (later abandoned)
1872 'God Sees the Truth But Waits', 'A Prisoner of the Caucasus'
1873 Begins *Anna Karenina*. Raises funds during famine in Bashkiriya, where he has bought an estate. Growing obsession with problems of death and religion; temptation to commit suicide
1874 Much occupied with educational theory
1875 Beginning of active revolutionary movement
1875–7 Instalments of *Anna Karenina* published
1877 Turgenev's *Virgin Soil*
Journal publication of *Anna Karenina* completed (published in book form in 1878)
1877–8 Russo-Turkish War
1878 Reconciliation with Turgenev, who visits him at Yasnaya Polyana. Works on 'The Decembrists' and again abandons it. Works on *A Confession* (completed 1882, but banned by the religious censor and published in Geneva in 1884)
1879 Dostoyevsky's *The Brothers Karamazov*
1880 Works on *A Critique of Dogmatic Theology*
1881 Assassination of Tsar Alexander II. With accession of Alexander III, the government returns to reactionary policies
Death of Dostoyevsky
Writes to Tsar Alexander III asking him to pardon his father's assassins
1882 Student riots in St Petersburg and Kazan Universities.
Jewish pogroms and repressive measures against minorities

Religious works, including new translation of the Gospels. Begins *The Death of Ivan Ilyich* and *What Then Must We Do?* Studies Hebrew

1883 Deathbed letter from Turgenev urging Tolstoy not to abandon his art

1884 Family relations strained, first attempt to leave home. *What I Believe* banned

Collected works published by his wife

1885–6 Tension with his wife over new beliefs. Works closely with Vladimir Chertkov, with whom (and others) he founds a publishing house, The Intermediary, to produce edifying literature for the common folk. Many popular stories written 1885–6, including 'What Men Live By', 'Where Love Is, God Is', 'Strider'

1886 Walks from Moscow to Yasnaya Polyana in five days. Works on land during the summer. Denounced as a heretic by Archbishop of Kherson

The Death of Ivan Ilyich, 'How Much Land Does a Man Need?', *What Then Must We Do?*

1887 Meets Leskov

'On Life'

1888 Chekhov's *The Steppe*

Renounces meat, alcohol and tobacco. Growing friction between his wife and Chertkov. *The Power of Darkness*, banned in 1886, performed in Paris

1889 Finishes *The Kreutzer Sonata*. Begins *Resurrection* (works on it for ten years)

1890 *The Kreutzer Sonata* banned, though on appeal by his wife to the Tsar publication was permitted in Collected Works

1891 Convinced that personal profits from writing are immoral, renounces copyright on all works published after 1881 and all future works. His family thus suffers financially, though his wife retains copyright in all the earlier works. Helps to organize famine relief in Ryazah Province. Attacks smoking and alcohol in 'Why Do Men Stupefy Themselves?'

1892 Organizes famine relief: *The Fruits of Enlightenment* (published 1891) produced in Maly Theatre, Moscow

1893 Finishes *The Kingdom of God Is Within You*

1894 Accession of Tsar Nicholas II. Strikes in St Petersburg
Writes preface to Maupassant collection of stories. Criticizes *Crime and Punishment*

1895 Meets Chekhov. *The Power of Darkness* produced in Maly Theatre, Moscow
'Master and Man'

1896 Chekhov's *The Seagull*
Sees production of *Hamlet* and *King Lear* at Hermitage Theatre, severely critical of Shakespeare
What is Art?

1897 Appeals to authorities on behalf of Dukhobors, a pacifist religious sect, to whom permission is granted to emigrate to Canada

1898 Formation of Social Democratic Party. Dreyfus Affair in France
Works for famine relief

1899 Widespread student riots
Serial publication of *Resurrection* (in book form in 1900)

1900 Meets Maxim Gorky, whom he calls a 'real man of the people'

1901 Foundation of Socialist Revolutionary Party
Excommunicated from Orthodox Church for writing works 'repugnant to Christ and the Church'. Seriously ill, convalesces in Crimea; visitors include Chekhov and Gorky

1902 Finishes *What Is Religion?* Writes to Tsar Nicholas II on evils of autocracy and ownership of property

1903 Protests against Jewish pogroms in Kishinev
'After the Ball'

1904 Russo-Japanese War. Russian fleet destroyed in Tsushima Straits. Assassination of V. K. Plehve, Minister of the Interior
Death of Chekhov
Death of second-eldest brother Sergey. Pamphlet on Russo-Japanese war published in England

1905 Attempted revolution in Russia (Tolstoy attacks all sides involved)
Potemkin mutiny. S. Yu. Witte becomes Prime Minister
Anarchical publicist pamphlets
Introduction to Chekhov's 'Darling'

1906 *Shakespeare and the Drama*

1908 Tolstoy's secretary N. N. Gusev exiled

'I Cannot Be Silent', a protest against capital punishment

1909 Increased animosity between his wife and Chertkov, she threatens suicide

1910 Corresponds with Mahatma Gandhi concerning the doctrine of non-violent resistance to evil. His wife threatens suicide; demands all Tolstoy's diaries for past ten years, but Tolstoy puts them in bank vault. Final breakdown of relationship with her. 28 October: leaves home. 7 November: dies at Astapovo railway station. Buried at Yasnaya Polyana

1911 'The Devil', 'Father Sergius', *Hadji Murat*, 'The Forged Coupon'

Introduction

A simple story of Tolstoy's life goes something like this: Leo Tolstoy (1828–1910) was a Russian aristocrat and eminent novelist who led a risqué early life, drinking and gambling, and visiting brothels. In midlife he converted to Christianity, put the writing of novels behind him for the most part, devoting his life to God-centred activity, which included a kind of social activism. He became, in effect, a prophet, espousing Christian values, pacifism, vegetarianism, abstinence from alcohol and tobacco, even sex. He became a champion of the poor as well, and his ideas about land reform and wealth distribution were considered radical at the time.

Needless to say, this portrait is simplistic and misleading. Tolstoy's life, as a whole, was much more complex than this easy portrait suggests. It was also much more integrated.

As for his early behaviour, one must recall that gambling and whoring were common vices among his peers. In any case, he indulged heavily in both. He grew up on his family estate in Tula as well as in Moscow, where the family moved so that the children could be educated. He later attended, but never graduated from, Kazan University, where he studied languages and law. Soon after this, he joined an artillery brigade in the Caucasus, hoping to broaden his experience. He commanded an army unit during the Crimean War, where he witnessed the infamous siege of Sevastopol (1854–5). His observations of battle informed *Sevastopol Sketches* – a remarkable volume of stories that confirmed his position as a writer of major talent. He had already published *Childhood* (1852) as well as *Boyhood* (1854) and would soon follow with *Youth* (1857) –

an autobiographical trilogy that stands among the treasures of Russian literature.

As anyone who glances at the vast shelf of books he left behind will know, Tolstoy was immensely prolific, writing stories and novels, plays, sketches, essays, diaries and letters throughout his long life. The novels, of course, made him a luminous figure in the literary world. *War and Peace* (1869) and *Anna Karenina* (1878) remain among the centrepieces of Western literature, on a par with the best of Dante, Shakespeare, Goethe and Dickens. But – as suggested above – Tolstoy was not content to think of himself as simply a novelist. He wanted more, for himself and his readers.

He married the nineteen-year-old Sofya Andreyevna Behrs in 1862, when he was thirty-four. They had thirteen children, and life at the ancestral home – Yasnaya Polyana – seemed good, at least to any observer from outside. But Tolstoy was not happy. All happy families, as he famously observed, are alike; all unhappy families are unhappy in their own ways. In his case, Tolstoy felt a spiritual longing that could not be satisfied in conventional ways. His noble rank upset him, as he wondered why he should live in luxury when millions suffered in hideous, degrading poverty. He came to dislike the State, ruled by a despotic tsar and his secret police. He also grew hostile to the Orthodox Church, which linked itself inexorably with the State, supporting its oppression of the people – at least in Tolstoy's view.

A turn in his career came with *A Confession* (1882), where he concluded that God did indeed exist. He wrote: '"He exists," said I to myself. And I had only for an instant to admit that, and at once life rose within me, and I felt the possibility and joy of being.' This seminal book was soon followed by others, including *The Kingdom of God Is Within You* (1893) – a thoughtful work of self-examination and religious meditation. Tolstoy began a systematic study of the Gospels, which resulted in various books, such as *A Critique of Dogmatic Theology* (1880) and *What I Believe* (1882). There were other works in this vein, too, most of them repetitive, all of them putting forward a version of Christian anarchism. In the 1890s, Tolstoy translated and 'harmonized' the four Gospels, taking out the supernatural elements (not unlike Thomas Jefferson had done before him in the *Jefferson Bible*, as it is called – a compilation not published until many years after Jefferson's death, as it cast Jesus as a great teacher without divine attributes). Two late works on religion are excerpted here: *What Is Religion, and Wherein Lies Its Essence?* (1902) and *The Law of Love and the Law of Violence* (1908). These are powerful tracts, and they show Tolstoy in full flower as a spiritual guide.

With typical single-mindedness, Tolstoy hurled himself into these religious and philosophical studies, writing numerous letters on religious or social topics to friends and followers, some of them the self-proclaimed 'Tolstoyans' who gathered around him or supported him from afar. In effect, Tolstoy became a prophet, putting forward a view of Christianity that stripped Jesus of his supernatural status and focused on his social vision. The key to Christianity, for Tolstoy, was the idea of non-resistance to evil, as formulated in several of the works included in this collection, such as the famous 'Letter on Non-Resistance to Ernest Howard Crosby' (1896) or '"Thou Shalt Not Kill"' (1900). Love was all that mattered, as Tolstoy explained in a vigorous essay published as 'An Appeal to the Clergy' (1902).

Tolstoy refused to accede to traditional Christian beliefs, which he regarded as 'meaningless and contradictory assertions' that had been put forward as religious truth. For him, all that one had to do was connect to one's original sense of God: 'Every man comes into the world with a consciousness of his dependence on a mysterious, all-powerful Source which has given him life, and a consciousness of his equality with all men, the equality of all men with one another, a desire to love and be loved, and a consciousness of the need of striving toward perfection.' He urged the clergy, in his avid 'appeal', to resist the notion that this Source is really 'an angry, unjust God, who executes and tortures people'. This God was not Tolstoy's God.

Overall, Tolstoy's religious vision was encompassing, affecting his views on society and politics, war and peace, and extending to personal behaviour as well. Rather famously, he argued for a vegetarian diet – as seen in *The First Step* (1891), excerpted here. In another development, he became increasingly puritanical about sex. In a strange, late novella called *The Kreutzer Sonata* (1890), he actually argued for sexual abstinence within marriage, noting that the physical attraction between men and women often led to tragedy. Yet even this bizarre work has its champions, including Anton Chekhov, who wrote in praise of it: 'You will scarcely find anything as powerful in seriousness of conception and beauty of execution.'

The political implications of Tolstoy's Christianity evolved as he moved through his last three decades. In general, he opposed violent revolution as a way to end the violence of governments. As he said, history had shown that one did not overthrow a government without violent consequences. In this, he had learned a good deal from his reading of Buddhist and Hindu scriptures. He understood the principle of *karma*, and he understood that violence only led to further violence. One had somehow to break this destructive cycle. It was this kind of thinking that brought him into alignment with the philosophies of Henry David Thoreau and Gandhi. Indeed, he corresponded with the young Gandhi, as seen in a letter, included in this volume, from September 1910, written not long before Tolstoy died.

Tolstoy seems to have been by nature depressive, even self-loathing. In his diaries he reflected this struggle, from early to later years. In January 1903, for instance, he wrote as follows:

> At present I suffer the torments of hell itself. I remember vividly the horrors, the sins, of my earlier life, and these recollections do not just fade; they circulate as poison in my blood. I hear that people often feel sorry about the fact that, after death, all sense of individual consciousness dies as well. I'm delighted that it does not! It would anguish me if I could recall after death all the evil I'd done in my earlier life; indeed, all of that remains painful to my conscience. What a good thing that death obliterates these recollections, that what survives is consciousness alone.

Of course one might well ask what 'consciousness' means if the term excludes memory; but Tolstoy probably wants to suggest that, after death, a kind of eternal present occurs. In any case, what apparently prompted this outburst of self-recrimination was a letter from Paul Biryukov, a friend and disciple, asking for help in writing his biography. Tolstoy apparently could not face his own past, even though he had done so in various novels.

As seen above, it is convenient to think about two Tolstoys, but such thinking distorts the reality. In truth, Tolstoy had a powerful sense of guilt from early in his life, an exquisitely afflicted conscience, as well as a powerful wish to focus on spiritual matters. At the age of twenty-seven, for example, he wrote in his diary about a conversation he had had with a young friend on the ideas of divinity and faith. This dialogue, he said, 'had summoned a tremendous idea, whose realization is something to which I could be persuaded to devote my whole life'. In a sense, he did just that.

From the outset in his novels one finds an acute sense of moral obligation. This enhances the work, making it distinctly 'Tolstoyan'. And, of course, Tolstoy continued to labour in the vineyards of fiction into his last decades. *The Death of Ivan Ilych* appeared in 1886, and it counts among his best work, a superb novella that centres on the consciousness of death. The story interrogates in blunt ways the realities of our petty preoccupations with wealth and power. Tolstoy was using fiction here to explore the delights and agonies of human consciousness.

Only a few years before he died he wrote two novels: *Resurrection* (1899) and *Hadji Murat* (written between 1896 and 1904 and published soon after his death). The former is focused on Prince Nekhlyudov, a wealthy, lazy man who experiences shame when called to jury duty; in the courtroom he realizes that the girl on trial is someone he once seduced. That seduction ruined her, as she fell into prostitution, having been rejected by her family and friends. Now she is accused of a murder, although (as even the jury notes) she never meant to hurt anyone and never did. She is nevertheless found guilty through a legal error – even the legal system fails the Russian people. The idle prince experiences a change of heart, and this 'resurrection' affects his life profoundly, although Tolstoy seems unwilling to grant any supernatural workings of the Holy Spirit here. It is just a change of attitude that Nekhlyudov experiences. As he would, Tolstoy uses the novel to attack the Orthodox Church, although these attacks are some of its weakest parts. In all, the novel reflects Tolstoy's ongoing efforts at self-examination, self-reformation, and it fits well with his overall philosophy, which by this time had become thoroughly defined.

Hadji Murat is a very different sort of book. Here Tolstoy revisits the theatre of war. While not on a par with *War and Peace* (which it resembles at points), this final adventure in historical fiction is a tale of betrayal that, like the early *Sevastopol Sketches*, underscores the pointless horror of war. In the light of Tolstoy's later writing, it may be seen as a meditation on the way violence cannot be easily suppressed once it becomes a way of life, a means for solving problems. As with his earlier writing on war, the author draws on his deep reservoir of personal recollections; in this case he returns to his early days in the Caucasus, when he first heard about this legendary rebel commander caught up in the struggles between Russians and Chechens. There is also a note of defiance here: Murat was like the thistle Tolstoy alludes to at the outset of the novel: a survivor against all odds.

There is a touching simplicity about Tolstoy's later writings, especially in the genre of folk-tale, which appealed to him greatly. Some of his strongest later stories, such as 'Master and Man' (1895), fall into this category, being didactic, almost childlike in their affect and approach. As he would write in an article called 'Truth in Art' (1887),

> there are fairy tales, parables, and legends in which amazing things are described that didn't really happen and could never have happened; but these tales are nevertheless true, in part because they reveal that God's will has always been, is, and will be for ever. In short, they reveal the truth of the kingdom of heaven.

As late as 1905, Tolstoy was writing stories such as 'Alyosha Gorshok', a portrait of a simple peasant who found peace in a life devoted to the service of others – a peace that Tolstoy himself sought in his later years, without much luck. This story is included here with a few other late examples, such as 'Where Love Is, God Is' (1885), a striking piece of fiction.

As a supreme artist himself, Tolstoy was always interested in aesthetics, and his strong opinions are often on display in his writing. Two of his final statements on these topics will be found in *What Is Art?* (1896) and *Shakespeare and the Drama* (1906). Both reflect the author's preoccupation with morality as a criterion for judging the value of art. He believed that many writers and critics had excluded moral considerations from their criteria for 'good' art, and he decried this development – the idea of art for art's sake was anathema to him. He famously denounced Shakespeare, arguing that much in his plays was morally suspect, even reprehensible, and that the Elizabethan author had put his characters 'in tragic circumstances which are impossible'. We cannot, of course, agree with him that 'Shakespeare may be whatever you wish but he was not an artist.' Nevertheless, he had read through the plays carefully, and his ideas – however easily dismissed as eccentric – are consistent with his aesthetic views.

Some of Tolstoy's letters became well known and were translated into many languages and passed around among a circle of admirers. A few of these are included here as stand-alone essays, such as the 'Letter to a Non-Commissioned Officer' (1899) and two letters on the American political economist Henry George (1839–97), known for his original ideas about land taxes. (George published *Progress and Poverty* in 1879 – a book about social inequality that plunged into theories of economic cycles.) For the most part, Tolstoy's highly distinctive style of letter-writing is on display in the selection of late letters included here.

The same preoccupations occur in the letters and diaries, which are among the finest by any Western author. Tolstoy had a huge correspondence, with several thousand letters still extant. One can learn a great deal about the life and times from these letters, which range widely from love letters to reports on his experiences in the Caucasus and the Crimean War. In early letters, he describes his travels in Europe, and he sometimes discusses his theories on education – always a major preoccupation, as seen in the late 'Letter on Education' (1902), included in this volume. He frequently corresponded with fellow authors, including foreign ones, such as George Bernard Shaw. The letters of his last decades are preoccupied with religious and social questions; he often wrote, of course, to 'Tolstoyans' like Vladimir Chertkov, his chief disciple, who became the dogged enemy of his wife, Sofya – as they both struggled towards the end to push Tolstoy one way or another. These late letters also reveal, with extraordinary honesty, Tolstoy's torment as he attempted (without much luck) to put his ideals into practice.

Tolstoy was not, in fact, alone in keeping diaries. Especially in the final year, everyone around him – his wife and children, his secretary, his doctor and his disciples – all furiously wrote in their journals about the crisis at hand: Tolstoy pulled one way by his wife and another way by Chertkov and the Tolstoyans, who wanted him to abandon his bourgeois life, to give up the copyright to his works (putting them into the public domain, so that nobody would profit from them). The tension between them grew increasingly toxic, and Tolstoy was finally moved to abandon the house where he was born, Yasnaya Polyana, and to take to the road as a kind of wandering saint. The journey did not last long, as he fell ill within weeks and died in a railway station at Astapovo, surrounded by his closest allies. Sofya chased after him, but she was not allowed into the stationmaster's cottage where he lay dying, and where he expired.

This operatic drama is the subject of my novel, *The Last Station*, which has been turned into a film with Christopher Plummer and Helen Mirren as the Tolstoys. Paul Giamatti plays Chertkov, while James McAvoy plays Tolstoy's young secretary, Valentin Bulgakov, who arrives in the final year at Yasnaya Polyana to assist the master in his work and, by chance, to observe the final debacle. The tragedy of the Tolstoys remains a vivid instance of powerful but conflicting values, centred on a great writer, in whose heart the terrible clash must play out and end, of course, as it will – in the throes and ecstasies of death, in the beautiful, hard expanse of memory as it gathers in those who follow.

Jay Parini

Further Reading

BY TOLSTOY

Tolstoy's Letters, in two volumes. Selected, edited and translated by R. F. Christian (New York: Charles Scribners Sons, 1978).

Tolstoy's Diaries, in two volumes. Edited and translated by R. F. Christian (New York: Charles Scribners Sons, 1985).

Leo Tolstoy, *A Confession and Other Religious Writings*. Translated, with an Introduction, by Jane Kentish (London: Penguin, 1987).

Leo Tolstoy, *Collected Shorter Fiction*, in two volumes. Translated by Louise and Aylmer Maude and Nigel J. Cooper (New York: Knopf, 2001).

The Lion and the Honeycomb: The Religious Writings of Tolstoy. Edited by A. N. Wilson, translated by Richard Chandler (London: Collins, 1987).

ABOUT TOLSTOY

Bayley, John, *Tolstoy and the Novel* (London: Chatto & Windus, 1966).

Christian, R. F., *Tolstoy: A Critical Introduction* (Cambridge: Cambridge University Press, 1969).

Jones, Malcolm (ed.), *New Essays on Tolstoy* (Cambridge: Cambridge University Press, 1978).

Knowles, A. V. (ed.), *Leo Tolstoy: The Critical Heritage* (London: Routledge, 1978).

Troyat, Henri, *Tolstoy: A Biography* (New York: Doubleday, 1967).

Wilson, A. N., *Tolstoy: A Biography* (New York: Norton, 1988).

A Note on the Translations

The translations in this volume represent the work of many hands. Among Tolstoy's earliest translators were Leo Wiener – a professor at Harvard in the late nineteenth century – and Aylmer Maude, who was Tolstoy's friend and biographer. Maude is generally considered the best of the early translators of Tolstoy, along with Constance Garnett (mother of the novelist David Garnett), who visited the author in Russia in the 1890s and published many versions of his work. In the case of Wiener and Garnett, I have taken occasional liberties, hoping to improve upon their work by shifting the diction in ways that will make the language more palatable for contemporary readers. Later translators included here are R. F. Christian, a professor at the University of St Andrews and a major Tolstoy scholar, and Jane Kentish, who translated many of Tolstoy's religious writings for a Penguin selection that appeared in 1987. Michael R. Katz translated the late story, 'Alyosha Gorshok'.

LAST STEPS

The Late Writings of Leo Tolstoy

FROM *A CONFESSION* [1882]

I

I was baptized and brought up in the Orthodox Christian faith. I had been taught it in childhood and throughout my boyhood and youth. But when I abandoned the second course of the university at the age of eighteen, I no longer believed any of the things I had been taught.

Judging by certain memories, I never seriously believed them, but had simply relied on what I was taught and on what was professed by the grown-up people around me, and that reliance was very unstable.

I remember that before I was eleven a grammar school pupil, Vladimir Milyutin (long since dead), visited us one Sunday and announced as the latest novelty a discovery made at his school. This discovery was that there is no God and that all we are taught about Him is a mere invention (this was in 1838). I remember how interested my elder brothers were in this information. They called me to their council and we all, I remember, became very animated, and accepted it as something very interesting and quite possible.

I remember also that when my elder brother, Dmitry, who was then at the university, suddenly, in the passionate way natural to him, devoted himself to religion and began to attend all the Church services, to fast and to lead a pure and moral life, we all – even our elders – unceasingly held him up to ridicule and for some unknown reason called him 'Noah'. I remember that Musin-Pushkin, the then Curator of Kazan University, when inviting us to dance at his home, ironically persuaded my brother (who was declining the invitation) by the argument that even David danced before the Ark. I sympathized with these jokes made by my elders, and drew from them the conclusion that though it is necessary to learn the catechism and go to church, one must not take such things too seriously. I remember also that I read Voltaire when I was very young, and that his raillery, far from shocking me, amused me very much.

My lapse from faith occurred as is usual among people at our level of education. In most cases, I think, it happens thus: a man lives like everybody else, on the basis of principles not merely having nothing in common with religious doctrine, but generally opposed to it; religious doctrine does not play a part in life, in intercourse with others it is never encountered, and in a man's own life he never has to reckon with it. Religious doctrine is professed far away from life and independently of it. If it is encountered, it is only as an external phenomenon disconnected from life.

Then as now, it was and is quite impossible to judge by a man's life and conduct whether he is a believer or not. If there be a difference between a man who publicly professes orthodoxy and one who denies it, the difference is not in favour of the former. Then as now, the public profession of orthodoxy occurred chiefly among people who were dull and cruel and who considered themselves very important. Ability, honesty, reliability, good-nature and moral conduct, were most common among unbelievers.

The schools teach the catechism and send the pupils to church and government officials must produce certificates of having received communion. But a man of our circle who has finished his education and is not in the government service may even now (and formerly it was still easier for him to do so) live for ten or twenty years without once remembering that he is living among Christians and is himself reckoned a member of the orthodox Christian Church.

So that, now as formerly, religious doctrine, accepted on trust and supported by external pressure, thaws away gradually under the influence of knowledge and experience of life which conflict with it, and a man very often lives on, imagining that he still holds intact the religious doctrine imparted to him in childhood whereas in fact not a trace of it remains.

S., a clever and truthful man, once told me the story of how he ceased to believe. On a hunting expedition, when he was already twenty-six, he once, at the place where they put up for the night, knelt down in the evening to pray – a habit retained from childhood. His elder brother, who was at the hunt with him, was lying on some hay and watching him. When S. had finished and was settling down for the night, his brother said to him: 'So you still do that?'

They said nothing more to one another. But from that day S. ceased to say his prayers or go to church. And now he has not prayed, received communion, or gone to church, for thirty years. And this not because he knows his brother's convictions and has joined him in them, nor because he has decided anything in his own soul, but simply because the word spoken by his brother was like the push of a finger on a wall that was ready to fall by its own weight. The word only showed that where he thought there was faith, in reality there had long been an empty space, and that therefore the utterance of words and the making of signs of the cross and genuflections while praying were quite senseless actions. Becoming conscious of their senselessness he could not continue them.

So it has been and is, I think, with the great majority of people. I am speaking of people of our educational level who are sincere with themselves, and not of those who make the profession of faith a means of attaining worldly aims. (Such people are the most fundamental infidels, for if faith is for them a means of attaining any worldly aims, then certainly it is not faith.) These people of our education are so placed that the light of knowledge and life has caused an artificial erection to melt away, and they have either already noticed this and swept its place clear, or they have not yet noticed it.

The religious dogma taught me from childhood disappeared in me as in others, but with this difference, that as from the age of fifteen I began to read philosophical works, my rejection of the doctrine became a conscious one at a very early age. From the time I was sixteen I ceased to say my prayers and ceased to go to church or to fast of my own volition. I did not believe what had been taught me in childhood but I believed in something. What it was I believed in I could not at all have said. I believed in a God, or rather I did not deny God – but I could not have said what sort of God. Neither did I deny Christ and his teaching, but what his teaching consisted in I again could not have said.

Looking back on that time, I now see clearly that my faith – my only real faith – that which apart from my animal instincts gave impulse to my life – was a belief in perfecting myself. But in what this perfecting consisted and what its object was, I could not have said. I tried to perfect myself mentally – I studied everything I could, anything life threw in my way; I tried to perfect my will, I drew up rules I tried to follow; I perfected myself physically, cultivating my strength and agility by all sorts of exercises, and accustoming myself to endurance and patience by all kinds of privations. And all this I considered to be the pursuit of perfection. The beginning of it all was of course moral perfection, but that was soon replaced by perfection in general: by the desire to be better not in my own eyes or those of God but in the eyes of other people. And very soon this effort again changed into a desire to be stronger than others: to be more famous, more important and richer than others.

XII

Awareness of the error in reasonable knowledge helped me to free myself from the temptation of idle thinking. The conviction that knowledge of truth can only be found by living led me to doubt the rightness of my life; but I was saved only by the fact that I was able to tear myself from my exclusiveness and to see the real life of the plain working people, and to understand that it alone is real life. I understood that if I wish to understand life and its meaning, I must not live the life of a parasite, but must live a real life, and – taking the meaning given to life by real humanity and merging myself in that life – verify it.

During that time this is what happened to me. During that whole year, when I was asking myself almost every moment whether I should not end matters with a noose or a bullet – all that time, together with the course of thought and observation about which I have spoken, my heart was oppressed with a painful feeling, which I can only describe as a search for God.

I say that that search for God was not reasoning, but a feeling, because that search proceeded not from the course of my thoughts – it was even directly contrary to them – but proceeded from the heart. It was a feeling of fear, orphanage, isolation in a strange land, and a hope of help from someone.

Though I was quite convinced of the impossibility of proving the existence of a Deity (Kant had shown, and I quite understood him, that it could not be proved), I yet sought for God, hoped that I should find Him, and from old habit addressed prayers to that which I sought but had not found. I went over in my mind the arguments of Kant and Schopenhauer showing the impossibility of proving the existence of a God, and I began to verify those arguments and to refute them. Cause, said I to myself, is not a category of thought such as are Time and Space. If I exist, there must be some cause for it, and a cause of causes. And that first cause of all is what men have called 'God'. And I paused on that thought, and tried with all my being to recognize the presence of that cause. And as soon as I acknowledged that there is a force in whose power I am, I at once felt that I could live. But I asked myself: What is that cause, that force? How am I to think of it? What are my relations to that which I call 'God'? And only the familiar replies occurred to me: 'He is the Creator and Preserver.' This reply did not satisfy me, and I felt I was losing within me what I needed for my life. I became terrified and began to pray to Him whom I sought, that He should help me. But the more I prayed the more apparent it became to me that He did not hear me, and that there was no one to whom to address myself. And with despair in my heart that there is no God at all, I said: 'Lord, have mercy, save me! Lord, teach me!' But no one had mercy on me, and I felt that my life was coming to a standstill.

But again and again, from various sides, I returned to the

same conclusion that I could not have come into the world without cause or reason or meaning; I could not be such a fledgling fallen from its nest as I felt myself to be. Or, granting that I be such, lying on my back crying in the high grass, even then I cry because I know that a mother has borne me within her, has hatched me, warmed me, fed me, and loved me. Where is she – that mother? If I have been deserted, who has deserted me? I cannot hide from myself that someone bore me, loving me. Who was that someone? Again 'God'? He knows and sees my searching, my despair, and my struggle.

'He exists,' said I to myself. And I had only for an instant to admit that, and at once life rose within me, and I felt the possibility and joy of being. But again, from the admission of the existence of a God I went on to seek my relation with Him; and again I imagined *that* God – our Creator in Three Persons who sent His Son, the Saviour – and again *that* God, detached from the world and from me, melted like a block of ice, melted before my eyes, and again nothing remained, and again the spring of life dried up within me, and I despaired and felt that I had nothing to do but to kill myself. And the worst of all was, that I felt I could not do it.

Not twice or three times, but tens and hundreds of times, I reached those conditions, first of joy and animation, and then of despair and consciousness of the impossibility of living.

I remember that it was in early spring: I was alone in the wood listening to its sounds. I listened and thought ever of the same thing, as I had constantly done during those last three years. I was again seeking God.

'Very well, there is no God,' said I to myself; 'there is no one who is not my imagination but a reality like my whole life. He does not exist, and no miracles can prove His existence, because the miracles would be my imagination, besides being irrational.

'But my *perception* of God, of Him whom I seek,' I asked myself, 'where has that perception come from?' And again at this thought the glad waves of life rose within me. All that was around me came to life and received a meaning. But my joy did not last long. My mind continued its work.

'The conception of God is not God,' said I to myself. 'The

conception is what takes place within me. The conception of God is something I can evoke or can refrain from evoking in myself. That is not what I seek. I seek that without which there can be no life.' And again all around me and within me began to die, and again I wished to kill myself.

But then I turned my gaze upon myself, on what went on within me, and I remembered all those cessations of life and reanimations that have recurred within me hundreds of times. I remembered that I only lived at those times when I believed in God. As it was before, so it was now; I need only be aware of God to live; I need only forget Him, or disbelieve Him, and I died.

What is this animation and dying? I do not live when I lose belief in the existence of God. I should long ago have killed myself had I not had a dim hope of finding Him. I live, really live, only when I feel Him and seek Him. 'What more do you seek?' exclaimed a voice within me. 'This is He. He is that without which one cannot live. To know God and to live is one and the same thing. God is life.'

'Live seeking God, and then you will not live without God.' And more than ever before, all within me and around me lit up, and the light did not again abandon me.

And I was saved from suicide. When and how this change occurred I could not say. As imperceptibly and gradually the force of life in me had been destroyed and I had reached the impossibility of living, a cessation of life and the necessity of suicide, so imperceptibly and gradually did that force of life return to me. And strange to say the strength of life which returned to me was not new, but quite old – the same that had borne me along in my earliest days.

I quite returned to what belonged to my earliest childhood and youth. I returned to the belief in that Will which produced me and desires something of me. I returned to the belief that the chief and only aim of my life is to be better, i.e. to live in accord with that Will, and I returned to the belief that I can find the expression of that Will in what humanity has produced for its guidance: that is to say, I returned to a belief in God, in moral perfection, and in a tradition transmitting the meaning of life. There was only this difference, that then all this was accepted unconsciously, while now I knew that without it I could not live.

What happened to me was something like this: I was put into a boat (I do not remember when) and pushed off from an unknown shore, shown the direction of the opposite shore, had oars put into my unpractised hands, and was left alone. I rowed as best I could and moved forward; but the further I advanced towards the middle of the stream the more rapid grew the current bearing me away from my goal and the more frequently did I encounter others, like myself, borne away by the stream. There were a few rowers who continued to row, there were others who had abandoned their oars; there were large boats and immense vessels full of people. Some struggled against the current, others yielded to it. And the further I went the more, seeing the progress down the current of all those who were adrift, I forgot the direction given me. In the very centre of the stream, amid the crowd of boats and vessels which were being borne down stream, I quite lost my direction and abandoned my oars. Around me on all sides, with mirth and rejoicing, people with sails and oars were borne down the stream, assuring me and each other that no other direction was possible. And I believed them and floated with them. And I was carried far; so far that I heard the roar of the rapids in which I must be shattered, and I saw boats shattered in them. And I recollected myself. I was long unable to understand what had happened to me. I saw before me nothing but destruction, towards which I was rushing and which I feared. I saw no safety anywhere and did not know what to do; but, looking back, I perceived innumerable boats which unceasingly and strenuously pushed across the stream, and I remembered about the shore, the oars and the direction, and began to pull back upwards against the stream and towards the shore.

That shore was God; that direction was tradition; the oars were the freedom given me to pull for the shore and unite with God. And so the force of life was renewed in me and I again began to live.

XV

How often I envied the peasants their illiteracy and ignorance! Those statements in the creeds which to me were evident absurdities, for them contained nothing false; they could accept them and could believe in the truth – the truth I believed in. Only to me, unhappy man, was it clear that with truth falsehood was interwoven by finest threads, and that I could not accept it in that form.

So I lived for about three years. At first, when I was only slightly associated with truth as a catechumen and was only scenting out what seemed to me clearest, these encounters struck me less. When I did not understand anything, I said, 'It is my fault, I am sinful'; but the more I became imbued with the truths I was learning, the more they became the basis of my life, the more oppressive and the more painful became these encounters and the sharper became the line between what I do not understand because I am not able to understand it, and what cannot be understood except by lying to oneself.

In spite of my doubts and sufferings I still clung to the Orthodox Church. But questions of life arose which had to be decided; and the decision of these questions by the Church – contrary to the very bases of the belief by which I lived – obliged me at last to renounce communion with Orthodoxy as impossible. These questions were: first the relation of the Orthodox Eastern Church to other Churches – to the Catholics and to the so-called sectarians. At that time, in consequence of my interest in religion, I came into touch with believers of various faiths: Catholics, Protestants, Old-Believers, Molokans* and others. And I met among them many men of lofty morals who were truly religious. I wished to be a brother to them. And what happened? That teaching which promised to unite all in one faith and love – that very teaching, in the person of its best representatives, told me that these men were all living a lie; that what gave them their power of life was a temptation of the

* A sect that rejects sacraments and ritual. [A. M.]

devil; and that we alone possess the only possible truth. And I saw that all who do not profess an identical faith with themselves are considered by the Orthodox to be heretics, just as the Catholics and others consider the Orthodox to be heretics. And I saw that the Orthodox (though they try to hide this) regard with hostility all who do not express their faith by the same external symbols and words as themselves; and this is naturally so; first, because the assertion that you are in falsehood and I am in truth, is the most cruel thing one man can say to another; and secondly, because a man loving his children and brothers cannot help being hostile to those who wish to pervert his children and brothers to a false belief. And that hostility is increased in proportion to one's greater knowledge of theology. And to me who considered that truth lay in union by love, it became self-evident that theology was itself destroying what it ought to produce.

This offence is so obvious to us educated people who have lived in countries where various religions are professed and have seen the contempt, self-assurance and invincible contradiction with which Catholics behave to the Orthodox Greeks and to the Protestants, and the Orthodox to Catholics and Protestants, and the Protestants to the two others, and the similar attitude of Old-Believers, Pashkovites (Russian Evangelicals), Shakers and all religions – that the very obviousness of the temptation at first perplexes us. One says to oneself: it is impossible that it is so simple and that people do not see that if two assertions are mutually contradictory, then neither of them has the sole truth which faith should possess. There is something else here, there must be some explanation. I thought there was, and sought that explanation and read all I could on the subject, and consulted all whom I could. And no one gave me any explanation, except the one which causes the Sumsky Hussars to consider the Sumsky Hussars the best regiment in the world, and the Yellow Uhlans to consider that the best regiment in the world is the Yellow Uhlans. The ecclesiastics of all the different creeds, through their best representatives, told me nothing but that they believed themselves to have the truth and the others to be in error, and that all they could do was to pray for them.

I went to archimandrites, bishops, elders, monks of the strictest orders, and asked them; but none of them made any attempt to explain the matter to me except one man, who explained it all and explained it so that I never asked anyone any more about it. I said that for every unbeliever turning to a belief (and all our young generation are in a position to do so) the question that presents itself first is, why is truth not in Lutheranism nor in Catholicism, but in Orthodoxy? Educated in the high school he cannot help knowing what the peasants do not know – that the Protestants and Catholics equally affirm that their faith is the only true one. Historical evidence, twisted by each religion in its own favour, is insufficient. Is it not possible, said I, to understand the teaching in a loftier way, so that from its height the differences should disappear, as they do for one who believes truly? Can we not go farther along a path like the one we are following with the Old-Believers? They emphasize the fact that they have a differently shaped cross and different alleluias and a different procession round the altar. We reply: You believe in the Nicene Creed, in the seven sacraments, and so do we. Let us hold to that, and in other matters do as you please. We have united with them by placing the essentials of faith above the unessentials. Now with the Catholics can we not say: You believe in so and so and in so and so, which are the chief things, and as for the Filioque clause and the Pope – do as you please. Can we not say the same to the Protestants, uniting with them in what is most important?

My interlocutor agreed with my thoughts, but told me that such conceptions would bring reproach of the spiritual authorities for deserting the faith of our forefathers, and this would produce a schism; and the vocation of the spiritual authorities is to safeguard in all its purity the Greco-Russian Orthodox faith inherited from our forefathers.

And I understood it all. I am seeking a faith, the power of life; and they are seeking the best way to fulfil in the eyes of men certain human obligations, and fulfilling these human affairs they fulfil them in a human way. However much they may talk of their pity for their erring brethren, and of addressing prayers for them to the throne of the Almighty – to carry out human purposes violence is necessary, and it has always been applied and is and will be applied. If of two religions each considers itself true and the other false, then men desiring to attract others to the truth will preach their own doctrine. And if a false teaching is preached to the inexperienced sons of their Church – which is the truth – then that Church cannot but burn the books and remove the man who is misleading its sons. What is to be done with a sectarian – burning, in the opinion of the Orthodox, with the fire of false doctrine – who in the most important affair of life, in faith, misleads the sons of the Church? What can be done with him except to cut off his head or to incarcerate him? Under the Tsar Alexis Mikhaylovich people were burned at the stake, that is to say, the severest method of punishment of the time was applied, and in our day also the severest method of punishment is applied – detention in solitary confinement.*

The second relation of the Church to a question of life was with regard to war and executions.

At that time Russia was at war. And Russians, in the name of Christian love, began to kill their fellow men. It was impossible not to think about this, and not to see that killing is an evil repugnant to the first principles of any faith. Yet prayers were said in the churches for the success of our arms, and the teachers of the Faith acknowledged killing to be an act resulting from the Faith. And besides the murders during the war, I saw, during the disturbances which followed the war, Church dignitaries and teachers and monks of the lesser and stricter orders who approved the killing of helpless, erring youths. And I took note of all that is done by men who profess Christianity, and I was horrified.

[Translated by Aylmer Maude]

* At the time this was written capital punishment was considered to be abolished in Russia. [A. M.]

FROM *THE FIRST STEP*
[1891]

VIII

There has been and there can be no good life without abstinence. No good life is thinkable without abstinence. Every attainment of a good life must begin through it.

There is a ladder of virtues, and we must begin with the first rung, in order to ascend to the next; and the first virtue which must be attained by a man, if he wants to attain the next, is what the ancients called ἐγκράτεια or σωφροσύνη, that is, reflection or self-possession.

If in the Christian teaching abstinence is included in the concept of self-renunciation, the consecutiveness none the less remains the same, and the attainment of no Christian virtues is possible without abstinence, not because somebody has thought it out so, but because such is the essence of the matter.

Abstinence is the first step of every good life.

But even abstinence is not attained at once, but by degrees.

Abstinence is a man's liberation from the lusts, their subjection to reason, σωφροσύνη. But there are many various lusts in man, and for the struggle with them to be successful he must begin with the basal ones, those on which other, more complex ones grow up, and not with the complex, which have grown up on the basal ones. There are complex passions, as the passion for adorning the body, games, amusements, gossiping, curiosity, and many others; and there are basal passions, such as gluttony, idleness, carnal love. In the struggle with the passions it is impossible to begin at the end, with the struggle with the complex passions; we must begin with the basal ones, and that, too, in a definite order. This order is determined both by the essence of the thing and by the tradition of human wisdom.

A glutton is not able to struggle against idleness, and a gluttonous and idle man is unable to struggle with the sexual lust. And so, according to all teachings, the striving after abstinence began with the struggle against the lust of gluttony, began with fasting. But in our society, where every serious relation to the attainment of the good life is lost to such a degree and has been lost for so long a time that the very first virtue, abstinence, without which no others are possible, is considered superfluous, there is also lost the consecutiveness which is indispensable for the attainment of this first virtue, and many have forgotten all about fasting, and it has been decided that fasting is a foolish superstition, and that fasting is not at all necessary.

And yet, just as the first condition of a good life is abstinence, so the first condition of an abstemious life is fasting.

A man may wish to be good, dream of goodness, without fasting; but in reality it is just as impossible to be good without fasting, as it is to walk without getting up on one's feet.

Fasting is an indispensable condition of a good life. But gluttony has always been the first symptom of the reverse, of a bad life, and unfortunately this symptom has particular force in the life of the majority of the men of our time.

Glance at the faces and at the figures of the men of our circle and time – on many of these faces with pendent chins and cheeks, obese limbs and large bellies, lies the ineffaceable imprint of a life of dissipation. Nor can it be otherwise. Look closely at our life, at that by which the majority of the men of our society are moved; ask yourself what is the chief interest of this majority. No matter how strange this may appear to us, who are accustomed to conceal our true interests and to put forth false, artificial ones, the chief interest of the life of the majority of men of our time is the gratification of the sense of taste, the pleasure of eating, gluttony. Beginning with the poorest and ending with the wealthiest classes of society, gluttony, I think, is the chief aim, the chief pleasure of our life. The poor working people form an exception only to the extent to which want keeps them from surrendering themselves to this passion. The moment they have time and means for it, they, emulating the higher classes, provide themselves with what tastes best and is sweetest, and eat and drink as much as they can. The more they eat, the more they consider themselves, not only happy, but even strong and healthy. And in this conviction they are maintained by the cultured people, who look upon food in precisely this manner. The cultured classes imagine happiness and health to lie in savoury, nutritive, easily digested food (in which opinion they are confirmed by the doctors, who assert that the most expensive food, meat, is the most wholesome), though they try to conceal this.

Look at the life of these people, listen to their talk. What kind of exalted subjects interests them? Philosophy, and science, and art, and poetry, and the distribution of wealth, and the welfare of the people, and the education of youth; but all this is for the vast majority a lie. All this interests them only between business, between the real business, between breakfast and dinner, while the stomach is full, and it is not possible to eat any more. The one living, real interest, the interest of the majority of men and women, is eating, especially after their first youth. How to eat, what to eat, when, where?

Not one solemnity, not one joy, not one christening, not one opening of anything takes place without eating.

Look at people in their travels. In them you can see it best. 'The museums, the libraries, the parliament – how interesting! And where shall we dine? Who sets the best table?' Yes, just look at the people, as they come down to dinner, dressed up, besprinkled with perfume, to a table adorned with flowers, how joyously they rub their hands and smile!

If we could look into their souls – what do the majority of men long for? For an appetite for breakfast, for dinner. In what does the severest punishment from childhood consist? In being reduced to bread and water. What artisan receives the greatest wages? The cook. In what does the chief interest of the lady of the house consist? Toward what does in the majority of cases the conversation incline between the ladies of the middle class? And if the conversation of the people of the higher classes does not incline toward it, the cause of it is not because they are more cultured and busy with higher interests, but only because they have a housekeeper or a steward who is busy with this and guarantees their dinners. But try to deprive them of this comfort, and you will see in what their cares lie. Everything reduces itself to the question of eating, the price of grouse, the best means for boiling coffee, baking sweet tarts, etc. People assemble, whatever the occasion may be – christening, funeral, wedding, dedication of a church, farewell, reception, celebration of a memorable day, the death or birth of a great scholar, thinker, teacher of morality – people assemble, claiming to be busy with some exalted subjects. So they say; but they dissemble: they all know that there will be something to eat, good, savoury food, and something to drink, and it is this mainly which has brought them together. For several days previous to this animals have been slaughtered and cut up for this very purpose, baskets with supplies have been brought from the gastronomic shops, and cooks, their assistants, scullions, peasants of the buffet, especially dressed up in clean starched aprons and caps, have been 'working'. So, too, chefs, who receive five hundred roubles per month and more, have been working and giving orders. The cooks have been chopping, mixing, washing, arranging, adorning. With the same solemnity and importance there has been working a similar superintendent of service, counting, reflecting, casting his glance, like an artist. The gardener has been working for the flowers. The dishwashers . . . A whole army of men work, the products of thousands of work-days are devoured, and all this in order that the people assembled may have a chance to talk of the memorable great teacher of science or morality, or to recall a deceased friend, or to say farewell to a young couple who are entering upon a new life.

In the lower and middle classes it is evident that a holiday, funeral, wedding, means gluttony. It is thus that they understand the matter in these classes. Gluttony to such an extent takes the place of the motive of assemblage that in Greek and French 'wedding' and 'feast' have the same meaning. But in the higher circle, amidst refined people, great art is employed in order to conceal this and to make it appear that the eating is a secondary matter, that it exists only for decency's sake. They can conveniently represent this in such a way, because for the most part they are in the real sense of the word satiated – they are never hungry.

They pretend that they have no need of a dinner, of eating, and that it is even a burden to them. But try, instead of the refined dishes expected by them, to give them, I do not say bread and water, but porridge and noodles, and you will see what a storm this will provoke, and how the real facts will come to the surface, namely, that in the gathering of these men the chief interest is not the one which they put forth, but the interest of eating.

See what people deal in; walk through the city and see what is being sold: attire and articles of food.

In reality this ought to be so and cannot be otherwise. We cannot stop thinking of eating, keep this lust within its limits, only when we submit to the necessity of eating; but when a man, only submitting to this necessity, that is, to the fulness of the stomach, stops eating, then it cannot be otherwise. If a man has taken a liking to the pleasure of eating, has allowed himself to love this pleasure, and finds that this pleasure is good (as the vast majority of men of our society and the cultured find, although they pretend the opposite), then there is no limit to its increase, there are no limits beyond which it cannot grow. The gratification of a need has its limits; but enjoyment has none. For the gratification of a need it is indispensable and sufficient to eat bread, porridge or rice; for the increase of enjoyment there is no end to dishes and to seasonings.

Bread is an indispensable and sufficient food (the proof of this: millions of strong, lithe, healthy men, who work much, live on nothing but bread). But it is better to eat bread with some preparation. It is good to soak bread in water with meat boiled in it. It is still better to put vegetables into this water, and still better a lot of different vegetables. It is not bad to eat meat itself. But it is better to eat, not boiled, but roasted meat. And still better, meat slightly broiled with butter, and with the blood, and only certain parts of it. Add to this vegetables and mustard. And wash it down with wine, best of all red wine.

You do not feel like eating anything else, but you can still devour some fish, if it is seasoned with sauce, and you can wash it down with white wine. One would think that no other fat or savoury food would go down. But you may still eat something sweet, in the summer ice-cream, in the winter preserves, jams, etc. And this is a dinner, a modest dinner. The pleasure of this dinner may be greatly, very greatly increased. And people do increase it, and there is no limit to this increase: there are appetizers, and *entremets*, and desserts, and all kinds of combinations of savoury food, and adornments, and music during the dinner.

And, strange to say, the people who every day eat such dinners, in comparison with which Belshazzar's feast, which called forth the remarkable threat, is nothing, are naïvely convinced that they can with it all lead a moral life.

IX

Fasting is an indispensable condition of a good life; but in fasting, as in abstinence, there appears the question, with what to begin the fasting, how to fast, how often to eat, what not to eat. And as it is impossible seriously to busy oneself with anything, without having acquired the consecutiveness necessary for it, so it is impossible to fast, without knowing with what to begin the fast, with what to begin the abstinence from food.

Fasting! But there is the choice to be made as to what to begin with. This idea seems ridiculous and extravagant to the majority of men.

I remember with what pride, on account of his originality, an Evangelical Protestant, who was attacking the asceticism of monasticism, said to me, 'My Christianity is not with fasts and privations, but with beefsteaks.' Christianity and virtue in general with beefsteaks!

So many savage and immoral things have eaten their way into our life, especially into that lower sphere of the first step toward a good life, the relation to food, to which very few people have paid any attention, that it is difficult for us even to comprehend the boldness and madness of the assertion in our time of a Christianity or virtue with beefsteaks.

The only reason why we are not horrified at this assertion is that with us has happened the unusual thing that we look and do not see, that we listen and do not hear. There is no stench, no sound, no monstrosity, to which a man cannot get used, so that he no longer notices what is startling to a man who is not used to it. The same is true in the moral sphere. Christianity and morality with beefsteaks!

The other day I visited the slaughter-house in our city of Tula. The slaughter-house is built according to a new, perfected method, as it is built in large cities, so that the animals killed shall suffer as little as possible. This was on a Friday, two days before Pentecost. There were there a large number of cattle.

Before that, a long time before, when reading the beautiful book, *Ethics of Diet*, I had made up my mind to visit the slaughter-house, in order with my own eyes to see the facts of the case, which are mentioned whenever vegetarianism is mentioned. But I felt uneasy, as one always feels uneasy when going to see sufferings which are sure to be there, but which one cannot prevent, and so I kept putting it off.

But lately I met on the road a butcher, who had been home and now was going back to Tula. He is not yet an experienced butcher, and his duty consists in stabbing with a dagger. I asked him whether he did not feel sorry that he had to kill the animals. And as the answer always is, so he answered, 'Why be sorry? This has to be done.' But when I told him that eating meat was not necessary, he agreed with me, and then he also agreed with me that it was a pity to kill. 'What is to be done? I have to make a living,' he said. 'At first I was afraid to kill. My father never killed a chicken in all his life.'

The majority of Russians cannot kill; they feel pity, which they express by the word 'afraid'. He, too, had been afraid, but had stopped. He explained to me that the busiest day is Friday, when the work lasts until evening.

Lately, too, I had a talk with a soldier, a butcher, and he, too, was surprised in the same way at my assertion that it is a pity to kill; and, as always, he said that this was the law; but later he agreed with me, 'Especially when it is a tame, kind animal. The dear animal comes up to you, believing you. It is truly a pity!'

One day we returned from Moscow on foot, and some drivers of drays, going from Serpukhov to a forest to get a merchant's timber, gave us a lift. It was Maundy Thursday. I was riding in the first *telega* with a strong, red-faced, coarse driver, who was apparently very drunk. As we entered a village, we saw that from the last yard they were pulling a fattened, shorn, pink-coloured pig, to get it killed. The pig squealed in a desperate voice, which resembled that of a man. Just as we passed by, they began to kill the pig. One of the men drew the knife down its throat. It squealed louder and more penetratingly than before, tore itself loose, and ran away, shedding its blood. I am near-sighted and so did not see all the details; all I saw was the pink-coloured flesh of the pig, which resembled that of a man, and I heard the desperate squeal; but the driver saw all the details, and he looked in that direction without taking his eyes off. The pig was caught and thrown down, and they began to finish the killing. When its squeal died down, the driver drew a deep sigh.

'Is it possible men will not have to answer for this?' he muttered.

So strong is people's disgust at any kind of a murder; but by example, by encouraging men's greed, by the assertion that this is permitted by God, and chiefly by habit, people have been brought to a complete loss of this natural feeling.

On Friday I went to Tula, and, upon meeting an acquaintance of mine, a meek, kindly man, I invited him to go with me.

'Yes, I have heard that it is well arranged, and I should like to see it, but if they slaughter there I sha'n't go in.'

'Why not? It is precisely what I want to see. If meat is to be eaten, cattle have to be killed.'

'No, no, I cannot.'

What is remarkable in this case is, that this man is a hunter and himself kills birds and animals.

We arrived. Even before entering we could smell the oppressive, detestable, rotten odour of joiner's glue or of glue paint.

The farther we went, the stronger was this odour. It is a very large, red brick building, with vaults and high chimneys. We entered through the gate. On the right was a large fenced yard, about a quarter of a *desyatina* in size – this is the cattle-yard, to which the cattle for sale are driven two days in the week – and at the edge of this space was the janitor's little house; on the left were what they call the chambers, that is, rooms with round gates, concave asphalt floors, and appliances for hanging up and handling the carcasses. By the wall of the little house, and to the right of it, sat six butchers in aprons, which were covered with blood, with blood-bespattered sleeves rolled up over muscular arms. They had finished their work about half an hour ago, so that on that day we could see only the empty chambers. In spite of the gates being opened on two sides, there was in each chamber an oppressive odour of warm blood; the floor was cinnamon-coloured and shining, and in the depressions of the floor stood coagulated black gore.

One of the butchers told us how they slaughtered, and showed us the place where this is done. I did not quite understand him, and formed a false, but very terrible conception of how they slaughtered, and I thought, as is often the case, that the reality would produce a lesser effect upon me than what I had imagined. But I was mistaken in this.

The next time I came to the slaughter-house in time. It was on Friday before Pentecost. It was a hot June day. The odour of glue and of blood was even more oppressive and more noticeable in the morning than during my first visit. The work was at white heat. The dusty square was all full of cattle, and the cattle were driven into all the stalls near the chambers.

In the street in front of the building stood carts with steers, heifers and cows tied to the cart stakes and shafts. Butchers' carts, drawn by good horses, loaded with live calves with dangling heads, drove up and unloaded; and similar carts with upturned and shaking legs of the carcasses of steers, with their heads, bright red lungs and dark red livers drove away from the slaughter-house. Near the fence stood the mounts of the cattle-dealers. The cattle-dealers themselves, in their long coats, with whips and knouts in their hands, walked up and down in the yard, either marking one man's cattle with tar paint, or haggling, or attending to the transfer of bulls and steers from the square to the stalls, from which the cattle entered the chambers. These men were obviously all absorbed in money operations and calculations, and the thought that it is good or bad to kill these animals was as far from them as the thought as to what was the chemical composition of the blood with which the floor of the chambers was covered.

No butchers could be seen in the yards: they were all working in the chambers. During this day about one hundred steers were killed. I entered a chamber and stopped at the door. I stopped, both because the chamber was crowded with the carcasses which were being shifted, and because the blood ran underfoot and dripped from above, and all the butchers who were there were smeared in it, and, upon entering inside, I should certainly have been smeared with blood. They were taking down one carcass, which was suspended; another was being moved to the door; a third, a dead ox, was lying with his white legs turned up, and a butcher with his strong fist was ripping the stretched-out hide.

Through the door opposite to the one where I was standing they were at that time taking in a large, red, fattened ox. Two men were pulling him. And they had barely brought him in, when I saw a butcher raise a dagger over his head and strike him. The ox dropped down on his belly, as though he had been knocked off all his four legs at once, immediately rolled over on one side, and began to kick with his legs and with his whole back. One of the butchers immediately threw himself on the fore part of the ox, from the end opposite his kicking legs, took hold of his horns, bent his head to the ground, and from beneath the head there spurted the dark red blood, under the current of which a boy besmeared in blood placed a tin basin. All the time while they were doing this, the ox kept jerking his head, as though trying to get up, and kicked with all his four legs in the air. The basin filled rapidly, but the ox was still alive and, painfully contracting and expanding his belly, kicked with his fore legs and hind legs, so that the butchers had to get out of his way. When one basin was filled, the boy carried it on his head to the albumen plant, while another boy set down another basin, which also began to fill up. But the ox kept contracting and expanding his belly and jerked with his hind legs. When the blood stopped flowing, the butcher raised the head of the ox and began to flay him. The ox continued kicking. The head was bared and began to look red with white veins, and assumed the position given to it by the butchers; on both sides of it hung the hide. The ox continued to kick. Then another butcher caught the ox by a leg, which he broke and cut off. Convulsions ran up and down the belly and the other legs. The other legs, too, were cut off, and they were thrown where all the legs belonging to one owner were thrown. Then the carcass was pulled up to a block and tackle and was stretched out, and there all motion stopped.

Thus I stood at the door and looked at a second, a third, a fourth ox. With all of them the same happened; the same flayed head with pinched tongue and the same kicking back. The only difference was that the butcher did not always strike in the right place to make the ox fall. It happened that the butcher made a mistake, and the ox jumped up, bellowed, and, shedding blood, tried to get away. But then he was pulled under a beam and struck a second time, after which he fell.

I later walked up from the side of the door, through which they brought in the oxen. Here I saw the same, only at closer range, and, therefore, more clearly. I saw here, above all else, what I had not seen through the other door – how they compelled the oxen to walk through this door. Every time when they took an ox out of the stall and pulled him by a rope, which was attached to his horns, the ox, scenting the blood, became stubborn and bellowed, and sometimes jerked back. It was impossible for two men to pull him in by force, and so a butcher every time went behind and took the ox by the tail, which he twisted until the gristle cracked and the tail broke, and the ox moved on.

The oxen of one owner were all finished, and they brought up the cattle of another. The first from this lot of the other owner was a bull. He was a fine-looking, thoroughbred black bull, with white spots on his body and white legs – a young, muscular, energetic animal. They began to pull him; he dropped his head and absolutely refused to move. But the butcher who was walking behind took hold of his tail, as a machinist puts his hand on the throttle, and twisted it; the cartilage cracked; and the bull rushed ahead, knocking the men who were pulling at the rope off their feet, and again stood stubbornly still, looking askance with his white, bloodshot eyes. But again the tail cracked, and the bull rushed forward and was where he was wanted. The butcher walked up, took his aim, and struck him. But the stroke did not fall in the right place. The bull jumped up, tossed his head, bellowed, and, all covered with blood, tore himself loose and rushed back. All the people at the doors started back; but the accustomed butchers, with a daring which was the result of the peril, briskly took hold of the rope and again of the tail, and again the bull found himself in the chamber, where his head was pulled under the beam, from which he no longer tore himself away. The butcher briskly looked for the spot where the hair scatters in the form of a star, and, having found it, in spite of the blood, struck him, and the beautiful animal, which was full of life, came down with a crash and kicked with its head and legs, while they let off the blood and flayed the head.

'Accursed devil, he did not even fall the right way,' growled the butcher as he cut the hide from his head.

Five minutes later the red, instead of black, head, without the hide, with glassy, fixed eyes, which but five minutes before had glistened with such a beautiful colour, was suspended on the beam.

Then I entered the division where they butcher the smaller animals. It is a very large and long chamber, with an asphalt floor and with tables with backs, on which they butcher sheep and calves. Here the work was all finished; in the long chamber, which was saturated with the odour of blood, there were only two butchers. One was blowing into the leg of a dead wether and patting the blown-up belly; the other, a young lad, with a blood-bespattered apron, was smoking a bent cigarette. There was no one else in the gloomy, long chamber, which was saturated with the oppressive odour. Immediately after me there came in one who looked like an ex-soldier, who brought a black yearling lamb, with spots on his neck, which he put down on one of the tables, as though on a bed. The soldier, apparently an acquaintance of theirs, greeted them and asked them when their master gave them days off. The young lad with the cigarette walked up with a knife, which he sharpened at the edge of the table, and answered that they had their holidays free. The live plump lamb was lying quietly as though dead, only briskly wagging his short tail and breathing more frequently than usual. The soldier lightly, without effort, held down his head, which was rising up; the young lad, continuing the conversation, took the lamb's head with his left hand and quickly drew the knife down his throat. The lamb shivered, and the little tail became arched and stopped wagging. While waiting for the blood to run off, the young lad puffed at the cigarette, which had nearly gone out. The blood began to flow, and the lamb began to be convulsed. The conversation was continued without the least interruption.

And those hens and chickens, which every day in a thousand kitchens, with heads cut off, shedding blood, jump about comically and terribly, flapping their wings?

And behold, a tender, refined lady will devour the corpses of these animals with the full conviction of her righteousness, asserting two propositions, which mutually exclude one another:

The first, that she is so delicate – and of this she is assured by her doctor – that she is unable to live on vegetable food alone, but that her weak organism demands animal food; and the second, that she is so sensitive that she not only cannot cause any sufferings to any animal, but cannot even bear the sight of them.

And yet, this poor lady is weak for the very reason, and for no other, that she has been taught to subsist on food which is improper for man; and she cannot help but cause the animals suffering, because she devours them.

X

We cannot pretend that we do not know this. We are not ostriches, and we cannot believe that, if we do not look, there will not be what we do not wish to see. This is the more impossible, when we do not wish to see what we wish to eat. And, above all else, if it were only indispensable! But let us assume that it is not indispensable, but necessary for some purpose. It is not.* It is good only for bringing out animal sensations, breeding lust, fornication, drunkenness. This is constantly confirmed by the fact that good, uncorrupted young men and women and girls, feel, without knowing how one thing follows from the other, that virtue is not compatible with beefsteak, and as soon as they wish to be good, they give up animal food.

What, then, do I wish to say? Is it this, that men, to be moral, must stop eating meat? Not at all.

What I wanted to say is that for a good life a certain order of good acts is indispensable; that if the striving after the good life is serious in a man, it will inevitably assume one certain order, and that in this order the first virtue for a man to work on is abstinence, self-possession. And in striving after abstinence, a man will inevitably follow one certain order, and in this order the first subject will be abstinence in food, fasting. But in fasting, if he seriously and sincerely seeks a good life, the first from which a man will abstain will always be the use of animal food, because, to say nothing of the excitation of the passions, which this food produces, its use is directly immoral, since it demands an act which is contrary to our moral sense – murder – and is provoked only by the desire and craving for good eating.

* Let those who doubt it read those numerous books, composed by scholars and physicians, in which it is proved that meat is not necessary for man's alimentation. And let them not listen to those old-fashioned doctors, who defend the necessity of subsisting on meat, only because their predecessors and they themselves have recognized it as necessary for a long time – they defend it with stubbornness, with malice, as everything old and obsolete is always defended. [L. T.]

Why abstinence from animal food will be the first work of fasting and a moral life has excellently been said, not by one man, but by the whole of humanity, in the persons of its best representatives in the course of the whole conscious life of humanity.

'But why, if the illegality, that is, the immorality, of animal food has for so long a time been known to humanity, have men not yet come to recognize this law?' is what those men will ask who are generally guided, not so much by their reason, as by public opinion. The answer to this question is this, that the moral progress of humanity, which forms the basis of every progress, always takes place slowly; but that the symptom of the true, not the accidental, progress is its unceasingness and constant acceleration.

And such is the motion of vegetarianism. This motion is expressed in all the thoughts of the writers on this subject, and in the life of humanity itself, which more and more passes unconsciously from meat eating to vegetable food, and consciously in the motion of vegetarianism, which has been manifesting itself with especial force and is assuming ever greater dimensions. This motion has for the last ten years been growing faster and faster; there appear every year more and more books and periodicals which deal with this subject; we constantly meet more and more men who reject animal food; and the number of vegetarian restaurants and hotels is growing every year abroad, especially in Germany, England and America.

This motion must be particularly pleasing to those who live striving after the realization of the kingdom of God upon earth, not because vegetarianism in itself is an important step toward this kingdom (all true steps are both important and not important), but because it serves as a sign of this, that the striving after man's moral perfection is serious and sincere, since it has assumed the proper invariable order, which begins with the first step.

We cannot help but rejoice in this, just as people could not help but rejoice who, striving to get to the top of a house, had been vainly and in disorder trying to climb the walls from various sides, and now at last assemble near the first rung of the ladder, knowing that there is no way of getting to the top but by beginning at this first rung of the ladder.

[Translated by Leo Wiener]

WHERE LOVE IS, GOD IS [1885]

In a certain town there lived a cobbler, Martin Avdeitch by name. He had a tiny room in a basement, the one window of which looked out on to the street. Through it one could only see the feet of those who passed by, but Martin recognized the people by their boots. He had lived long in the place and had many acquaintances. There was hardly a pair of boots in the neighbourhood that had not been once or twice through his hands, so he often saw his own handiwork through the window. Some he had re-soled, some patched, some stitched up, and to some he had even put fresh uppers. He had plenty to do, for he worked well, used good material, did not charge too much, and could be relied on. If he could do a job by the day required, he undertook it; if not, he told the truth and gave no false promises; so he was well known and never short of work.

Martin had always been a good man; but in his old age he began to think more about his soul and to draw nearer to God. While he still worked for a master, before he set up on his own account, his wife had died, leaving him with a three-year-old son. None of his elder children had lived, they had all died in infancy. At first Martin thought of sending his little son to his sister's in the country, but then he felt sorry to part with the boy, thinking: 'It would be hard for my little Kapiton to have to grow up in a strange family; I will keep him with me.'

Martin left his master and went into lodgings with his little son. But he had no luck with his children. No sooner had the boy reached an age when he could help his father and be a support as well as a joy to him than he fell ill and, after being laid up for a week with a burning fever, died. Martin buried his son, and gave way to despair so great and overwhelming that he murmured against God. In his sorrow he prayed again and again that he too might die, reproaching God for having taken the son he loved, his only son, while he, old as he was, remained alive. After that Martin left off going to church.

One day an old man from Martin's native village, who had been a pilgrim for the last eight years, called in on his way from Troitsa Monastery. Martin opened his heart to him, and told him of his sorrow.

'I no longer even wish to live, holy man,' he said. 'All I ask of God is that I soon may die. I am now quite without hope in the world.'

The old man replied: 'You have no right to say such things, Martin. We cannot judge God's ways. Not our reasoning, but God's will, decides. If God willed that your son should die and you should live, it must be best so. As to your despair – that comes because you wish to live for your own happiness.'

'What else should one live for?' asked Martin.

'For God, Martin,' said the old man. 'He gives you life, and you must live for Him. When you have learnt to live for Him, you will grieve no more, and all will seem easy to you.'

Martin was silent awhile, and then asked: 'But how is one to live for God?'

The old man answered: 'How one may live for God has been shown us by Christ. Can you read? Then buy the Gospels, and read them: there you will see how God would have you live. You have it all there.'

These words sank deep into Martin's heart, and that same day he went and bought himself a Testament in large print, and began to read.

At first he meant only to read on holidays, but having once begun he found it made his heart so light that he read every day. Sometimes he was so absorbed in his reading that the oil in his lamp burnt out before he could tear himself away from the book. He continued to read every night, and the more he read the more clearly he understood what God required of him, and how he might live for God. And his heart grew lighter and lighter. Before, when he went to bed he used to lie with a heavy heart, moaning as he thought of his little Kapiton; but now he only repeated again and again: 'Glory to Thee, glory to Thee, O Lord! Thy will be done!'

From that time Martin's whole life changed. Formerly, on holidays he used to go and have tea at the public-house, and did not even refuse a glass or two of vodka. Sometimes, after having had a drop with a friend, he left the public-house not drunk, but rather merry, and would say foolish things: shout at a man, or abuse him. Now, all that sort of thing passed away from him. His life became peaceful and joyful. He sat down to his work in the morning, and when he had finished his day's work he took the lamp down from the wall, stood it on the table, fetched his book from the shelf, opened it, and sat down to read. The more he read the better he understood, and the clearer and happier he felt in his mind.

It happened once that Martin sat up late, absorbed in his book. He was reading Luke's Gospel; and in the sixth chapter he came upon the verses:

'And unto him that smiteth thee on the one cheek offer also the other; and him that taketh away thy cloke forbid not to take thy coat also. Give to every man that asketh of thee; and of him that taketh away thy goods ask them not again. And as ye would that men should do to you, do ye also to them likewise.'

He also read the verses where our Lord says:

'And why call ye me, Lord, Lord, and do not the things which I say? Whosoever cometh to me, and heareth my sayings, and doeth them, I will shew you to whom he is like: He is like a man which built an house, and digged deep, and laid the foundation on a rock: and when the flood arose, the stream beat vehemently upon that house, and could not shake it: for it was founded upon a rock. But he that heareth, and doeth not, is like a man that without a foundation built an house upon the earth; against which the stream did beat vehemently, and immediately it fell; and the ruin of that house was great.'

When Martin read these words his soul was glad within him. He took off his spectacles and laid them on the book, and leaning his elbows on the table pondered over what he had read. He tried his own life by the standard of those words, asking himself:

'Is my house built on the rock, or on sand? If it stands on the rock, it is well. It seems easy enough while one sits here alone, and one thinks one has done all that God commands; but as soon as I cease to be on my guard, I sin again. Still I will persevere. It brings such joy. Help me, O Lord!'

He thought all this, and was about to go to bed, but was loth to leave his book. So he went on reading the seventh chapter – about the centurion, the widow's son and the answer to John's disciples – and he came to the part where a rich Pharisee invited the Lord to his house; and he read how the woman who was a sinner, anointed his feet and washed them with her tears, and how he justified her. Coming to the forty-fourth verse, he read:

'And he turned to the woman, and said unto Simon, Seest thou this woman? I entered into thine house, thou gavest me no water for my feet: but she hath washed my feet with tears, and wiped them with the hairs of her head. Thou gavest me no kiss: but this woman since the time I came in hath not ceased to kiss my feet. My head with oil thou didst not anoint: but this woman hath anointed my feet with ointment.'

He read these verses and thought: 'He gave no water for his feet, gave no kiss, his head with oil he did not anoint . . .' And Martin took off his spectacles once more, laid them on his book, and pondered.

'He must have been like me, that Pharisee. He too thought only of himself – how to get a cup of tea, how to keep warm and comfortable; never a thought of his guest. He took care of himself, but for his guest he cared nothing at all. Yet who was the guest? The Lord himself! If he came to me, should I behave like that?'

Then Martin laid his head upon both his arms and, before he was aware of it, he fell asleep.

'Martin!' he suddenly heard a voice, as if someone had breathed the word above his ear.

He started from his sleep. 'Who's there?' he asked.

He turned round and looked at the door; no one was there.

He called again. Then he heard quite distinctly: 'Martin, Martin! Look out into the street tomorrow, for I shall come.'

Martin roused himself, rose from his chair and rubbed his eyes, but did not know whether he had heard these words in a dream or awake. He put out the lamp and lay down to sleep.

Next morning he rose before daylight, and after saying his prayers he lit the fire and prepared his cabbage soup and buck-wheat porridge. Then he lit the samovar, put on his apron, and sat down by the window to his work. As he sat working Martin thought over what had happened the night before. At times it seemed to him like a dream, and at times he thought that he had really heard the voice. 'Such things have happened before now,' thought he.

So he sat by the window, looking out into the street more than he worked, and whenever anyone passed in unfamiliar boots he would stoop and look up, so as to see not the feet only but the face of the passer-by as well. A house-porter passed in new felt boots; then a water-carrier. Presently an old soldier of Nicholas's reign came near the window spade in hand. Martin knew him by his boots, which were shabby old felt ones, goloshed with leather. The old man was called Stepanitch: a neighbouring tradesman kept him in his house for charity, and his duty was to help the house-porter. He began to clear away the snow before Martin's window. Martin glanced at him and then went on with his work.

'I must be growing crazy with age,' said Martin, laughing at his fancy. 'Stepanitch comes to clear away the snow, and I must needs imagine it's Christ coming to visit me. Old dotard that I am!'

Yet after he had made a dozen stitches he felt drawn to look out of the window again. He saw that Stepanitch had leaned his spade against the wall, and was either resting himself or trying to get warm. The man was old and broken down, and had evidently not enough strength even to clear away the snow.

'What if I called him in and gave him some tea?' thought Martin. 'The samovar is just on the boil.'

He stuck his awl in its place, and rose; and putting the samovar on the table, made tea. Then he tapped the window with his fingers. Stepanitch turned and came to the window. Martin beckoned to him to come in, and went himself to open the door.

'Come in,' he said, 'and warm yourself a bit. I'm sure you must be cold.'

'May God bless you!' Stepanitch answered. 'My bones do ache to be sure.' He came in, first shaking off the snow, and lest he should leave marks on the floor he began wiping his feet; but as he did so he tottered and nearly fell.

'Don't trouble to wipe your feet,' said Martin; 'I'll wipe up the floor – it's all in the day's work. Come, friend, sit down and have some tea.'

Filling two tumblers, he passed one to his visitor, and, pouring his own out into the saucer, began to blow on it.

Stepanitch emptied his glass, and, turning it upside down, put the remains of his piece of sugar on the top. He began to express his thanks, but it was plain that he would be glad of some more.

'Have another glass,' said Martin, refilling the visitor's tumbler and his own. But while he drank his tea Martin kept looking out into the street.

'Are you expecting anyone?' asked the visitor.

'Am I expecting anyone? Well, now, I'm ashamed to tell you. It isn't that I really expect anyone; but I heard something last night which I can't get out of my mind. Whether it was a vision, or only a fancy, I can't tell. You see, friend, last night I was reading the Gospel, about Christ the Lord, how he suffered, and how he walked on earth. You have heard tell of it, I dare say.'

'I have heard tell of it,' answered Stepanitch; 'but I'm an ignorant man and not able to read.'

'Well, you see, I was reading of how he walked on earth. I came to that part, you know, where he went to a Pharisee who did not receive him well. Well, friend, as I read about it, I thought how that man did not receive Christ the Lord with proper honour. Suppose such a thing could happen to such a man as myself, I thought, what would I not do to receive him! But that man gave him no reception at all. Well, friend, as I was thinking of this, I began to doze, and as I dozed I heard someone call me by name. I got up, and thought I heard someone whispering, "Expect me; I will come tomorrow." This happened twice over. And to tell you the truth, it sank so into my mind that, though I am ashamed of it myself, I keep on expecting him, the dear Lord!'

Stepanitch shook his head in silence, finished his tumbler and laid it on its side; but Martin stood it up again and refilled it for him.

'Here, drink another glass, bless you! And I was thinking, too, how he walked on earth and despised no one, but went mostly among common folk. He went with plain people, and chose his disciples from among the likes of us, from workmen like us, sinners that we are. "He who raises himself," he said, "shall be humbled; and he who humbles himself shall be raised." "You call me Lord," he said, "and I will wash your feet." "He who would be first," he said, "let him be the servant of all; because," he said, "blessed are the poor, the humble, the meek, and the merciful."'

Stepanitch forgot his tea. He was an old man, easily moved to tears, and as he sat and listened the tears ran down his cheeks.

'Come, drink some more,' said Martin. But Stepanitch crossed himself, thanked him, moved away his tumbler, and rose.

'Thank you, Martin Avdeitch,' he said, 'you have given me food and comfort both for soul and body.'

'You're very welcome. Come again another time. I am glad to have a guest,' said Martin.

Stepanitch went away; and Martin poured out the last of the tea and drank it up. Then he put away the tea things and sat down to his work, stitching the back seam of a boot. And as he stitched he kept looking out of the window, waiting for Christ, and thinking about him and his doings. And his head was full of Christ's sayings.

Two soldiers went by: one in Government boots, the other in boots of his own; then the master of a neighbouring house, in shining goloshes; then a baker carrying a basket. All these passed on. Then a woman came up in worsted stockings and peasant-made shoes. She passed the window, but stopped by the wall. Martin glanced up at her through the window, and saw that she was a stranger, poorly dressed, and with a baby in her arms. She stopped by the wall with her back to the wind, trying to wrap the baby up though she had hardly anything to wrap it in. The woman had only summer clothes on, and even they were shabby and worn. Through the window Martin heard the baby crying, and the woman trying to soothe it, but unable to do so. Martin rose, and going out of the door and up the steps he called to her.

'My dear, I say, my dear!'

The woman heard, and turned round.

'Why do you stand out there with the baby in the cold? Come inside. You can wrap him up better in a warm place. Come this way!'

The woman was surprised to see an old man in an apron, with spectacles on his nose, calling to her, but she followed him in.

They went down the steps, entered the little room, and the old man led her to the bed.

'There, sit down, my dear, near the stove. Warm yourself, and feed the baby.'

'Haven't any milk. I have eaten nothing myself since early morning,' said the woman, but still she took the baby to her breast.

Martin shook his head. He brought out a basin and some bread. Then he opened the oven door and poured some cabbage soup into the basin. He took out the porridge pot also, but the porridge was not yet ready, so he spread a cloth on the table and served only the soup and bread.

'Sit down and eat, my dear, and I'll mind the baby. Why, bless me, I've had children of my own; I know how to manage them.'

The woman crossed herself, and sitting down at the table began to eat, while Martin put the baby on the bed and sat down by it. He chucked and chucked, but having no teeth he could not do it well and the baby continued to cry. Then Martin tried poking at him with his finger; he drove his finger straight at the baby's mouth and then quickly drew it back, and did this again and again. He did not let the baby take his finger in its mouth, because it was all black with cobbler's wax. But the baby first grew quiet watching the finger, and then began to laugh. And Martin felt quite pleased.

The woman sat eating and talking, and told him who she was, and where she had been.

'I'm a soldier's wife,' said she. 'They sent my husband somewhere, far away, eight months ago, and I have heard nothing of him since. I had a place as cook till my baby was born, but then they would not keep me with a child. For three months now I have been struggling, unable to find a place, and I've had to sell all I had for food. I tried to go as a wet-nurse, but no one would have me; they said I was too starved-looking and thin. Now I have just been to see a tradesman's wife (a woman from our village is in service with her) and she has promised to take me. I thought it was all settled at last, but she tells me not to come till next week. It is far to her place, and I am fagged out, and baby is quite starved, poor mite. Fortunately our landlady has pity on us, and lets us lodge free, else I don't know what we should do.'

Martin sighed. 'Haven't you any warmer clothing?' he asked.

'How could I get warm clothing?' said she. 'Why, I pawned my last shawl for sixpence yesterday.'

Then the woman came and took the child, and Martin got up. He went and looked among some things that were hanging on the wall, and brought back an old cloak.

'Here,' he said, 'though it's a worn-out old thing, it will do to wrap him up in.'

The woman looked at the cloak, then at the old man, and taking it, burst into tears. Martin turned away, and groping under the bed brought out a small trunk. He fumbled about in it, and again sat down opposite the woman. And the woman said:

'The Lord bless you, friend. Surely Christ must have sent me to your window, else the child would have frozen. It was mild when I started, but now see how cold it has turned. Surely it must have been Christ who made you look out of your window and take pity on me, poor wretch!'

Martin smiled and said, 'It is quite true; it was He made me do it. It was no mere chance made me look out.'

And he told the woman his dream, and how he had heard the Lord's voice promising to visit him that day.

'Who knows? All things are possible,' said the woman. And she got up and threw the cloak over her shoulders, wrapping it round herself and round the baby. Then she bowed, and thanked Martin once more.

'Take this for Christ's sake,' said Martin, and gave her sixpence to get her shawl out of pawn. The woman crossed herself, and Martin did the same, and then he saw her out.

After the woman had gone, Martin ate some cabbage soup, cleared the things away, and sat down to work again. He sat and worked, but did not forget the window, and every time a shadow fell on it he looked up at once to see who was passing. People he knew and strangers passed by, but no one remarkable.

After a while Martin saw an apple-woman stop just in front of his window. She had a large basket, but there did not seem to be many apples left in it; she had evidently sold most of her stock. On her back she had a sack full of woodchips, which she was taking home. No doubt she had gathered them at some place where building was going on. The sack evidently hurt her, and she wanted to shift it from one shoulder to the other, so she put it down on the footpath and, placing her basket on a post, began to shake down the woodchips in the sack. While she was doing this a boy in a tattered cap ran up, snatched an apple out of the basket, and tried to slip away; but the old woman noticed it, and, turning, caught the boy by his sleeve. He began to struggle, trying to free himself, but the old woman held on with both hands, knocked his cap off his head, and seized hold of his hair. The boy screamed and the old woman scolded. Martin dropped his awl, not waiting to stick it in its place, and rushed out of the door. Stumbling up the steps, and dropping his spectacles in his hurry, he ran out into the street. The old woman was pulling the boy's hair and scolding him, and threatening to take him to the police. The lad was struggling and protesting, saying, 'I did not take it. What are you beating me for? Let me go!'

Martin separated them. He took the boy by the hand and said, 'Let him go, Granny. Forgive him for Christ's sake.'

'I'll pay him out, so that he won't forget it for a year! I'll take the rascal to the police!'

Martin began entreating the old woman.

'Let him go, Granny. He won't do it again. Let him go for Christ's sake!'

The old woman let go, and the boy wished to run away, but Martin stopped him

'Ask the Granny's forgiveness!' said he. 'And don't do it another time. I saw you take the apple.'

The boy began to cry and to beg pardon.

'That's right. And now here's an apple for you,' and Martin took an apple from the basket and gave it to the boy, saying, 'I will pay you, Granny.'

'You will spoil them that way, the young rascals,' said the old woman. 'He ought to be whipped so that he should remember it for a week.'

'Oh, Granny, Granny,' said Martin, 'that's our way – but it's not God's way. If he should be whipped for stealing an apple, what should be done to us for our sins?'

The old woman was silent.

And Martin told her the parable of the lord who forgave his servant a large debt, and how the servant went out and seized his debtor by the throat. The old woman listened to it all, and the boy, too, stood by and listened.

'God bids us forgive,' said Martin, 'or else we shall not be forgiven. Forgive everyone; and a thoughtless youngster most of all.'

The old woman wagged her head and sighed.

'It's true enough,' said she, 'but they are getting terribly spoilt.'

'Then we old ones must show them better ways,' Martin replied.

'That's just what I say,' said the old woman. 'I have had seven of them myself, and only one daughter is left.' And the old woman began to tell how and where she was living with her daughter, and how many grandchildren she had. 'There now,' she said, 'I have but little strength left, yet I work hard for the sake of my grandchildren; and nice children they are, too. No one comes out to meet me but the children. Little Annie, now, won't leave me for any one. "It's grandmother, dear grandmother, darling grandmother." ' And the old woman completely softened at the thought.

'Of course, it was only his childishness, God help him,' said she, referring to the boy.

As the old woman was about to hoist her sack on her back, the lad sprang forward to her, saying, 'Let me carry it for you, Granny. I'm going that way.'

The old woman nodded her head, and put the sack on the boy's back, and they went down the street together, the old woman quite forgetting to ask Martin to pay for the apple. Martin stood and watched them as they went along talking to each other.

When they were out of sight Martin went back to the house. Having found his spectacles unbroken on the steps, he picked up his awl and sat down again to work. He worked a little, but could soon not see to pass the bristle through the holes in the leather; and presently he noticed the lamplighter passing on his way to light the street lamps.

'Seems it's time to light up,' thought he. So he trimmed his lamp, hung it up, and sat down again to work. He finished off one boot and, turning it about, examined it. It was all right. Then he gathered his tools together, swept up the cuttings, put away the bristles and the thread and the awls, and, taking down the lamp, placed it on the table. Then he took the Gospels from the shelf. He meant to open them at the place he had marked the day before with a bit of morocco, but the book opened at another place. As Martin opened it, his yesterday's dream came back to his mind, and no sooner had he thought of it than he seemed to hear footsteps, as though someone were moving behind him. Martin turned round, and it seemed to him as if people were standing in the dark corner, but he could not make out who they were. And a voice whispered in his ear: 'Martin, Martin, don't you know me?'

'Who is it?' muttered Martin.

'It is I,' said the voice. And out of the dark corner stepped Stepanitch, who smiled and vanishing like a cloud was seen no more.

'It is I,' said the voice again. And out of the darkness stepped the woman with the baby in her arms, and the woman smiled and the baby laughed, and they too vanished.

'It is I,' said the voice once more. And the old woman and the boy with the apple stepped out and both smiled, and then they too vanished.

And Martin's soul grew glad. He crossed himself, put on his spectacles, and began reading the Gospel just where it had opened; and at the top of the page he read:

'I was an hungred, and ye gave me meat: I was thirsty, and ye gave me drink: I was a stranger, and ye took me in.'

And at the bottom of the page he read:

'Inasmuch as ye have done it unto one of the least of these my brethren, ye have done it unto me' (Matthew 25:35, 40).

And Martin understood that his dream had come true; and that the Saviour had really come to him that day, and he had welcomed him.

[Translated by Aylmer Maude]

FROM *THE KINGDOM OF GOD IS WITHIN YOU* [1893]

'The Doctrine of Non-Resistance to Evil by Force Must Inevitably be Accepted by Men of the Present Day'

VIII

It is often said that if Christianity is a truth, it should have been accepted by everyone at the very moment when it appeared and ought to have transformed men's lives for the better. But this is like saying that if the seed were fertile it should at once bring forth stalk, flower, and fruit.

The Christian religion is not a legal system that, being imposed by violence, may transform men's lives. Christianity is a fresh and higher conception of life. A new conception of life cannot be imposed on people; it can only be freely assimilated. And it can only be freely assimilated in two ways: one spiritual and internal, the other experimental and external.

Some people – a minority – by a kind of prophetic instinct understand the truth of the doctrine, surrender themselves to it, and adopt it. Others – the majority – only through a long course of mistakes, experiments, and suffering are brought to recognize the truth of the doctrine and the necessity of adopting it.

And by this experimental external method the majority of Christian men have now been brought to this necessity of assimilating the doctrine. One sometimes wonders what brought on the corruption of Christianity, which is now the greatest obstacle to its acceptance in its true significance.

If Christianity had been presented to people in its true, uncorrupted form, it would not have been accepted by the majority, who would have been as untouched by it as the nations of Asia are now. The peoples who accepted it in its corrupt form were subjected to its slow but certain influence, and by a long course of errors and experiments and their resultant sufferings have now been brought to the necessity of assimilating it in its true significance.

The corruption of Christianity and its acceptance in its corrupt form by the majority of men was necessary, as the seed should remain hidden in the earth in order to germinate.

Christianity is at once a doctrine of truth and a prophecy. Eighteen centuries ago Christianity revealed to men the truth in which they ought to live, and at the same time foretold what human life would become if men would not live by it but continued to live by their previous principles, and what it would become if they accepted the Christian doctrine and carried it out in their lives.

Laying down in the Sermon on the Mount the principles by which to guide men's lives, Christ said, 'Therefore whosoever heareth these sayings of mine, and doeth them, I will liken him unto a wise man, which built his house upon a rock: And the rain descended, and the floods came, and the winds blew, and beat upon that house: and it fell not: for it was founded upon a rock. And everyone that heareth these sayings of mine, and doeth them not, shall be likened unto a foolish man, which built his house upon the sand: And the rain descended, and the floods came, and the winds blew, and beat upon that house; and it fell: and great was the fall of it' (Matthew 7:24–7).

And now after eighteen centuries the prophecy has been fulfilled. Not having followed Christ's teaching generally and its application to social life in non-resistance to evil, men have been brought in spite of themselves to the inevitable destruction foretold by Christ for those who do not fulfil his teaching.

People often think the question of non-resistance to evil by force is a theoretical one, which can be neglected. Yet this question is presented by life itself to all men, and calls for some answer from every thinking man. Ever since Christianity has been outwardly professed, this question is for men in their social life like the question that presents itself to a traveller when the road on which he has been journeying divides into two branches. He must go on and he cannot say, 'I will not think about it, but will go on just as I did before.' There was one road, now there are two, and he must make his choice.

In the same way since Christ's teaching has been known by men they cannot say, 'I will live as before and will not decide the question of resistance or non-resistance to evil by force.' At every new struggle that arises one must inevitably decide: will I, or will I not, resist by force what I regard as evil?

The question of resistance or non-resistance to evil arose when the first conflict between men took place, since every conflict is nothing else than resistance by force to what each of the combatants regards as evil. But before Christ, men did not see that resistance by force to what each regards as evil, simply because one thinks evil what the other thinks good, is only one of the methods of settling the dispute, and that there is another method, that of not resisting evil by force at all.

Before Christ's teaching, it seemed to men that the only means of settling a dispute was by resistance to evil by force. And they acted accordingly, each of the combatants trying to convince himself and others that what each respectively regards as evil is actually, absolutely evil.

And to do this from the earliest time men have devised definitions of evil and tried to make them binding on everyone. And such definitions of evil sometimes took the form of laws, supposed to have been received by supernatural means, sometimes of the commands of rulers or assemblies to whom infallibility was attributed. Men resorted to violence against others, and convinced themselves and others that they were directing their violence against evil recognized as such by all.

This means was employed from the earliest times, especially by those who had gained possession of authority, and for a long while its irrationality was not detected.

But the longer men lived in the world and the more complex their relations became, the more evident it was that to resist by force what each regarded as evil was irrational, that conflict was in no way lessened thereby, and that no human definitions can succeed in making what some regard as evil be accepted as such by others.

Already at the time Christianity arose, it was evident to a great number of people in the Roman Empire where it arose, that what was regarded as evil by Nero and Caligula could not be regarded as evil by others. Even at that time men had begun to understand that human laws, though given out for divine laws, were compiled by men, and cannot be infallible, whatever the external majesty with which they are invested, and that erring men are not rendered infallible by assembling together and calling themselves a senate or any other name. Even at that time this was felt and understood by many. And it was then that Christ preached his doctrine, which consisted not only of the prohibition of resistance to evil by force, but gave a new conception of life and a means of putting an end to conflict between all men, not by making it the duty of one section only of mankind to submit without conflict to what is prescribed to them by certain authorities, but by making it the duty of all – and consequently of those in authority – not to resort to force against anyone in any circumstances.

This doctrine was accepted at the time by only a very small number of disciples. The majority of men, especially all who were in power, even after the nominal acceptance of Christianity, continued to maintain for themselves the principle of resistance by force to what they regarded as evil. So it was under the Roman and Byzantine emperors, and so it continued to be afterwards.

The insufficiency of the principle of the authoritative definition of evil and resistance to it by force, evident as it was in the early ages of Christianity, becomes still more obvious through the division of the Roman Empire into many states of equal authority, through their hostilities and the internal conflicts that broke out within them.

But men were not ready to accept the solution given by Christ, and the old definitions of evil, which ought to be resisted, continued to be laid down by means of making laws binding on all and enforced by forcible means. The authority who decided what ought to be regarded as evil and resisted by force was at one time the Pope, at another an emperor or king, an elective assembly or a whole nation. But both within and without the state there were always men to be found who did not accept as binding on themselves the laws given out as the decrees of a god, or made by men invested with a sacred character, or the institutions supposed to represent the will of the nation; and there were men who thought good what the existing authorities regarded as bad, and who struggled against the authorities with the same violence as was employed against them.

The men invested with religious authority regarded as evil what the men and institutions invested with temporal authority regarded as good and vice versa, and the struggle grew more and more intense. And the longer men used violence as the means of settling their disputes, the more obvious it became that it was an unsuitable means, since there could be no external authority able to define evil recognized by all.

Things went on like this for eighteen centuries, and at last reached the present position in which it is absolutely obvious that there is, and can be, no external definition of evil binding upon all. Men have come to the point of ceasing to believe in the possibility or even desirability of finding and establishing such a general definition. It has come to men in power ceasing to attempt to prove that what they regard as evil is evil, and simply declaring that they regard as evil what they don't like, while their subjects no longer obey them because they accept the definition of evil laid down by them, but simply obey because they cannot help themselves. It was not because it was a good thing, necessary and beneficial to men, and the contrary course would have been an evil, but simply because it was the will of those in power that Nice was incorporated into France, and Lorraine into Germany, and Bohemia into Austria, and that Poland was divided, and Ireland and India ruled by the English government, and that the Chinese are attacked and the Africans slaughtered, and the Chinese prevented from immigrating by the Americans, and the Jews persecuted by the Russians, and that landowners appropriate lands they do not cultivate and capitalists enjoy the fruits of the labour of others.

It has come to the present state of things; one set of men commit acts of violence no longer on the pretext of resistance to evil, but simply for their profit or their caprice, and another set submit to violence, not because they suppose, as was supposed in former times, that this violence was practised upon them for the sake of securing them from evil, but simply because they cannot avoid it.

If the Roman, or the man of medieval times, or the average Russian of fifty years ago, as I remember him, was convinced without a shade of doubt that the violence of authority was indispensable to preserve him from evil; that taxes, dues, serfdom, prisons, scourging, knouts, executions, the army and war were what ought to be – we know now that one can seldom find a man who believes that all these means of violence preserve anyone from any evil whatever, and indeed does not clearly perceive that most of these acts of violence to which he is exposed, and in which he has some share, are in themselves a great and useless evil.

There is no one today who does not see the uselessness and injustice of collecting taxes from the toiling masses to enrich idle officials; or the senselessness of inflicting punishments on weak or depraved persons in the shape of transportation from one place to another, or of imprisonment in a fortress where, living in security and indolence, they only become weaker and more depraved; or the worse than uselessness and injustice, the positive insanity and barbarity of preparations for war and of wars, causing devastation and ruin, and having no kind of justification. Yet these forms of violence continue and are supported by the very people who see their uselessness, injustice, and cruelty, and suffer from them. If fifty years ago the idle rich man and the illiterate labourer were both alike convinced that their state of everlasting holiday for one and everlasting toil for the other was ordained by God Himself, we know very well that nowadays, thanks to the growth of population and the diffusion of books and education, it would be hard to find in Europe or even in Russia, either among rich or poor, a man to whom in one shape or another a doubt as to the justice of this state of things had never presented itself. The rich know that they are guilty in the very fact of being rich, and try to expiate their guilt by sacrifices to art and science, as of old they expiated their sins by sacrifices to the Church. And even the larger half of the working people openly declares that the existing order is iniquitous and bound to be destroyed or reformed. One set of religious people of whom there are millions in Russia, the so-called sectaries, consider the existing social order as unjust and to be destroyed on the ground of the Gospel teaching taken in its true sense. Others regard it as unjust on the ground of the socialistic, communistic or anarchistic theories, which are springing up in the lower strata of the working people. Violence no longer rests on the belief in its utility, but only on the fact of its having existed so long, and being organized by the ruling classes who profit by it, so that those who are under their authority cannot extricate themselves from it. The governments of our day – all of them, the most despotic and the liberal alike – have become what Herzen* so well called 'Genghis Khan with the telegraph'; that is to say, organizations of violence based on no principle but the grossest tyranny, and at the same time taking advantage of all the means invented by science for the peaceful collective social activity of free and equal men, used by them to enslave and oppress their fellows.

Governments and the ruling classes no longer take their stand on right or even on the semblance of justice, but on a skilful organization carried to such a point of perfection by the aid of science that everyone is caught in the circle of violence and has no chance of escaping from it. This circle is made up now of four methods of working upon men, joined together like the links of a chain ring.

The first and oldest method is intimidation. This consists in representing the existing state organization – whatever it may be, a free republic or the most savage despotism – as something sacred and immutable, and therefore following any efforts to alter it with the most cruel punishments. This method is in use now – as it has been from olden times – wherever there is a government: in Russia against the so-called Nihilists, in

* Alexander Herzen (1812–70) – a Russian socialist thinker. [J. P.]

America against Anarchists, in France against Imperialists, Legitimists, Communards and Anarchists.

Railways, telegraphs, telephones, photographs, and the great perfection of the means of getting rid of men for years, without killing them, by solitary confinement, where, hidden from the world, they perish and are forgotten, and the many other modern inventions employed by government, give such power that when once authority has come into certain hands, the police, open and secret, the administration and prosecutors, jailers and executioners of all kinds, do their work so zealously that there is no chance of overturning the government, however cruel and senseless it may be.

The second method is corruption. It consists in plundering the industrious working people of their wealth by means of taxes and distributing it in satisfying the greed of officials, who are bound in return to support and keep up the oppression of the people. These bought officials, from the highest government ministers to the poorest copying clerks, make up an unbroken network of men bound together by the same interest – that of living at the expense of the people. They become the richer the more submissively they carry out the will of the government; and at all times and places, sticking at nothing, in all departments support by word and deed the violence of government, on which their own prosperity also rests.

The third method is what I can only describe as hypnotizing the people. This consists in checking the moral development of men, and by various suggestions keeping them back in the ideal of life, outgrown by mankind at large, on which the power of government rests. This hypnotizing process is organized at the present in the most complex manner and, starting from their earliest childhood, continues to act on men until the day of their death. It begins in their earliest years in the compulsory schools, created for this purpose, in which the children have instilled into them the ideas of life of their ancestors, which are in direct antagonism with the conscience of the modern world. In countries where there is a state religion, they teach the children the senseless blasphemies of the Church catechisms, together with the duty of obedience to their superiors. In republican states they teach them the savage superstition of patriotism and the same pretended obedience to the governing authorities.

The process is kept up during later years by the encouragement of religious and patriotic superstitions.

The religious superstition is encouraged by establishing, with money taken from the people, temples, processions, memorials and festivals, which, aided by painting, architecture, music and incense, intoxicate the people, and above all by the support of the clergy, whose duty consists in brutalizing the people and keeping them in a permanent state of stupefaction by their teaching, the solemnity of their services, their sermons, and their interference in private life – at births, deaths and marriages. The patriotic superstition is encouraged by the creation, with money taken from the people, of national fêtes, spectacles, monuments and festivals to dispose men to attach importance to their own nation, and to the aggrandizement of the state and its rulers, and to feel antagonism and even hatred for other nations. With these objects under despotic governments there is direct prohibition against printing and disseminating books to enlighten the people, and everyone who might rouse the people from their lethargy is exiled or imprisoned. Moreover, under every government without exception everything is kept back that might emancipate and everything encouraged that tends to corrupt the people, such as literary works tending to keep them in the barbarism of religious and patriotic superstition, all kinds of sensual amusements, spectacles, circuses, theatres, and even the physical means of inducing stupefaction, as tobacco and alcohol, which form the principal source of revenue of states. Even prostitution is encouraged, and not only recognized, but also even organized by the government in the majority of states. So much for the third method.

The fourth method consists in selecting from all the men who have been stupefied and enslaved by the three former methods a certain number, exposing them to special and intensified means of stupefaction and brutalization, and so making them into a passive instrument for carrying out all the cruelties and brutalities needed by the government. This result is attained by taking them at the youthful age, when men have not had time to form clear and definite principles of morals, and removing them from all natural and human conditions of life, home, family, kindred and useful labour. They are shut up together in barracks, dressed in special clothes, and worked upon by cries, drums, music and shining objects to go through certain daily actions invented for this purpose, and by this means are brought into an hypnotic condition in which they cease to be men and become mere senseless machines, submissive to the hypnotizer. These physically vigorous young men (in these days of universal conscription, all young men), hypnotized, armed with murderous weapons, always obedient to the governing authorities and ready for any act of violence at their command, constitute the fourth and principal method of enslaving men.

By this method the circle of violence is completed.

Intimidation, corruption and hypnotizing bring people into a condition in which they are willing to be soldiers; the soldiers give the power of punishing and plundering them (and purchasing officials with the spoils), and hypnotizing them and converting them in time into these same soldiers again.

The circle is complete, and there is no chance of breaking through it by force.

Some persons maintain that freedom from violence, or at least a great diminution of it, may be gained by the oppressed forcibly overturning the oppressive government and replacing it by a new one under which such violence and oppression will be unnecessary, but they deceive themselves and others, and their efforts do not better the position of the oppressed, but only make it worse. Their conduct only tends to increase the despotism of government. Their efforts only afford a plausible pretext for government to strengthen its power.

Even if we admit that under a combination of circumstances specially unfavourable for the government, as in France in 1870, any government might be forcibly overturned and the power transferred to other hands, the new authority would rarely be less oppressive than the old one; on the contrary, always having to defend itself against its dispossessed and exasperated enemies, it would be more despotic and cruel, as has always been the rule in all revolutions.

While socialists and communists regard the individualistic, capitalistic organization of society as an evil, and the anarchists regard as an evil all government whatever, there are royalists, conservatives and capitalists who consider any socialistic or communistic organization or anarchy as an evil, and all these parties have no means other than violence to bring men to agreement. Whichever of these parties was successful in bringing their schemes to pass must resort to support its authority to all the existing methods of violence, and even invent new ones.

The oppressed would be another set of people, and coercion would take some new form; but the violence and oppression would be unchanged or even more cruel, since hatred would be intensified by the struggle, and new forms of oppression would have been devised. So it has always been after all revolutions and all attempts at revolution, all conspiracies, and all violent changes of government. Every conflict only strengthens the means of oppression in the hands of those who happen at a given moment to be in power.

The position of our Christian society, and especially the ideals most current in it, prove this in a strikingly convincing way.

There remains now only one sphere of human life not encroached upon by government authority – that is the domestic, economic sphere, the sphere of private life and labour. And even this is now – thanks to the efforts of communists and socialists – being gradually encroached upon by government, so that labour and recreation, dwellings, dress and food will gradually, if the hopes of the reformers are successful, be prescribed and regulated by government.

The slow progress of eighteen centuries has brought the Christian nations again to the necessity of deciding the question they have evaded – the question of the acceptance or non-acceptance of Christ's teaching, and the question following upon it in social life of resistance or non-resistance to evil by force. But there is this difference, that whereas formerly men could accept or refuse to accept the solution given by Christ, now that solution cannot be avoided, since it alone can save men from the slavery in which they are caught like a net.

But it is not only the misery of the position that makes this inevitable.

While the pagan organization has been proved more and more false, the truth of the Christian religion has been growing more and more evident.

Not in vain have the best men of Christian humanity, who apprehended the truth by spiritual intuition, for eighteen centuries testified to it in spite of every menace, every privation and every suffering. By their martyrdom they passed on the truth to the masses, and impressed it on their hearts.

Christianity has penetrated into the consciousness of humanity, not only negatively by the demonstration of the impossibility of continuing in the pagan life, but also through its simplification, its increased clearness and freedom from the superstitions intermingled with it, and its diffusion through all classes of the population.

Eighteen centuries of Christianity have not passed without an effect even on those who accepted it only externally. These centuries have brought people so far that even while they continue to live the pagan life that is no longer consistent with the development of humanity, they not only see clearly all the wretchedness of their position, but in the depths of their souls they believe (they can only live through this belief) that the only salvation from this position is to be found in fulfilling the Christian doctrine in its true significance. As to the time and manner of salvation, opinions are divided according to the intellectual development and the prejudices of each society. But every person in the modern world recognizes that our salvation lies in fulfilling the law of Christ. Some believers in the supernatural character of Christianity hold that salvation will come when all men are brought to believe in Christ, whose second coming is at hand. Other believers in supernatural Christianity hold that salvation will come through the Church, which will draw all men into its fold, train them in the Christian virtues, and transform their lives. A third section, who do not admit the divinity of Christ, hold that the salvation of mankind will be brought about by slow and gradual progress, through which the pagan principles of our existence will be replaced by the principles of liberty, equality and fraternity – that is, by Christian principles. A fourth section, who believe in the social revolution, hold that salvation will come when through a violent revolution men are forced into community of property, abolition of government and collective instead of individual industry – that is to say, the realization of one side of the Christian doctrine. In one way or another all men of our day in their inner consciousness condemn the existing effete pagan order, and admit, often unconsciously and while regarding themselves as hostile to Christianity, that our salvation is only to be found in the application of the Christian doctrine, or parts of it, in its true significance to our daily life.

Christianity cannot, as its founder said, be realized by the majority of men all at once; it must grow like a huge tree from a tiny seed. And so it has grown, and now has reached its full development, not yet in actual life, but in the conscience of men of today.

Now not only the minority, who have always comprehended Christianity by spiritual intuition, but also all the vast majority who seem so far from it in their social existence, recognize its true significance.

Look at individual men in their private life, listen to their standards of conduct in their judgement of one another; hear not only their public utterances, but the counsels given by parents and guardians to the young in their charge; and you will see that, far as their social life based on violence may be from realizing Christian truth, in their private life what is considered good by all without exception is nothing but the Christian virtues; what is considered as bad is nothing but the anti-Christian vices. Those who consecrate their lives self-sacrificingly to the service of humanity are regarded as the best men. The selfish, who make use of the misfortunes of others for their own advantage, are regarded as the worst of men.

Though some non-Christian ideals, such as strength, courage and wealth, are still worshipped by a few who have not been penetrated by the Christian spirit, these ideals are out of date and are abandoned, if not by all, at least by all those regarded as the best people. There are no ideals, other than the Christian ideals, which are accepted by all and regarded as binding on all.

The position of our Christian humanity, if you look at it from the outside with all its cruelty and degradation of men, is terrible indeed. But if one looks at it within, in its inner consciousness, the spectacle it presents is absolutely different.

All the evil of our life seems to exist only because it has been so for so long; those who do the evil have not had time yet to learn how to act otherwise, though they do not want to act as they do.

All the evil seems to exist through some cause independent of the conscience of men.

Strange and contradictory as it seems, all men of the present day hate the very social order they are themselves supporting.

I think it is Max Müller* who describes the amazement of an Indian convert to Christianity, who after absorbing the essence of the Christian doctrine came to Europe and saw the actual life of Christians. He could not recover from his astonishment at the complete contrast between the reality and what he had expected to find among Christian nations. If we feel no astonishment at the contrast between our convictions and our conduct, that is because the influences, tending to obscure the contrast, produce an effect upon us too. We need only look at our life from the point of view of that Indian, who understood Christianity in its true significance, without any compromises or concessions, we need but look at the savage brutalities of which our life is full, to be appalled at the contradictions in the midst of which we live often without observing them.

We need only recall the preparations for war, the machine guns, the silver-gilt bullets, the torpedoes, and – the Red Cross; the solitary prison cells, the experiments of execution by electricity – and the care of the hygienic welfare of prisoners; the philanthropy of the rich, and their life, which produces the poor they are benefiting.

* Max Müller (1823–1900) – a German philologist and Orientalist. [J. P.]

And these inconsistencies are not, as it might seem, because men pretend to be Christians while they are really pagans, but because of something lacking in men, or some kind of force hindering them from being what they already feel themselves to be in their consciousness, and what they genuinely wish to be. Men of the present day do not merely pretend to hate oppression, inequality, class distinction and every kind of cruelty to animals as well as human beings. They genuinely detest all this, but they do not know how to put a stop to it, or perhaps cannot decide to give up what preserves it all, and seems to them necessary.

Indeed, ask every man separately whether he thinks it laudable and worthy of a man of this age to hold a position from which he receives a salary disproportionate to his work; to take from the people – often in poverty – taxes to be spent on constructing cannons, torpedoes and other instruments of butchery, so as to make war on people with whom we wish to be at peace, and who feel the same wish in regard to us; or to receive a salary for devoting one's whole life to constructing these instruments of butchery, or to preparing oneself and others for the work of murder. And ask him whether it is laudable and worthy of a man, and suitable for a Christian, to employ himself, for a salary, in seizing wretched, misguided, often illiterate and drunken, creatures because they appropriate the property of others – on a much smaller scale than we do – or because they kill men in a different fashion from that in which we undertake to do it – and shutting them in prison for it, ill treating them and killing them; and whether it is laudable and worthy of a man and a Christian to preach for a salary to the people not Christianity, but superstitions that one knows to be stupid and pernicious; and whether it is laudable and worthy of a man to rob his neighbour for his gratification of what he wants to satisfy his simplest needs, as the great landowners do; or to force him to exhausting labour beyond his strength to augment one's wealth, as do factory owners and manufacturers; or to profit by the poverty of men to increase one's gains, as merchants do. And everyone taken separately, especially if one's remarks are directed at someone else, not himself, will answer, 'No!' And yet the very man who sees all the baseness of those actions, of his own free will, uncoerced by anyone, often even for no pecuniary profit, but only from childish vanity, for a china cross, a scrap of ribbon, a bit of fringe he is allowed to wear, will enter military service, become a magistrate or justice of the peace, commissioner, archbishop or beadle, though in fulfilling these offices he must commit acts the baseness and shamefulness of which he cannot fail to recognize.

I know that many of these men will confidently try to prove that they have reasons for regarding their position as legitimate and quite indispensable. They will say in their defence that authority is given by God, that the functions of the State are indispensable for the welfare of humanity, that property is not opposed to Christianity, that the rich young man was only commanded to sell all he had and give to the poor if he wished to be perfect, that the existing distribution of property and our commercial system must always remain as they are, and are to the advantage of all, and so on. But, however much they try to deceive themselves and others, they all know that what they are doing is opposed to all the beliefs that they profess, and in the depths of their souls, when they are left alone with their conscience, they are ashamed and miserable at the recollection of it, especially if the baseness of their action has been pointed out to them. A man of the present day, whether he believes in the divinity of Christ or not, cannot fail to see that to assist in the capacity of tsar, government minister, governor or commissioner in taking from a poor family its last cow for taxes to be spent on cannons, or on the pay and pensions of idle officials, who live in luxury and are worse than useless; or in putting into prison some man we have ourselves corrupted, and throwing his family on the streets; or in plundering and butchering in war; or in inculcating savage and idolatrous superstitions in the place of the law of Christ; or in impounding the cow found on one's land, though it belongs to a man who has no land; or to cheat the workman in a factory, by imposing fines for accidentally spoiled articles; or making a poor man pay double the value for anything simply because he is in the direst poverty – not a man of the present day can fail to know that all these actions are base and disgraceful, and that they need not do them. They all know it. They know that what they are doing is wrong, and would not do it for anything in the world if they had the power of resisting the forces that shut their eyes to the criminality of their actions and impel them to commit them.

In nothing is the pitch of inconsistency modern life has attained to so evident as in universal conscription, which is the last resource and the final expression of violence.

Indeed, it is only because this state of universal armament has been brought about gradually and imperceptibly, and because governments have exerted, in maintaining it, every resource of intimidation, corruption, brutalization and violence, that we do not see its flagrant inconsistency with the Christian ideas and sentiments by which the modern world is permeated.

We are so accustomed to the inconsistency that we do not see all the hideous folly and immorality of men voluntarily choosing the profession of butchery as though it were an honourable career, of poor wretches submitting to conscription, or in countries where compulsory service has not been introduced, of people voluntarily abandoning a life of industry to recruit soldiers and train them as murderers. We know that all of these men are either Christians, or profess humane and liberal principles, and they know that they thus become partly responsible – through universal conscription, personally responsible – for the most insane, aimless and brutal murders. And yet they all do it.

More than that, in Germany, where compulsory service first originated, Caprivi* has given expression to what had been hitherto so assiduously concealed – that is, that the men that the soldiers will have to kill are not foreigners alone, but their own countrymen, the very working people from whom they themselves are taken. And this admission has not opened people's eyes, has not horrified them! They still go like sheep to the slaughter, and submit to everything required of them.

And that is not all. The Emperor of Germany† has lately

* Leo von Caprivi (1831–99) – German statesman and chancellor. [J. P.]
† Wilhelm II (1859–1941) – last German emperor. [J. P.]

shown still more clearly the duties of the army, by thanking and rewarding a soldier for killing a defenceless citizen who made his approach incautiously. By rewarding an action always regarded as base and cowardly even by men on the lowest level of morality, Wilhelm II has shown that a soldier's chief duty – the one most appreciated by the authorities – is that of executioner; and not a professional executioner who kills only condemned criminals, but one ready to butcher any innocent man at the word of command.

And even that is not all. In 1892, the same Wilhelm, the *enfant terrible* of state authority, who says plainly what other people only think, in addressing some soldiers gave public utterance to the following speech, which was reported next day in thousands of newspapers: 'Conscripts!' he said, 'you have sworn fidelity to *me* before the altar and the minister of God! You are still too young to understand all the importance of what has been said here; let your care before all things be to obey the orders and instructions given you. You have sworn fidelity to *me*, lads of my guard; *that means that you are now my soldiers, that you have given yourselves to me body and soul.* For you there is now but one enemy, *my* enemy. *In these days of socialistic sedition it may come to pass that I command you to fire on your own kindred, your brothers, even your own fathers and mothers – which God forbid!* – even then you are bound to obey my orders without hesitation.'

This man expresses what all sensible rulers think, but studiously conceal. He says openly that the soldiers are in *his* service, at *his* disposal, and must be ready for *his* advantage to murder even their brothers and fathers.

In the most brutal words he frankly exposes all the horrors and criminality for which men prepare themselves in entering the army, and the depths of ignominy to which they fall in promising obedience. Like a bold hypnotizer, he tests the degree of insensibility of the hypnotized subject. He touches his skin with a red-hot iron; the skin smokes and scorches, but the sleeper does not awake.

This miserable man, imbecile and drunk with power, outrages in this utterance everything that can be sacred for a man of the modern world. And yet all the Christians, liberals and cultivated people, far from resenting this outrage, did not even observe it.

The last, the most extreme test is put before men in its coarsest form. And they do not seem even to notice that it is a test, that there is any choice about it. They seem to think there is no course open but slavish submission. One would have thought these insane words, which outrage everything a man of the present day holds sacred, must rouse indignation. But there has been nothing of the kind.

All the young men through the whole of Europe are exposed year after year to this test, and with very few exceptions they renounce all that a man can hold sacred, all express their readiness to kill their brothers, even their fathers, at the bidding of the first crazy creature dressed up in a livery with red and gold trimming, and only wait to be told where and when they are to kill. And they actually are ready.

Every savage has something he holds sacred, something for which he is ready to suffer, and something he will not consent to do. But what is it that is sacred to the civilized man of today? They say to him, 'You must become my slave, and this slavery may force you to kill even your own father'; and he, often very well educated, trained in all the sciences at the university, quietly puts his head under the yoke. They dress him up in a clown's costume and order him to cut capers, turn, twist, bow and kill. He does it all submissively. And when they let him go, he seems to shake himself and go back to his former life, and he continues to discourse upon the dignity of man, liberty, equality and fraternity as before.

'Yes, but what is one to do?' people often ask in genuine perplexity. 'If everyone would stand out it would be something, but by myself, I shall only suffer without doing any good to anyone.'

And that is true. A man with the social conception of life cannot resist. The aim of his life is his personal welfare. It is better for his personal welfare for him to submit, and he submits.

Whatever they do to him, however they torture or humiliate

him, he will submit, for, alone, he can do nothing; he has no principle for the sake of which he could resist violence alone. And those who control them never allow them to unite together. It is often said that the invention of terrible weapons of destruction will put an end to war. That is an error. As the means of extermination are improved, the means of reducing men who hold the state conception of life to submission can be improved to correspond. They may slaughter them by thousands, by millions, they may tear them to pieces, and still they will march to war like senseless cattle. Some will want beating to make them move, others will be proud to go if they are allowed to wear a scrap of ribbon or gold lace.

And of this mass of men so brutalized as to be ready to promise to kill their own parents, the social reformers – conservatives, liberals, socialists and anarchists – propose to form a rational and moral society. What sort of moral and rational society can be formed out of such elements? With warped and rotten planks you cannot build a house, however you put them together. And to form a rational moral society of such men is just as impossible a task. They can be formed into nothing but a herd of cattle, driven by the shouts and whips of the herdsmen. As indeed they are.

So, then, we have on one side men calling themselves Christians, and professing the principles of liberty, equality and fraternity, and along with that ready, in the name of liberty, to submit to the most slavish degradation; in the name of equality, to accept the crudest, most senseless division of men by externals merely into higher and lower classes, allies and enemies; and, in the name of fraternity, ready to murder their brothers.

The contradiction between life and conscience and the misery resulting from it have reached the extreme limit and can go no further. The state organization of life based on violence, the aim of which was the security of personal, family and social welfare, has come to the point of renouncing the very objects for which it was founded – it has reduced men to absolute renunciation and loss of the welfare it was to secure.

The first half of the prophecy has been fulfilled in the

generation of men who have not accepted Christ's teaching. Their descendants have been brought now to the absolute necessity of putting the truth of the second half to the test of experience.

[Translated by Constance Garnett]

FROM *WHAT IS ART?* [1896]

In order properly to define art, it is necessary, first, to cease to consider it as a means to pleasure and as one of the conditions of human life. Viewing it in this way we cannot fail to observe that art is one of the means of communication between people.

Every work of art causes the receiver to enter into a relationship both with him who produced, or is producing, the art, and with all those who, simultaneously, previously or subsequently, receive the same artistic impression.

Speech, transmitting the thoughts and experiences of men, serves as a means of union among them, and art acts in a similar manner. The peculiarity of this latter means of communication, distinguishing it from communication by means of words, consists in this, that whereas by words a man transmits his thoughts to another, by means of art he transmits his feelings.

The activity of art is based on the fact that a man, receiving through his sense of hearing or sight another man's expression of feeling, is capable of experiencing the emotion which moved the man who expressed it. To take the simplest example; one man laughs, and another who hears becomes merry; or a man weeps, and another who hears feels sorrow. A man is excited or irritated, and another man seeing him comes to a similar state of mind. By his movements or by the sounds of his voice, a man expresses courage and determination or sadness and calmness, and this state of mind passes on to others. A man suffers, expressing his sufferings by groans and spasms, and this suffering transmits itself to other people; a man expresses his feeling of admiration, devotion, fear, respect or love to certain objects, persons or phenomena, and others are infected by the same feelings of admiration, devotion, fear, respect or love to the same objects, persons and phenomena.

And it is upon this capacity of man to absorb another man's life experience that the activity of art is based.

If a man infects another or others directly, immediately, by his appearance or by the sounds he gives vent to at the very time he experiences the feeling; if he causes another man to yawn when he himself cannot help yawning, or to laugh or cry when he himself is obliged to laugh or cry, or to suffer when he himself is suffering – that does not amount to art.

Art begins when one person, with the object of joining another or others to himself in one and the same feeling, expresses that feeling by certain indications. To take the simplest example: a boy, having experienced, let us say, fear on encountering a wolf, relates that encounter; and, in order to evoke in others the feeling he has experienced, describes himself, his condition before the encounter, the surroundings, the woods, his own lightheartedness, and then the wolf's appearance, its movements, the distance between himself and the wolf, etc. All this is art only if the boy, when telling the story, again experiences the feelings he had lived through and infects the hearers and compels them to feel what the narrator had experienced. Even if the boy had not seen a wolf but had frequently been afraid of one, and if, wishing to evoke in others the fear he had felt, he invented an encounter with a wolf and recounted it so as to make his hearers share the feelings he experienced when he feared the wolf, that also would be art. And just in the same way it is art if a man, having experienced either the fear of suffering or the attraction of enjoyment (whether in reality or in imagination) expresses these feelings on canvas or in marble so that others are infected by them. And it is also art if a man feels or imagines to himself feelings of delight, gladness, sorrow, despair, courage or despondency and the transition from one to another of these feelings, and expresses these feelings by sounds so that the hearers are infected by them and experience them as they were experienced by the composer.

The feelings with which the artist infects others may be incredibly various – very strong or very weak, very important or very insignificant, very bad or very good: feelings of love for one's own country, self-devotion and submission to fate or to God expressed in a drama, raptures of lovers described in a novel, feelings of voluptuousness expressed in a picture, courage expressed in a triumphal march, merriment evoked by a dance, humour evoked by a funny story, the feeling of quietness transmitted by an evening landscape or by a lullaby, or the feeling of admiration evoked by a beautiful arabesque – it is all art.

If only the spectators or auditors are infected by the feelings which the author has felt, it is art.

To evoke in oneself a feeling one has once experienced, and having evoked it in oneself, then, by means of movements, lines, colours, sounds or forms expressed in words, so to transmit that feeling that others may experience the same feeling – this is the activity of art.

Art is a human activity consisting in this, that one man consciously, by means of certain external signs, hands on to others feelings he has lived through, and that other people are infected by these feelings and also experience them.

Art is not, as the metaphysicians say, the manifestation of some mysterious idea of beauty or God; it is not, as the aesthetical physiologists say, a game in which man lets off his excess of stored-up energy; it is not the expression of man's emotions by external signs; it is not the production of pleasing objects; and, above all, it is not pleasure; but it is a means of union among men, joining them together in the same feelings, and indispensable for the life and progress towards well-being of individuals and of humanity.

As, thanks to man's capacity to express thoughts by words, every man may know all that has been done for him in the realms of thought by all humanity before his day, and can in the present, thanks to this capacity to understand the thoughts of others, become a sharer in their activity and can himself hand on to his contemporaries and descendants the thoughts he has assimilated from others, as well as those which have arisen within himself; so, thanks to man's capacity to be infected with the feelings of others by means of art, all that is being lived through by his contemporaries is accessible to him, as well as the feelings experienced by men thousands of years ago, and he is also able to transmit his own feelings to others.

If people lacked this capacity to receive the thoughts conceived by the men who preceded them and to pass on to others their own thoughts, men would be like wild beasts, or like Kaspar Hauser.*

And if men lacked this other capacity of being infected by art, people might be almost more savage still, and, above all, more separated from, and more hostile to, one another.

And therefore the activity of art is a most important one, as important as the activity of speech itself and as generally diffused.

We are accustomed to understand art to be only what we hear and see in theatres, concerts and exhibitions, together with buildings, statues, poems, novels . . . But all this is but the smallest part of the art by which we communicate with each other in life. All human life is filled with works of art of every kind – from cradlesong, jest, mimicry, the ornamentation of houses, dress and utensils, up to church services, buildings, monuments and triumphal processions. It is all artistic activity. So that by art, in the limited sense of the word, we do not mean all human activity transmitting feelings, but only that part which we for some reason select from it and to which we attach special importance.

This special importance has always been given by all men to that part of this activity which transmits feelings flowing from their religious perception, and this small part of art they have specifically called art, attaching to it the full meaning of the word.

That was how men of old – Socrates, Plato and Aristotle – looked on art. Thus did the Hebrew prophets and the ancient Christians regard art; thus it was, and still is, understood by the Mohammedans, and thus it still is understood by religious folk among our own peasantry.

* Hauser was a wild orphan once thought to have been raised by wolves in German forests. [J. P.]

Some teachers of mankind – as Plato in his *Republic* and people such as the primitive Christians, the strict Mohammedans, and the Buddhists – have gone so far as to repudiate all art.

People viewing art in this way (in contradiction to the prevalent view of today which regards any art as good if only it affords pleasure) considered, and consider, that art (as contrasted with speech, which need not be listened to) is so highly dangerous in its power to infect people against their wills that mankind will lose far less by banishing all art than by tolerating each and every art.

Evidently such people were wrong in repudiating all art, for they denied that which cannot be denied – one of the indispensable means of communication, without which mankind could not exist. But not less wrong are the people of civilized European society of our class and day in favouring any art if it but serves beauty, i.e., gives people pleasure.

Formerly people feared lest among the works of art there might chance to be some causing corruption, and they prohibited art altogether. Now they only fear lest they should be deprived of any enjoyment art can afford, and patronize any art. And I think the last error is much grosser than the first and that its consequences are far more harmful.

Art, in our society, has been so perverted that not only has bad art come to be considered good, but even the very perception of what art really is has been lost. In order to be able to speak about the art of our society, it is, therefore, first of all necessary to distinguish art from counterfeit art.

There is one clear indication distinguishing real art from its counterfeit, namely, the infectiousness of art. If a man, without exercising effort and without altering his standpoint on reading, hearing or seeing another man's work, experiences a mental condition which unites him with that man and with other people who also partake of that work of art, then the object evoking that condition is a work of art. And however poetical, realistic, effectful or interesting a work may be, it is not a work of art if it does not evoke that feeling (quite distinct from all other feelings) of joy and of spiritual union with another (the author) and with others (those who are also infected by it).

It is true that this indication is an internal one, and that there are people who have forgotten what the action of real art is, who expect something else from art (in our society the great majority are in this state), and that therefore such people may mistake for this aesthetic feeling the feeling of diversion and a certain excitement which they receive from counterfeits of art. But though it is impossible to undeceive these people, just as it is impossible to convince a man suffering from Daltonism [colour blindness] that green is not red, yet, for all that, this indication remains perfectly definite to those whose feeling for art is neither perverted nor atrophied, and it clearly distinguishes the feeling produced by art from all other feelings.

The chief peculiarity of this feeling is that the receiver of a true artistic impression is so united to the artist that he feels as if the work were his own and not someone else's – as if what it expresses were just what he had long been wishing to express. A real work of art destroys, in the consciousness of the receiver, the separation between himself and the artist – not that alone, but also between himself and all whose minds receive this work of art. In this freeing of our personality from its separation and isolation, in this uniting of it with others, lies the chief characteristic and the great attractive force of art.

If a man is infected by the author's condition of soul, if he feels this emotion and this union with others, then the object which has effected this is art; but if there be no such infection, if there be not this union with the author and with others who are moved by the same work – then it is not art. And not only is infection a sure sign of art, but the degree of infectiousness is also the sole measure of excellence in art.

The stronger the infection, the better is the art as art, speaking now apart from its subject matter, i.e., not considering the quality of the feelings it transmits.

And the degree of the infectiousness of art depends on three conditions:

(1) On the greater or lesser individuality of the feeling transmitted;
(2) on the greater or lesser clearness with which the feeling is transmitted;
(3) on the sincerity of the artist, i.e., on the greater or lesser force with which the artist himself feels the emotion he transmits.

The more individual the feeling transmitted the more strongly does it act on the receiver; the more individual the state of soul into which he is transferred, the more pleasure does the receiver obtain, and therefore the more readily and strongly does he join in it.

The clearness of expression assists infection because the receiver, who mingles in consciousness with the author, is the better satisfied the more clearly the feeling is transmitted, which, as it seems to him, he has long known and felt, and for which he has only now found expression.

But most of all is the degree of infectiousness of art increased by the degree of sincerity in the artist. As soon as the spectator, hearer or reader feels that the artist is infected by his own production, and writes, sings or plays for himself, and not merely to act on others, this mental condition of the artist infects the receiver; and, contrariwise, as soon as the spectator, reader or hearer feels that the author is not writing, singing or playing for his own satisfaction – does not himself feel what he wishes to express – but is doing it for him, the receiver, a resistance immediately springs up, and the most individual and the newest feelings and the cleverest technique not only fail to produce any infection but actually repel.

I have mentioned three conditions of contagiousness in art, but they may be all summed up into one, the last, sincerity, i.e., that the artist should be impelled by an inner need to express his feeling. That condition includes the first; for if the artist is sincere he will express the feeling as he experienced it. And as each man is different from everyone else, his feeling will be individual for everyone else; and the more individual it is – the more the artist has drawn it from the depths of his nature –

the more sympathetic and sincere will it be. And this same sincerity will impel the artist to find a clear expression of the feeling which he wishes to transmit.

Therefore this third condition – sincerity – is the most important of the three. It is always complied with in peasant art, and this explains why such art always acts so powerfully; but it is a condition almost entirely absent from our upper-class art, which is continually produced by artists actuated by personal aims of covetousness or vanity.

Such are the three conditions which divide art from its counterfeits, and which also decide the quality of every work of art apart from its subject matter.

The absence of any one of these conditions excludes a work from the category of art and relegates it to that of art's counterfeits. If the work does not transmit the artist's peculiarity of feeling and is therefore not individual, if it is unintelligibly expressed, or if it has not proceeded from the author's inner need for expression – it is not a work of art. If all these conditions are present, even in the smallest degree, then the work, even if a weak one, is yet a work of art.

The presence in various degrees of these three conditions – individuality, clearness and sincerity – decides the merit of a work of art as art, apart from subject matter. All works of art take rank of merit according to the degree in which they fulfil the first, the second and the third of these conditions. In one the individuality of the feeling transmitted may predominate; in another, clearness of expression; in a third, sincerity; while a fourth may have sincerity and individuality but be deficient in clearness; a fifth, individuality and clearness but less sincerity; and so forth, in all possible degrees and combinations.

[Translated by Aylmer Maude]

LETTER ON NON-RESISTANCE TO ERNEST HOWARD CROSBY OF NEW YORK [1896]

DEAR MR CROSBY,

I am very glad to have news of your activity, and to hear that your work begins to attract attention. Fifty years ago Lloyd Garrison's Declaration of Non-Resistance* only estranged people from him; and Ballou's† fifty years' labour in the same direction was constantly met by a conspiracy of silence. I now read with great pleasure in the *Voice* admirable thoughts by American writers on this question of Non-Resistance. I need only demur to the notion expressed by Mr Bemis. It is an old but unfounded libel upon Christ to suppose that the expulsion of the cattle from the temple indicates that Jesus beat people with a whip and advised his disciples to behave in the same way.‡

The opinions expressed by these writers, especially by Heber Newton and G. D. Herron, are quite correct, but unfortunately they do not reply to the question Christ put to men, but to

* The Declaration of Non-Resistance drawn up by William Lloyd Garrison was adopted at a Peace Convention held in Boston, 18–20 September 1838. [A. M.]

† Adin Ballou (1803–1890), a Massachusetts Restorationist minister, founder of Hopedale Community (1842–56) and author of *Christian Non-Resistance*. [A. M.]

‡ Christ's use of a scourge is mentioned only in St John's Gospel. Our Revised Version, following the Greek, indicates that the scourge was for 'the sheep and the oxen'. [A. M.]

another question which has been substituted for it by those chief and most dangerous opponents of Christianity – the so-called 'orthodox' ecclesiastical authorities.

Mr Higginson says, 'I do not believe Non-Resistance admissible as a universal rule.' Heber Newton says that 'People's opinion as to the practical results of the application of Christ's teaching will depend on the extent of people's belief in his authority.' Carlos Martyn considers 'The transition stage in which we live is not suited for the application of the doctrine of Non-Resistance.' G. D. Herron holds 'That to obey the law of Non-Resistance we must learn how to apply it to life.' Mrs Livermore, thinking that the law of Non-Resistance can be fully obeyed only in the future, says the same.

All these views refer to the question, 'What would happen if people were all obliged to obey the law of Non-Resistance?' But, in the first place, it is impossible to oblige everyone to accept this law. Secondly, if it were possible to do so, such compulsion would in itself be a direct negation of the very principle set up. Oblige all men to refrain from violence! Who then would enforce the decision? Thirdly, and this is the chief point, the question as put by Christ is not at all, Can Non-Resistance become a general law for humanity? but, How must each man act to fulfil his allotted task, to save his soul, and to do the will of God? – which are all really one and the same thing.

Christian teaching does not lay down laws for everybody, and does not say to people, 'You all, for fear of punishment, must obey such and such rules, and then you will all be happy'; but it explains to each individual his position in relation to the world, and lets him see what results, for him individually, inevitably flow from that relation. Christianity says to man (and to each man separately) that his personal life can have no rational meaning if he counts it as belonging to himself, or as having for its aim worldly happiness for himself or for other people. This is so because the happiness he seeks is unattainable: (1) because, as all beings strive after worldly advantages, the gain of one is the loss of others, and it is most probable that each individual will incur much superfluous suffering in the course of his vain efforts to seize unattainable blessings; (2) because, even if a man get worldly advantages, the more he obtains the less they satisfy him and the more he hankers after fresh ones; (3) and chiefly because the longer a man lives, the more inevitable becomes the approach of old age, sickness and of death, destroying all possibility of worldly advantages.

So that if a man considers his life his own, to be spent in seeking worldly happiness for himself as well as for others, then that life can have no rational explanation for him.

Life has a rational meaning only when one understands that to consider our life our own, or to see its aim in worldly happiness for ourselves or for other people, is a delusion; that a man's life does not belong to him who has received it, but to Him who has given it; and its object should, therefore, be, not the attainment of worldly happiness either for one's self or for other individuals, but solely the fulfilment of the will of Him who created this life.

This conception alone gives life a rational meaning, and makes its aim (which is to fulfil the will of God) attainable. And, most important of all, only when enlightened by this conception does man see clearly the right direction for his own activity. Man is then no longer destined to suffer and to despair, as was inevitable under the former conception.

'The universe and I in it,' says to himself a man with this conception, 'exist by the will of God. I cannot know the whole of the universe (for in its immensity it transcends my comprehension), nor can I know my own position in it, but I do know with certainty what God, Who has sent me into the world (infinite in time and space, and therefore incomprehensible to me), demands from me. This is revealed to me (1) by the collective wisdom of the best men who have gone before me, i.e., by tradition, (2) by my own reason, and (3) by my heart, i.e., by the highest aspiration of my nature.

Tradition (the collective wisdom of our greatest forerunners) tells me that I should do unto others as I would that they should do unto me.

My reason shows me that only by all men acting thus is the highest happiness for all men attainable.

Only when I yield myself to that intuition of love which demands obedience to this law is my own heart happy and at rest. And not only can I then know how to act, but I can and do discern the work to co-operate for which my activity was designed and is required.

I cannot fathom God's whole design, for the sake of which the universe exists and lives; but the Divine work which is being accomplished in this world and in which I participate by living is comprehensible to me.

This work is the annihilation of discord and strife among men and among all creatures, and the establishment of the highest unity and concord and love.

It is the fulfilment of the promises of the Hebrew prophet who foretold a time when all men should be taught by truth, when spears should be turned into reaping-hooks, swords be beaten to ploughshares, and the lion lies down with the lamb.

So that a man of Christian intelligence not only knows what he has to do, but he also understands the work he is doing.

He has to act so as to co-operate towards the establishment of the kingdom of God on earth. For this a man must obey his intuition of God's will, i.e., must act lovingly towards others, as he would that others should act towards him.

Thus the intuitive demands of man's soul coincide with the external aim of life which he sees before him.

According to Christian teaching, man in this world is God's labourer. A labourer does not know his master's whole design, but he does know the immediate object which he is set to work at. He receives definite instructions what to do, and especially what not to do, lest he hinder the attainment of the very aims towards which his labour should tend. For the rest he has full liberty given him. And, therefore, for a man who has grasped the Christian conception of life, the meaning of his life is perfectly plain and reasonable, nor can he have a moment's hesitation as to *how* he should act, or *what* he should do to fulfil the object for which he lives.

And yet in spite of such a twofold indication (clear and indubitable to a man of Christian understanding) of what is the real aim and meaning of human life, and of what men should do and should not do, we find people (and people calling themselves Christians) who decide that, in such and such circumstances, men ought to abandon God's law and reason's guidance and to act in opposition to them, because (according to their conception) the effects of actions performed in submission to God's law may be detrimental or inconvenient.

According to the law contained alike in tradition, in our reason and in our hearts, man should always do unto others as he would that they should do unto him; he should always co-operate in the development of love and union among created beings. But, in the judgement of these far-sighted people, on the contrary, as long as in their opinion it is premature to obey this law, man should do violence – imprison or kill people – and thereby evoke anger and venom instead of loving union in the hearts of men. It is as though a bricklayer, set to do a particular task and knowing that he was co-operating with others to build a house, after receiving clear and precise instructions from the master himself how to build a certain wall, accepted orders from some fellow-bricklayers (who like himself knew neither the plan of the house, nor what would fit in with it) to cease building his wall, and, instead, to pull down a wall that other workmen had erected.

Astonishing delusion! A being who breathes today and has vanished tomorrow receives one definite indubitable law to guide him through the brief term of his life; but, instead of obeying that law, he prefers to fancy that he knows what is necessary, advantageous and well-timed for men and for all the world – this world which continually changes and evolves – and for the sake of some advantage (which each man pictures after his own fancy) he decides that he and other people should, temporarily, abandon the indubitable law given to him and to all men, and should act, not as he would that others should act towards him, nor to bring love into the world – but should do violence, imprison, kill and bring into the world enmity whenever it seems to him advisable to do so. And he decides to act thus, though he knows that the most horrible cruelties, martyrdoms and murders – from the Inquisition, and the murders and horrors of all the revolutions, down to the brutalities of contemporary Anarchists and their slaughter by the established authorities – have only occurred because people will imagine that they know what is necessary for mankind and for the world. But are there not always, at any given moment, two opposite parties, each of which declares that it is necessary to use force against the other? The 'law-and-order' party against the Anarchist, the Anarchist against the 'law-and-order' men; English against Americans, and Americans against English; Germans against English, and English against Germans, and so forth in all possible combinations and rearrangements.

A man enlightened by Christianity sees that he has no reason to abandon the law of God, given to enable him to walk sure-footedly through life, in order to follow the chance, inconstant and often contradictory demands of men. But besides this, if he has lived a Christian life for some time and has developed in himself a moral Christian sensibility, he literally cannot act as people demand of him. Not his reason alone but his feeling also makes it impossible.

To many people of our society it would be impossible to torture or kill a baby, even if they were told that by so doing they could save hundreds of other people. And in the same way, a man who has developed a Christian sensibility of heart finds a whole series of actions become impossible for him. For instance, a Christian who is obliged to take part in judicial proceedings in which a man may be sentenced to death, or who is obliged to take part in evictions or in debating a proposal leading to war, or to participate in preparations for war (not to mention war itself), is in a position parallel to that of a kindly man called on to torture or to kill a baby. It is not reason alone that forbids him to do what is demanded of him; he feels instinctively that he *cannot* do it. For certain actions are morally impossible, just as others are physically impossible. As a man cannot lift a mountain, and as a kindly man cannot kill an infant, so a man living a Christian life cannot take part in deeds of violence. Of what value to him, then, are arguments about the imaginary advantages of doing what it is morally impossible for him to do?

But how is a man to act when he sees clearly the evil of

following the law of love and its corollary law of Non-Resistance? How (to use the stock example) is a man to act when he sees a robber killing or outraging a child, and he can only save the child by killing the robber?

When such a case is put, it is generally assumed that the only possible reply is that one should kill the robber to save the child. But this answer is given so quickly and decidedly only because we are all so accustomed to the use of violence – not only to save a child, but even to prevent a neighbouring Government altering its frontier at the expense of ours, or someone from smuggling lace across that frontier, or even to defend our garden fruit from a passer-by.

It is assumed that to save the child the robber should be killed. But it is only necessary to consider the question, on what grounds a man (whether he be or be not a Christian) ought to act so, in order to come to the conclusion that such action has no reasonable foundation, and only seems to us necessary because up to two thousand years ago such conduct was considered right, and a habit of acting so was formed. Why should a non-Christian – not acknowledging God, nor regarding the fulfilment of His will as the aim of life – decide to kill the robber in order to defend the child? By killing the robber, he certainly kills; whereas he cannot know positively whether the robber would have killed the child or not. But letting that pass, who shall say whether the child's life was more needed, was better, than the robber's life?

Surely, if the non-Christian knows not God nor sees life's meaning in the performance of His will, the only rule for his actions must be a reckoning, a conception, of what is more profitable for him and for all men: a continuation of the robber's life or of the child's. To decide that, he needs to know what would become of the child whom he saves, and what – had he not killed him – would have been the future of the robber he kills. And as he cannot know this, the non-Christian has no sufficient rational ground for killing a robber to save a child.

If a man is a Christian, and consequently acknowledges God and sees the meaning of life in fulfilling His will, then, however ferocious the robber, however innocent and lovely the child, he has even less ground to abandon the God-given law and to do to the robber what the robber wishes to do to the child. He may plead with the robber, may interpose his own body between the robber and the victim, but there is one thing he cannot do: he cannot deliberately abandon the law he has received from God, the fulfilment of which alone gives meaning to his life. Very probably bad education, or his animal nature, may cause a man (Christian or non-Christian) to kill the robber, not only to save the child, but even to save himself or his purse, but it does not follow that he is right in acting thus, nor that he should accustom himself or others to think such conduct right.

What it does show is that, notwithstanding a coating of education and of Christianity, the habits of the Stone Age are yet so strong in man, that he still commits actions long since condemned by his reasonable conscience.

I see a robber killing a child, and I can save the child by killing the robber – therefore in certain cases violence must be used to resist evil. A man's life is in danger, and can be saved only by my telling a lie – therefore in certain cases one must lie. A man is starving, and one can save him only by stealing – therefore in certain cases one must steal.

I lately read a story by Coppée, in which an orderly kills his officer, whose life was insured, and thereby saves the honour and the family of the officer. Therefore in certain cases one must kill.

Such inventions, and the deductions from them, only prove that there are men who know that it is not well to steal, to lie or to kill, but who are still so unwilling that people should cease to do these things, that they use all their mental powers to invent excuses for such conduct. There is no moral law concerning which we may not devise a case in which it is difficult to decide what is more moral: to disobey the law or to obey it? But all such inventions fail to prove that the laws, 'thou shalt not lie, steal, or kill', are invalid.

It is the same with reference to the law of Non-Resistance. People know it is wrong to use violence, but they are so anxious to continue to live a life secured by the 'strong arm of the law', that – instead of devoting their intellects to the elucidation of the evils which have flowed and are still flowing from admitting that man has a right to use violence to his fellow-men – they prefer to exert their mental powers in defence of that error.

'*Fais ce que dois, advienne que pourra*' ('Do what's right, come what may') is an expression of profound wisdom. We each can know indubitably what we ought to do, but what results will follow from our actions none of us either knows or can know. Therefore it follows that, besides feeling the call of duty, we are farther driven to act as duty bids us, by the consideration that we have no other guidance, but are totally ignorant of what will result from our actions.

Christian teaching indicates what a man should do to perform the will of Him who sent him into life; but discussion as to what results we anticipate from such or such human actions has nothing to do with Christianity, but is just an example of the error Christianity eliminates.

None of us has ever yet met the imaginary robber with the imaginary child, but all the horrors which fill the annals of history and of our own times came and come from this one thing – that people will believe that they can foresee the results of hypothetical future actions.

The case is this: People once lived an animal life, and violated or killed whom they thought well to violate or to kill. They even ate each other; and public opinion approved of it. Thousands of years ago, as far back as the times of Moses, a day came when people realized that to violate or kill each other is bad. But there were people for whom the reign of force was advantageous, and these did not approve of the change, but assured themselves and others that to do deeds of violence and to kill people is not always bad, but that there are circumstances when it is necessary and even moral. And violence and even slaughter, though not so frequent or so cruel as before, continued – only with this difference, that those who committed or commended such acts excused themselves by pleading that they did it for the benefit of humanity.

It was just this sophistical justification of violence that Christ denounced. When two enemies fight, each may think his own conduct justified by the circumstances. Excuses can be made for every use of violence; and no infallible standard has ever been discovered by which to measure the worth of these excuses. Therefore Christ taught us to believe in no excuse for violence, and (contrary to what had been taught by them of old time) never to use violence.

One would have thought that those who professed Christianity would have been indefatigable in exposing deception in this matter, for such an exposure forms one of the chief features of Christianity. What really happened was just the reverse. People who profited by violence, and who did not wish to give up their advantages, took on themselves a monopoly of Christian preaching, and declared that as cases can be found in which Non-Resistance causes more harm than the use of violence (the imaginary robber killing the imaginary child), therefore Christ's doctrine of Non-Resistance need not always be followed, and that one may deviate from his teaching to defend one's life or the life of others, to defend one's country, to save society from lunatics or criminals, and in many other cases. The answer to the question, In what cases should Christ's teaching be set aside? was left to the very people who employed violence. So that it ended by Christ's teaching, on the subject of not resisting evil by violence, being completely annulled. And, worst of all, the very people Christ denounced came to consider themselves the sole preachers and expositors of his doctrines. But the light shines through the darkness, and Christ's teaching is again exposing the pseudo-teachers of Christianity.

We may think about rearranging the world to suit our own taste – no one can prevent that – and we may try to do what seems to us pleasant or profitable, and with that object treat our fellow-creatures with violence on the pretext that we are doing good. But acting thus we cannot pretend to follow Christ's teaching, for Christ denounced just this deception. Truth sooner or later reappears, and the false teachers are unmasked, which is just what is happening today.

Only let the question of man's life be rightly put, as Christ put it, and not as it has been perversely put by the Churches, and the whole structure of falsehood which the Churches have built over Christ's teaching will collapse of itself.

The real question is not whether it would be good or bad for a certain human society that people should follow the law of Love and the consequent law of Non-Resistance, but it is this, Do you, who today live and tomorrow will die – who are indeed tending deathward every moment – do you wish now, immediately and entirely, to obey the law of Him Who sent you into life, and Who clearly showed you His will alike in tradition and in your mind and heart; or do you prefer to resist His will? And as soon as the question is put thus, only one reply is possible – I wish now, this moment, without delay or hesitation, to the very utmost of my strength, neither waiting for anyone nor counting the cost, to do that which alone is clearly demanded by Him Who sent me into the world; and on no account, and under no conditions, do I wish to, or can I, act otherwise, for herein lies my only possibility of a rational and unharassed life.

[Translated by Aylmer Maude]

LETTERS ON HENRY GEORGE
[1897]

I

To T. M. Bondaref, who had written from Siberia asking for information about the Single-Tax.

This is Henry George's plan:

The advantage and convenience of using land is not everywhere the same; there will always be many applicants for land that is fertile, well situated, or near a populous place; and the better and more profitable the land, the more people will wish to have it. All such land should, therefore, be valued according to its advantages: the more profitable – dearer; the less profitable – cheaper. Land for which there are few applicants should not be valued at all, but allotted gratuitously to those who wish to work it themselves.

With such a valuation of the land – here in the Tula Government, for instance – good arable land might be estimated at about 5 or 6 roubles* the *desyatina*;† kitchen-gardens in the villages, at about 10 roubles the *desyatina*; meadows that are fertilized by spring floods at about 15 roubles, and so on. In towns the valuation would be 100 to 500 roubles the *desyatina*, and in crowded parts of Moscow or Petersburg, or at the landing-places of navigable rivers, it would amount to several thousands or even tens of thousands of roubles the *desyatina*.

When all the land in the country has been valued in this way, Henry George proposes that a law should be made by which,

* The rouble was a little more than 25 pence. [A. M.]
† The *desyatina* is nearly 2¾ acres. [A. M.]

after a certain date in a certain year, the land should no longer belong to any one individual, but to the whole nation – the whole people; and that everyone holding land should, therefore, pay to the nation (that is, to the whole people) the yearly value at which it has been assessed. This payment should be used to meet all public or national expenses, and should replace all other rates, taxes or customs dues.

The result of this would be that a landed proprietor who now holds, say, 2,000 *desyatina*, might continue to hold them if he liked, but he would have to pay to the treasury – here in the Tula Government, for instance (as his holding would include both meadow-land and homestead) – 12,000 or 15,000 roubles a year; and, as no large landowners could stand such a payment, they would all abandon their land. But it would mean that a Tula peasant, in the same district, would pay a couple of roubles per *desyatina* less than he pays now, and could have plenty of available land near by, which he would take up at 5 or 6 roubles per *desyatina*. Besides, he would have no other rates or taxes to pay, and would be able to buy all the things he requires, foreign or Russian, free of duty. In towns, the owners of houses and manufactories might continue to own them, but would have to pay to the public treasury the amount of the assessment on their land.

The advantages of such an arrangement would be:

1. That no one will be unable to get land for use.

2. That there will be no idle people owning land and making others work for them in return for permission to use that land.

3. That the land will be in the possession of those who use it, and not of those who do not use it.

4. That as the land will be available for people who wish to work on it, they will cease to enslave themselves as hands in factories and works, or as servants in towns, and will settle in the country districts.

5. That there will be no more inspectors and collectors of taxes in mills, factories, refineries and workshops, but there will only be collectors of the tax on land which cannot be stolen, and from which a tax can be most easily collected.

6. (And chiefly): That the non-workers will be saved from

the sin of exploiting other people's labour (in doing which they are often not the guilty parties, for they have from childhood been educated in idleness, and do not know how to work), and from the yet greater sin of all kinds of shuffling and lying to justify themselves in committing that sin; and the workers will be saved from the temptation and sin of envying, condemning and being exasperated with the non-workers, so that one cause of separation among men will be destroyed.

II

To a German Propagandist of Henry George's Views.

It is with particular pleasure that I hasten to answer your letter, and say that I have known of Henry George since the appearance of his *Social Problems*. I read that book and was struck by the justice of his main thought – by the exceptional manner (unparalleled in scientific literature), clear, popular and forcible, in which he stated his cause – and especially by (what is also exceptional in scientific literature) the Christian spirit that permeates the whole work. After reading it I went back to his earlier *Progress and Poverty*, and still more deeply appreciated the importance of its author's activity.

You ask what I think of Henry George's activity, and of his Single-Tax system. My opinion is the following:

Humanity constantly advances: on the one hand clearing its consciousness and conscience, and on the other hand rearranging its modes of life to suit this changing consciousness. Thus, at each period of the life of humanity, the double process goes on: the clearing up of conscience, and the incorporation into life of what has been made clear to conscience.

At the end of the eighteenth century and the commencement of the nineteenth, a clearing up of conscience took place in Christendom with reference to the labouring classes – who lived under various forms of slavery – and this was followed by a corresponding readjustment of the forms of social life, to suit this clearer consciousness: namely, the abolition of slavery, and the organization of free wage-labour in its place. At the present time an enlightenment of men's consciences is going on in relation to the way land is used; and soon, it seems to me, a practical application of this new consciousness must follow.

And in this process (the enlightenment of conscience as to the utilization of land, and the practical application of that new consciousness), which is one of the chief problems of our time, the leader and organizer of the movement was and is Henry George. In this lies his immense, his pre-eminent, importance. He has helped, by his excellent books, both to clear men's minds and consciences on this question, and to place it on a practical footing.

But in relation to the abolition of the shameful right to own landed estates, something is occurring similar to what happened (within our own recollection) with reference to the abolition of serfdom. The Government and the governing classes – knowing that their position and privileges are bound up with the land question – pretend that they are preoccupied with the welfare of the people, organizing savings banks for workmen, factory inspection, income taxes, even eight-hour working days – and carefully ignore the land question, or even, aided by compliant science, which will demonstrate anything they like, declare that the expropriation of the land is useless, harmful and impossible.

Just the same thing occurs, as occurred in connection with slavery. At the end of the eighteenth and the beginning of the nineteenth centuries, men had long felt that slavery was a terrible anachronism, revolting to the human soul; but pseudo-religion and pseudo-science demonstrated that slavery was not wrong, that it was necessary, or at least that it was premature to abolish it. The same thing is now being repeated with reference to landed property. As before, pseudo-religion and pseudo-science demonstrate that there is nothing wrong in the private ownership of landed estates, and that there is no need to abolish the present system.

One would think it would be plain to every educated man of our time that an exclusive control of land by people who do not work on it, but who prevent hundreds and thousands of poor families from using it, is a thing as plainly bad and shameful as it was to own slaves; yet we see educated, refined aristocrats – English, Austrian, Prussian and Russian – making use of this cruel and shameful right, and not only not feeling ashamed, but feeling proud of it.

Religion blesses such possessions, and the science of political economy demonstrates that the present state of things is the one that should exist for the greatest benefit of mankind.

The service rendered by Henry George is that he has not only mastered the sophistries with which religion and science try to justify private ownership of land, and simplified the question to the uttermost, so that it is impossible not to admit the wrongfulness of landownership – unless one simply stops one's ears – but he was also the first to show how the question can be practically solved. He first gave a clear and direct reply to the excuses, used by the enemies of every reform, to the effect that the demands of progress are unpractical and inapplicable dreams.

Henry George's plan destroys that excuse, by putting the question in such a form that a committee might be assembled tomorrow to discuss the project and to convert it into law. In Russia, for instance, the discussion of land purchase, or of nationalizing the land without compensation, could begin tomorrow; and the project might – after undergoing various vicissitudes – be carried into operation, as occurred thirty-three years ago* with the project for the emancipation of the serfs.

The need to alter the present system has been explained, and the possibility of the change has been shown (there may be alterations and amendments of the Single-Tax system, but its fundamental idea is practicable); and, therefore, it will be impossible for people not to do what their reason demands. It is only necessary that this thought should become public opinion; and in order that it may become public opinion it must be spread abroad and explained – which is just what you are doing, and is a work with which I sympathize with my whole soul, and in which I wish you success.

[Translated by Aylmer Maude]

* The Emancipation of the Serfs in Russia was decreed in 1861, and was accomplished during the following few years. [A. M.]

MODERN SCIENCE* [1898]

παντὶ λόγῳ λόγος ἴσος ἀντικεῖται.†

I think this article of Carpenter's on Modern Science should be particularly useful in Russian society, in which, more than in any other in Europe, a superstition is prevalent and deeply rooted which considers that humanity for its welfare does not need the diffusion of true religious and moral knowledge, but only the study of experimental science, and that such science will satisfy all the spiritual demands of mankind.

It is evident how harmful an influence (quite like that of religious superstition) so gross a superstition must have on men's moral life. And, therefore, the publication of the thoughts of writers who treat experimental science and its method critically is specially desirable in our society.

Carpenter shows that neither Astronomy, nor Physics, nor Chemistry, nor Biology, nor Sociology supplies us with true knowledge of actual facts; that all the laws discovered by those sciences are merely generalizations, having but an approximate value as laws, and *that* only as long as we do not know, or leave out of account, certain other factors; and that even these laws seem laws to us only because we discover them in a region so far away from us in time and space that we cannot detect their non-correspondence with actual fact.

Moreover, Carpenter points out that the method of science, which consists in explaining things near and important to us

* Written as preface to a Russian translation, by Count Sergius Tolstoy, of Edward Carpenter's essay, 'Modern science: a criticism', which forms part of the volume *Civilization: Its Cause and Cure*, published by Swan Sonnenschein and Co., London. [A. M.]

† To every argument an equal argument is matched. [A. M.]

by things more remote and indifferent, is a false method which can never bring us to the desired result.

He says that every science tries to explain the facts it is investigating by means of conceptions of a lower order. 'Each science has been (as far as possible) reduced to its lowest terms. Ethics has been made a question of utility and inherited experience. Political Economy has been exhausted of all conceptions of justice between man and man, of charity, affection and the instinct of solidarity, and has been founded on its lowest discoverable factor, namely, self-interest. Biology has been denuded of the force of personality in plants, animals and men; the "self" here has been set aside, and the attempt made to reduce the science to a question of chemical and cellular affinities, protoplasm and the laws of osmose. Chemical affinities, again, and all the wonderful phenomena of Physics are emptied down into a flight of atoms; and the flight of atoms (and of astronomic orbs as well) is reduced to the laws of dynamics.'

It is supposed that the reduction of questions of a higher order to questions of a lower order will explain the former. But an explanation is never obtained in this way, and what happens is merely that, descending in one's investigations ever lower and lower, from the most important questions to less important ones, science reaches at last a sphere quite foreign to man, with which he is barely in touch, and confines its attention to that sphere, leaving all unsolved the questions most important to him.

What takes place is as if a man, wishing to understand the use of an object lying before him – instead of coming close to it, examining it from all sides and handling it – were to retire further and further from it, until he was at such a distance from the object that all its peculiarities of colour and inequalities of surface had disappeared, and only its outline was still visible against the horizon; and as if, from there, he were to begin writing a minute description of the object, imagining that now, at last, he clearly understood it, and that this understanding, formed at such a distance, would assist a complete comprehension of it. And it is this self-deception that is partly exposed by Carpenter's criticism, which shows, first, that the knowledge afforded us by the natural sciences amounts merely to convenient generalizations, which certainly do not express actual facts; and, secondly, that the method of science by which facts of a higher order are reduced to facts of a lower order, will never furnish us with an explanation of the former.

But without predetermining the question whether experimental science will, or will not, by its methods, ever bring us to the solution of the most serious problems of human life, the activity of experimental science itself, in its relation to the eternal and most reasonable demands of man, is so anomalous as to amaze one.

People must live. But in order to live they must know how to live. And all men always obtained this knowledge – well or ill – and in conformity with it have lived, and progressed; and this knowledge of how men should live has from the days of Moses, Solon and Confucius been always considered a science – the very essence of science. And only in our time has it come to be considered that the science telling us how to live is not a science at all, but that only experimental science – commencing with Mathematics and ending in Sociology – is real science.

And a strange misunderstanding results.

A plain, reasonable working man supposes, in the old way which is also the common-sense way, that if there are people who spend their lives in study, whom he feeds and keeps while they think for him – then no doubt these men are engaged in studying things men need to know; and he expects of science that it will solve for him the questions on which his welfare, and that of all men, depends. He expects science to tell him how he ought to live: how to treat his family, his neighbours and the men of other tribes, how to restrain his passions, what to believe in and what not to believe in, and much else. And what does our science say to him on these matters?

It triumphantly tells him: how many million miles it is from the earth to the sun; at what rate light travels through space; how many million vibrations of ether per second are caused by light, and how many vibrations of air by sound; it tells of the chemical components of the Milky Way, of a new element – helium – of micro-organisms and their excrements, of the points on the hand at which electricity collects, of X-rays, and similar things.

'But I don't want any of those things,' says a plain and reasonable man – 'I want to know how to live.'

'What does it matter what you want?' replies science. 'What you are asking about relates to Sociology. Before replying to sociological questions, we have yet to solve questions of Zoology, Botany, Physiology, and, in general, of Biology; but to solve those questions we have first to solve questions of Physics, and then of Chemistry, and have also to agree as to the shape of the infinitesimal atoms, and how it is that imponderable and incompressible ether transmits energy.'

And people – chiefly those who sit on the backs of others, and to whom it is therefore convenient to wait – are content with such replies, and sit blinking, awaiting the fulfilment of these promises; but a plain and reasonable working man – such as those on whose backs these others sit while occupying themselves with science – the whole great mass of men, the whole of humanity, cannot be satisfied by such answers, but naturally ask in perplexity: 'But when will this be done? We cannot wait. You say yourselves that you will discover these things after some generations. But we are alive now – alive today and dead tomorrow – and we want to know how to live our life while we have it. So teach us!'

'What a stupid and uneducated man!' replies science. 'He does not understand that science exists not for use, but for *science*. Science studies whatever presents itself for study, and cannot select the subjects to be studied. Science studies *everything*. That is the characteristic of science.'

And scientists are really convinced that to be occupied with trifles, while neglecting what is more essential and important, is a characteristic not of themselves, but of science. The plain, reasonable man, however, begins to suspect that this characteristic pertains not to science, but to men who are inclined to occupy themselves with trifles and to attach great importance to those trifles.

'Science studies *everything*,' say the scientists. But, really, *everything* is too much. Everything is an infinite quantity of objects; it is impossible at one and the same time to study *all*. As a lantern cannot light up everything, but only lights up the place on which it is turned or the direction in which the man carrying it is walking, so also science cannot study everything, but inevitably only studies that to which its attention is directed. And as a lantern lights up most strongly the place nearest to it, and less and less strongly objects that are more and more remote from it, and does not at all light up those things its light does not reach, so also human science, of whatever kind, has always studied and still studies most carefully what seems most important to the investigators, less carefully what seems to them less important, and quite neglects the whole remaining infinite quantity of objects. And what for men has defined and still defines the subjects they are to consider most important, less important and unimportant, is the general understanding of the meaning and purpose of life (that is to say, the religion) possessed by those who occupy themselves with science. But men of science today – not acknowledging any religion, and having therefore no standard by which to choose the subjects most important for study, or to discriminate them from less important subjects and, ultimately, from that infinite quantity of objects which the limitations of the human mind, and the infinity of the number of those objects, will always cause to remain uninvestigated – have formed for themselves a theory of 'science for science's sake', according to which science is to study not what mankind needs, but *everything*.

And, indeed, experimental science studies everything, not in the sense of the totality of objects, but in the sense of disorder – chaos in the arrangement of the objects studied. That is to say, science does not devote most attention to what people most need, less to what they need less, and none at all to what is quite useless, but it studies anything that happens to come to hand. Though Comte's and other classifications of the sciences exist, these classifications do not govern the selection of subjects for study, but that selection is dependent on the human weaknesses common to men of science as well as to the rest of mankind. So that, in reality, scientists study not *everything*, as they imagine and declare, but they study what is more profitable and easier to study. And it is more profitable to study things that conduce to the well-being of the upper classes, with whom the men of science are connected; and it is easier to study things that lack life. Accordingly, many men of science study books, monuments and inanimate bodies.

Such study is considered the most real 'science'. So that in our day what is considered to be the most real 'science', the only one (as the Bible was considered the only book worthy of the name), is, not the contemplation and investigation of how to make the life of man more kindly and more happy, but the compilation and copying from many books into one of all that our predecessors wrote on a certain subject, the pouring of liquids out of one glass bottle into another, the skilful slicing of microscopic preparations, the cultivation of bacteria, the cutting up of frogs and dogs, the investigation of X-rays, the theory of numbers, the chemical composition of the stars, etc.

Meanwhile all those sciences which aim at making human life kindlier and happier – religious, moral and social science – are considered by the dominant science to be unscientific, and are abandoned to the theologians, philosophers, jurists, historians and political economists; who, under the guise of scientific investigation, are chiefly occupied in demonstrating that the existing order of society (the advantages of which they enjoy) is the very one which ought to exist, and that, therefore, it must not only not be changed, but must be maintained by all means.

Not to mention Theology and Jurisprudence, Political Economy, the most advanced of the sciences of this group, is remarkable in this respect. The most prevalent Political Economy (that of Karl Marx),* accepting the existing order of life as though it were what it ought to be, not only does not call on men to alter that order – that is to say, does not point out to them how they ought to live that their condition may improve – but, on the contrary, it demands an increase in the cruelty of the existing order of things, that its more-than-questionable predictions may be fulfilled, concerning what will happen if people continue to live as badly as they are now living.

And, as always occurs, the lower a human activity descends

* In Russia the rigid theories of Karl Marx, and the German type of Social Democracy, have had, and still have, more vogue than in England. [A. M.]

– the more widely it diverges from what it should be – the more its self-confidence increases. That is just what has happened with the science of today. True science is never appreciated by its contemporaries, but on the contrary is usually persecuted. Nor can this be otherwise. True science shows men their mistakes, and points to new, unaccustomed ways of life. And both these services are unpleasant to the ruling section of society. But present-day science not only does not run counter to the tastes and demands of the ruling section of society, but it quite complies with them: it satisfies idle curiosity, excites people's wonder, and promises them increase of pleasure. And so, whereas all that is truly great is calm, modest and unnoticed, the science of today knows no limits to its self-laudation.

'All former methods were erroneous, and all that used to be considered science was an imposture, a blunder, and of no account. Only our method is true, and the only true science is ours. The success of our science is such that thousands of years have not done what we have accomplished in the last century. In the future, travelling the same path, our science will solve all questions, and make all mankind happy. Our science is the most important activity in the world, and we, men of science, are the most important and necessary people in the world.'

So think and say the scientists of today, and the cultured crowd echo it, but really at no previous time and among no people has science – the whole of science with all its knowledge – stood on so low a level as at present. One part of it, which should study the things that make human life kind and happy, is occupied in justifying the existing evil order of society; another part is engaged in solving questions of idle curiosity.

'What? – Idle curiosity?' I hear voices ask in indignation at such blasphemy. 'What about steam, and electricity, and telephones, and all our technical improvements? Not to speak of their scientific importance, see what practical results they have produced! Man has conquered Nature and subjugated its forces' . . . with more to the same effect.

'But all the practical results of the victories over Nature have till now – for a considerable time past – gone to factories that injure the workmen's health; have produced weapons to kill men with, and increased luxury and corruption' – replies a plain, reasonable man – 'and, therefore, the victory of man over Nature has not only failed to increase the welfare of human beings, but has, on the contrary, made their condition worse.'

If the arrangement of society is bad (as ours is), and a small number of people have power over the majority and oppress it, every victory over Nature will inevitably only serve to increase that power and that oppression. That is what is actually happening.

With a science which aims not at studying how people ought to live, but at studying whatever exists – and which is therefore occupied chiefly in investigating inanimate things while allowing the order of human society to remain as it is – no improvements, no victories over Nature, can better the state of humanity.

'But medical science? You are forgetting the beneficent progress made by medicine. And bacteriological inoculations? And recent surgical operations?' exclaim the defenders of science – adducing as a last resource the success of medical science to prove the utility of all science. 'By inoculations we can prevent illness, or can cure it; we can perform painless operations: cut open a man's inside and clean it out, and can straighten hunched-backs,' is what is usually said by the defenders of present-day science, who seem to think that the curing of one child from diphtheria, among those Russian children of whom 50 per cent (and even 80 per cent in the Foundling Hospitals) die as a regular thing apart from diphtheria – must convince anyone of the beneficence of science in general.

Our life is so arranged that from bad food, excessive and harmful work, bad dwellings and clothes, or from want, not children only, but a majority of people, die before they have lived half the years that should be theirs. The order of things is such that children's illnesses, consumption, syphilis and alcoholism seize an ever-increasing number of victims, while a great part of men's labour is taken from them to prepare for wars, and every ten or twenty years millions of men are slaughtered in wars; and all this because science, instead of supplying correct religious, moral and social ideas, which would cause these ills to disappear of themselves, is occupied on the one hand in justifying the existing order, and on the other hand – with toys. And, in proof of the fruitfulness of science, we are told that it cures one in a thousand of the sick, who are sick only because science has neglected its proper business.

Yes, if science would devote but a small part of those efforts, and of that attention and labour which it now spends on trifles, to supplying men with correct religious, moral, social, or even hygienic ideas, there would not be a one-hundredth part of the diphtheria, the diseases of the womb or the deformities, the occasional cure of which now makes science so proud, though they are effected in clinical hospitals, the cost of whose luxurious appointments is too great for them to be at the service of all who need them.

It is as though men who had ploughed badly, and sown badly with poor seeds, were to go over the ground tending some broken ears of corn and trampling on others that grew alongside, and should then exhibit their skill in healing the injured ears, as a proof of their knowledge of agriculture.

Our science, in order to become science and to be really useful and not harmful to humanity, must first of all renounce its experimental method, which causes it to consider as its duty the study merely of what exists, and must return to the only reasonable and fruitful conception of science, which is, that the object of science is to show how people ought to live. Therein lies the aim and importance of science; and the study of things as they exist can only be a subject for science in so far as that study co-operates towards the knowledge of how men should live.

It is just to the admission of its bankruptcy by experimental science, and to the need of adopting another method, that Carpenter draws attention in this article.

[Translated by Aylmer Maude]

LETTER TO A NON-COMMISSIONED OFFICER [1899]

You are surprised that soldiers are taught that it is right to kill people in certain cases and in war, while in the books admitted to be holy by those who so teach, there is nothing like such a permission, but, on the contrary, not only is all murder forbidden but all insulting of others is forbidden also, and we are told not to do to others what we do not wish done to us. And you ask, Is there not some fraud in all this? And if so, then for whose sake is it committed?

Yes, there is a fraud, committed for the sake of those accustomed to live on the sweat and blood of other men, and who therefore have perverted, and still pervert, Christ's teaching, given to man for his good, but which has now, in its perverted form, become a chief source of human misery.

The thing has come about in this way:

The Government and all those of the upper classes near the Government who live by other people's work, need some means of dominating the workers, and find this means in the control of the army. Defence against foreign enemies is only an excuse. The German Government frightens its subjects about the Russians and the French; the French Government frightens its people about the Germans; the Russian Government frightens its people about the French and the Germans; and that is the way with all Governments. But neither Germans nor Russians nor Frenchmen desire to fight their neighbours or other people; but, living in peace, they dread war more than anything else in the world. The Government and the upper, governing classes, to excuse their domination of the labourers, behave like a gipsy who whips his horse before he turns a corner and then pretends he cannot hold it in. They stir up their own people and some foreign Government, and then pretend that for the well-being, or the defence, of their people they must declare war: which again brings profit only to generals, officers, officials, merchants, and, in general, to the rich. In reality war is an inevitable result of the existence of armies; and armies are only needed by Governments to dominate their own working classes.

The thing is a crime, but the worst of it is that the Government, in order to have a plausible basis for its domination of the people, has to pretend that it holds the highest religious teaching known to man (the Christian), and that it brings up its subjects in this teaching. That teaching, however, is in its very nature opposed not only to murder but to all violence, and therefore the Governments, in order to dominate the people and to be considered Christian, had to pervert Christianity and to hide its true meaning from the people, and thus deprive men of the well-being Christ offered them.

This perversion was accomplished long ago, in the time of that scoundrel the Emperor Constantine, who for doing it was enrolled among the saints.* All subsequent Governments, especially our Russian Government, do their utmost to preserve this perverted understanding, and to prevent people from seeing the real meaning of Christianity; because, having once seen the real meaning of Christianity, the people would perceive that the Governments, with their taxes, soldiers, prisons, gallows and false priests, are not only not the pillars of Christianity they profess to be, but are its greatest enemies.

In consequence of this perversion, those frauds which have surprised you are possible, and all those terrible misfortunes occur from which men suffer.

The people are oppressed and robbed, and are poor, ignorant, dying of hunger. Why? Because the land is in the hands of the

* Constantine the Great was decreed to be a god by the Roman Senate, and was made a Christian saint by the Eastern Church. [A. M.]

rich; and the people are enslaved in mills and in factories, obliged to earn money because taxes are demanded from them, and the price of their labour is diminished while the price of things they need is increased.

How are they to escape? By taking the land from the rich? But if this is done, soldiers will come, and will kill the rebels or put them in prison. Seize the mills and factories? The same will happen. Organize and maintain a strike? It is sure to fail. The rich will hold out longer than the workers, and the armies are always on the side of the capitalists. The people will never extricate themselves from the want in which they are kept as long as the army is in the hands of the governing classes.

But who compose these armies that keep the people in this state of slavery? Who are these soldiers that will fire at peasants who take the land, or at strikers who will not disperse, or at smugglers who bring in goods without paying taxes? Who put in prison and guard there those who refuse to pay taxes? The soldiers are these same peasants who are deprived of land, these same strikers who want better wages, these same taxpayers who want to be rid of these taxes.

And why do these people shoot at their brothers? Because it has been instilled into them that the oath they were obliged to take on entering the service is binding, and that though it is generally wrong to kill people, it is right to do so at the command of one's superiors. That is to say, the same fraud is played off upon them which has struck you. But here we meet the question, How is it that sensible people – often people who can read, and even educated people – believe such an evident lie? However little education a man may have, he cannot but know that Christ did not sanction murder, but taught kindness, meekness, forgiveness of injuries, love of one's enemies; and therefore he cannot help seeing that on the basis of Christian teaching he cannot pledge himself in advance to kill all whom he may be ordered to kill.

The question is, How can sensible people believe – as all now serving in the army have believed and still believe – such an evident falsehood? The answer is that it is not this one fraud by itself that takes people in, but they have from childhood been deprived of the proper use of their reason by a whole series of deceptions, a whole system of frauds, called the Orthodox Faith, which is nothing but the grossest idolatry. In this faith people are taught: that God is triple, that besides this triple God there is a Queen of Heaven,* and besides this Queen there are various saints whose corpses have not decayed,† and besides these saints there are icons‡ of the Gods and of the Queen of Heaven, to which one should offer candles and pray with one's hands; and that the most important and holy thing on earth is the pap§ which the priest makes of wine and white bread on Sundays, behind a partition; and that after the priest has whispered over it, the wine is no longer wine, and the white bread is not bread, but they are the blood and flesh of one of the triple Gods, etc. All this is so stupid and senseless that it is quite impossible to understand what it all means. And the very people who teach this faith do not ask you to understand it, but only tell you to believe it; and people trained to believe these things from childhood can believe any kind of nonsense that is told them. And when men have been so befooled that they believe that God hangs in the corner,¶ or sits in a morsel of pap which the priest gives out in a spoon; that to kiss a board or some relic and put candles in front of them, is useful for life here and hereafter – they are next called on to enter the military

* The Holy Virgin, the 'Mother of God' and 'Queen of Heaven', plays a prominent part in the Orthodox Eastern Church. [A. M.]

† One proof of holiness adduced as justifying admission to the rank of sainthood is the non-decomposition of the holy person's corpse. These miraculously preserved bodies are enshrined in chapels, monasteries and cathedrals, and are there visited by pilgrims, who offer up prayers at the shrine, place candles before it, and usually leave some contribution for the benefit of the establishment. [A. M.]

‡ The icons of the Eastern Church are not 'graven images', but are pictures painted in a conventional cadaverous manner on wood; these are often covered with an embossed metal cover allowing only the hands and face to be seen, and making the icon as much like an image as a picture. [A. M.]

§ The mixture of bread and wine administered by the priests of the Orthodox Eastern Church at the celebration of the Eucharist. [A. M.]

¶ This refers to the common practice of hanging an icon in the corner of each dwelling-room. These icons are called 'gods', and are prayed to in a way that often amounts to idolatry. [A. M.]

service, where they are humbugged to any extent; being first made to swear on the Gospel (in which swearing is prohibited) that they will do just what is forbidden in those Gospels, and then taught that to kill people at the word of those in command is not a sin, but that to refuse to obey those in command is a sin. So that the fraud played off on soldiers when it is instilled into them that they may, without sin, kill people at the wish of those in command, is not an isolated fraud, but is bound up with a whole system of deception without which this one fraud would not deceive them.

Only a man quite befooled by the false faith called Orthodoxy, palmed off upon him for true Christian faith, can believe that it is no sin for a Christian to enter the army, promising blindly to obey any man who ranks above him in the service, and, at the will of others, learning to kill, and committing that most terrible crime forbidden by all moral law.

A man free from the pseudo-Christian faith that is called Orthodoxy will not believe that.

And that is why the so-called Sectarians – Christians who have repudiated the Orthodox teaching, and acknowledge Christ's teaching as explained in the Gospels, and especially in the Sermon on the Mount – are not tricked by this deception, but have frequently refused, and still do refuse, to be soldiers, considering such an occupation incompatible with Christianity, and preferring to bear all kinds of persecution, as hundreds and thousands of people are doing: in Russia many of the Dukhobors and Molokans; in Austria the Nazarenes, and in Sweden, Switzerland and Germany some members of the Evangelical sects. The Government knows this, and is therefore exceedingly anxious that the general Church deception, without which its power could not be maintained, should be commenced with every child from early infancy and be continually maintained in such a way that none may escape it. The Government tolerates anything else: drunkenness and vice (and not only tolerates but even organizes drunkenness and vice – they help to stupefy people), but by all means in its power it hinders those who have escaped out of its trap from assisting others to escape.

The Russian Government perpetrates this fraud with special

craft and cruelty. It orders all its subjects to baptize their children during infancy into the false faith called Orthodoxy, and it threatens to punish them if they disobey. And when the children are baptized – that is, are reckoned as Orthodox – then, under threats of criminal penalties, they are forbidden to discuss the faith into which, without their wish, they were baptized; and for such discussion of that faith, as well as for renouncing it and changing to another, they are actually punished. So that it cannot be said of Russians in general that they believe the Orthodox Faith – they do not know whether they believe it or not. They were converted to it during infancy, and kept in it by violence – that is, by the fear of punishment. All Russians were entrapped into Orthodoxy by cunning fraud, and are kept in it by cruel force.

Using the power it wields, the Government perpetrates and maintains this fraud, and by means of it retains power.

And, therefore, the sole way to free people from their many miseries lies in freeing them from the false faith instilled into them by Government, and in their imbibing the true Christian teaching, which this false teaching hides. The true Christian teaching is very simple, clear, and obvious to all, as Christ said. But it is simple and accessible only when man is freed from that falsehood in which we were all educated, and which is passed off upon us as God's Truth.

Nothing useful can be poured into a vessel that is already full of what is useless. We must first empty out what is useless. So it is with the acquirement of true Christian teaching. We have first to understand that all the stories telling how God made the world 6,000 years ago; how Adam sinned and the human race fell, and how the Son of God (a God born of a virgin) came on earth and redeemed man; and all the fables in the Old Testament and in the Gospels, and all the lives of the saints with their stories of miracles and relics – are all nothing but a gross hash of Jewish superstitions and priestly frauds. Only to a man quite free from this deception can the clear and simple teaching of Christ, which needs no explanation, be accessible and comprehensible. That teaching tells us nothing of the beginning, or of the end, of the world, nor about God and His purpose, nor, in general, about things which we cannot and need not know; but it speaks only of what man must do to save himself – that is, how best to live the life he has come into, in this world, from birth to death. For that purpose it is only necessary to act towards others as we wish them to act towards us. In *that* is all the law and the prophets, as Christ said. And to act in this way we need neither icons, nor relics, nor church services, nor priests, nor catechisms, nor Governments, but, on the contrary, we need perfect freedom from all that; for to do to others as we wish them to do to us is only possible when a man is free from the fables which the priests give out as the only truth, and when he is not bound by promises to act as other people may order. Only such a man will be capable of fulfilling – not his own will nor that of other men, but – the will of God.

And the will of God is not that we should fight and oppress the weak, but that we should acknowledge all men to be our brothers and should serve one another.

These are the thoughts your letter has aroused in me. I shall be very glad if they help to clear up the questions you are thinking about.

[Translated by Aylmer Maude]

FROM *NEED IT BE SO?* [1900]

I

Amidst fields there stands, surrounded by a wall, a foundry, with smoking chimneys, clattering chains, furnaces, a railway siding and scattered little houses of the managers and labourers. In this foundry and in the mines belonging to it the working people swarm like ants; some of them, in passages two hundred feet underground, are at work from morning until night, or from night until morning, mining the ore; others in the darkness, bending over, take this ore or clay to the shaft and take back empty cars, and again fill them, working for twelve or fourteen hours a day throughout the week.

In the foundry itself, some work at the furnace in an oppressive heat, others work at the trough of the melted ore and slag; others again, the engineers, stokers, smiths, brickmakers, carpenters, are at work in shops, also from twelve to fourteen hours a day throughout the week.

On Sunday all these men receive their wages, wash themselves, or sometimes even do not wash themselves, go to the inns and saloons which on all sides surround the foundry, and which entice the working people, and early on Monday morning they go back to their work.

Near this same foundry peasants plough somebody else's field with lean, worn-out horses. These peasants get up with the dawn, if they have not passed the night in the pasture, that is, near a swamp, the only place where they can feed their horses; they get up with the dawn, come home, harness the horses, and, taking with them a slice of bread, go out to plough somebody else's field.

Other peasants are sitting not far away from the foundry, on the highway, and, having made themselves a shield from matting, are breaking rock for the highway. The legs of these men are bruised, their hands are all calluses, their whole bodies are dirty, and not only their faces, hair and beards, but even their lungs are permeated with lime dust.

Taking a small unbroken stone from a heap, these men put it between the soles of their feet, which are covered with bast shoes and wrapped in rags, and strike this stone with a heavy mallet, until the stone breaks: when the stone has broken, they take the smaller parts and strike them until these are broken fine; and again they take whole stones, and again. – And thus these men work from early summer dawn until night – fifteen, sixteen hours, resting only for two hours after dinner, and twice, at breakfast and at noon, strengthening themselves with bread and water.

And thus do these men live in the mines and in the foundry, and the ploughmen, and the stone-breakers, from early youth until old age; and in similar work above their strength live their wives and their mothers, suffering from diseases of the womb; and thus live their fathers and their children, poorly fed, poorly dressed, doing work which is above their strength and ruins their health, from morning until evening, from childhood until old age.

And past the foundry, past the stone-breakers, past the ploughing peasants, meeting and overtaking ragged men and women with their wallets, who are wandering from place to place and begging in the name of Christ, there races a carriage, with tinkling bells, drawn by four matched chestnut horses of good height, the worst of which is worth the whole farm of any of the peasants who are admiring the four-in-hand. In the carriage are seated two ladies, displaying brightly coloured parasols, ribbons and hat feathers, each of which costs more than the horse with which a peasant ploughs his field; in the front seat sits an officer, shining in the sun with lace and buttons, and dressed in a freshly laundered blouse; on the box sits a ponderous coachman, in blue silk shirt-sleeves and velvet sleeveless coat. He came very near crushing some women pilgrims, and almost knocked a peasant, who, dressed in a dirty shirt, was jolting in his empty cart, into the ditch.

'You see this?' says the coachman, showing the whip to the peasant, who was not quick enough in turning aside, and the peasant with one hand pulls the rein and with the other timidly pulls his cap off his lousy head.

Back of the carriage, glinting in the sun with the nickel-plated parts of their machines, noiselessly race two men and one woman on bicycles, and they laugh merrily, as they overtake and frighten the wandering women, who make the sign of the cross.

On the side-path of the highway pass two riders – a man on an English cob, and a lady on an ambler. To say nothing of the cost of the horses and the saddles, the one black hat with the lilac veil cost two months' work of the stone-breakers, and for the fashionable English whip as much was paid as in a week will be earned by that young lad, who is happy that he has hired out to work underground in the mine, and who is getting out of the way, while admiring the sleek forms of the horses and riders, and the fat, imported, immense dog in an expensive collar, which is running with protruding tongue back of them.

Not far from this company there travel in a cart a dressed-up, smiling maid, with curls, wearing a white apron, and a fat, ruddy man, with well-groomed side-whiskers, who is whispering something to the maid. In the cart may be seen a samovar, bundles in napkins, and an ice-cream freezer.

These are the servants of the people who are travelling in the carriage, on horseback and on bicycles. The present day is nothing out of the ordinary. Thus they live the whole summer, going out for pleasure almost every day, and at times, as now, taking with them tea, beverages and sweets, in order to eat and drink, not in the same, but in some new place.

These people are three families which are passing the summer in the country. One is the family of a proprietor, the owner of two thousand *desyatinas* of land, another that of an official, who receives a salary of three thousand roubles, and the third – the wealthiest family – the children of a manufacturer.

All these people are not in the least surprised or touched by the sight of all this poverty and hard labour by which they are surrounded. They think that all this must be so. They are interested in something quite different.

'No, that is impossible,' says the lady on horseback, looking back at the dog, 'I cannot see that!' and she stops the carriage. All talk together in French and laugh, and they put the dog into the carriage and proceed, covering the stone-breakers and the itinerants with clouds of lime dust.

And the carriage, the riders, the bicyclists have flashed by like beings from another world; and the people in the foundry, the stone-breakers, the ploughmen continue their hard, monotonous work for somebody else, which will end with their lives.

'Some people have a fine time!' they think, as they watch the travellers off. And their painful existence appears still more painful to them.

2

What is this? Have these labouring people done something very criminal that they are punished thus? Or is this the lot of all men? And have those who passed by in the carriages and on the bicycles done something particularly useful and important that they are thus rewarded? Not in the least! On the contrary, those who are working with such tension are for the most part moral, continent, modest, industrious people; while those who passed by are for the most part corrupted, lustful, impudent, idle people. This is so, because such a structure of life is considered natural and regular in the world of men who assert that they are professing Christ's law of love of our neighbour, or that they are people of culture, that is, perfected people.

Such a structure exists, not only in that corner of Tula County, which presents itself vividly to me, because I frequently see it, but everywhere, not only in Russia – from St Petersburg to Batum – but also in France – from Paris to Auvergne – and in Italy – from Rome to Palermo – and in Germany, in Spain, in America, in Australia, and even in India and in China. Everywhere two or three people in a thousand live in such a way that, without doing anything for themselves, they in one day consume in food and drink as much as would support hundreds of people for a year; they wear clothes which cost thousands; live in palaces, where thousands of labouring people could find room; spend on their whims thousands of roubles and millions of work-days; others again, getting neither enough sleep nor enough food, work above their strength, ruining their bodily and their spiritual health for these few elect.

For one class of women, when they are about to bear children, they send for a midwife, a doctor, sometimes for two doctors for one lying-in woman, and their layettes contain a hundred baby-shirts and swaddling-clothes with silk ribbons, and they get ready little wagons swinging on springs; the other class of women, the vast majority, bear children in any chance place and in any chance manner, without aid, swaddle them in rags, put them into bast cradles on straw, and are glad when they die.

The children of one class, while the mother is lying in bed for nine days, are taken care of by the midwife, the nurse, the wet-nurse; the children of the other class are not taken care of, because there is no one to do so, and the mother herself gets up immediately after childbirth, makes the fires in the oven, milks the cow, and sometimes washes the clothes for herself, her husband and her children. One class of children grows up among toys, amusements and instructions; the other children at first crawl with their bared bellies over thresholds, become maimed, are eaten up by pigs, and at five years of age begin to work above their strength. The first are taught all the scientific wisdom which is adapted to their age; the others learn vulgar curses and the most savage of superstitions. The first fall in love, carry on love-affairs, and then marry, after they have experienced all the pleasures of love; the others are married off to those whom the parents choose, between the ages of sixteen and twenty years, for the purpose of receiving additional aid. The first eat and drink the best and the most expensive things in the world, feeding their dogs on white bread and beef; the second eat nothing but bread and kvas, nor do they get enough bread, and what they get is stale, so that they may not eat too much of it. The first change their fine underwear every day, so as not to get soiled; the second, who are constantly doing work for others, change their coarse, ragged, lousy underwear once in two weeks, or do not change it at all, but wear it until it falls to pieces. The first sleep between clean sheets, on feather beds; the second sleep on the ground, covering themselves with their tattered caftans.

The first drive out with well-fed horses, for no work, but simply for pleasure; the second work hard with ill-fed horses, and walk, if they have any business to attend to. The first wonder what to do, in order to occupy their leisure time; the second find no time to clean themselves, to wash, to take a rest, to say a word, to visit their relatives. The first read four languages and every day amuse themselves with the greatest variety of things; the second do not know how to read at all and know no other amusement than drunkenness. The first know everything and believe in nothing; the second know nothing and believe any nonsense that they are told. When the first get sick, they travel from place to place in search of the best curative air, to say nothing of all kinds of waters, every kind of attention, and every kind of cleanliness and medicine; the second lie down on the oven in a smoky hut, and with unwashed sores, and with the absence of any food but stale bread, and of all air but such as is infected by ten members of the family, and by the calves and sheep, rot alive and die before their time.

Must it be so?

If there is a higher reason and a love which guide the world, if there is a God, He cannot have wished to see such division among men, when one class of them do not know what to do with the surplus of their wealth and senselessly squander the fruit of the labours of other men, and the others grow sick and die before their time, or live an agonizing life, working above their strength.

If there is a God, this cannot and must not be. But if there is no God, such a structure of life, in which the majority of men must waste their lives, so that a small number of men may enjoy an abundance, which only corrupts this minority and weighs heavily upon it, is, from the simplest human point of view, insipid, because it is disadvantageous for all men.

[Translated by Leo Wiener]

'THOU SHALT NOT KILL'
[1900]

'Thou shalt not kill.' – Exodus 20:13

'The disciple is not above his master: but every one that is perfect shall be as his master.' – Luke 6:40

'For all they that take the sword shall perish with the sword.' – Matthew 26:52

'Therefore all things whatsoever ye would that men should do to you, do ye even so to them.' – Matthew 7:12

When kings are executed after trial, as in the case of Charles I, Louis XVI and Maximilian of Mexico; or when they are killed in Court conspiracies, like Peter III, Paul, and various sultans, shahs and khans – little is said about it; but when they are killed without a trial and without a Court conspiracy – as in the case of Henry IV of France, Alexander II, the Empress of Austria, the late Shah of Persia and, recently, Humbert – such murders excite the greatest surprise and indignation among kings and emperors and their adherents, just as if they themselves never took part in murders, nor profited by them, nor instigated them. But, in fact, the mildest of the murdered kings (Alexander II or Humbert, for instance), not to speak of executions in their own countries, were instigators of, and accomplices and partakers in, the murder of tens of thousands of men who perished on the field of battle; while more cruel kings and emperors have been guilty of hundreds of thousands, and even millions, of murders.

The teaching of Christ repeals the law, 'An eye for an eye,

and a tooth for a tooth'; but those who have always clung to that law, and still cling to it, and who apply it to a terrible degree – not only claiming 'an eye for an eye', but without provocation decreeing the slaughter of thousands, as they do when they declare war – have no right to be indignant at the application of that same law to themselves in so small and insignificant a degree that hardly one king or emperor is killed for each hundred thousand, or perhaps even for each million who are killed by the order and with the consent of kings and emperors. Kings and emperors not only should not be indignant at such murders as those of Alexander II and Humbert, but they should be surprised that such murders are so rare, considering the continual and universal example of murder that they give to mankind.

The crowd are so hypnotized that they see what is going on before their eyes, but do not understand its meaning. They see what constant care kings, emperors and presidents devote to their disciplined armies; they see the reviews, parades and manœuvres the rulers hold, about which they boast to one another; and the people crowd to see their own brothers, brightly dressed up in fools' clothes, turned into machines to the sound of drum and trumpet, all, at the shout of one man, making one and the same movement at one and the same moment – but they do not understand what it all means. Yet the meaning of this drilling is very clear and simple: it is nothing but a preparation for killing.

It is stupefying men in order to make them fit instruments for murder. And those who do this, who chiefly direct this and are proud of it, are the kings, emperors and presidents. And it is just these men – who are specially occupied in organizing murder and who have made murder their profession, who wear military uniforms and carry murderous weapons (swords) at their sides – that are horrified and indignant when one of themselves is murdered.

The murder of kings – the murder of Humbert – is terrible, but not on account of its cruelty. The things done by command of kings and emperors – not only past events such as the massacre of St Bartholomew, religious butcheries, the terrible repressions of peasant rebellions, and Paris *coups d'état*, but the present-day Government executions, the doing-to-death of prisoners in solitary confinement, the Disciplinary Battalions, the hangings, the beheadings, the shootings and slaughter in wars – are incomparably more cruel than the murders committed by Anarchists. Nor are these murders terrible because undeserved. If Alexander II and Humbert did not deserve death, still less did the thousands of Russians who perished at Plevna, or of Italians who perished in Abyssinia. Such murders are terrible, not because they are cruel or unmerited, but because of the unreasonableness of those who commit them.

If the regicides act under the influence of personal feelings of indignation evoked by the sufferings of an oppressed people, for which they hold Alexander or Carnot or Humbert responsible; or if they act from personal feelings of revenge, then – however immoral their conduct may be – it is at least intelligible; but how is it that a body of men (Anarchists, we are told) such as those by whom Bresci was sent, and who are now threatening another emperor – how is it that they cannot devise any better means of improving the condition of humanity than by killing people whose destruction can no more be of use than the decapitation of that mythical monster on whose neck a new head appeared as soon as one was cut off? Kings and emperors have long ago arranged for themselves a system like that of a magazine-rifle: as soon as one bullet has been discharged another takes its place. *Le roi est mort, vive le roi!* So what is the use of killing them?

Only on a most superficial view can the killing of these men seem a means of saving the nations from oppression and from wars destructive of human life.

One only need remember that similar oppression and similar war went on, no matter who was at the head of the Government – Nicholas or Alexander, Frederick or Wilhelm, Napoleon or Louis, Palmerston or Gladstone, McKinley or anyone else – in order to understand that it is not any particular person who causes these oppressions and these wars from which the nations suffer. The misery of nations is caused not by particular persons, but by the particular order of Society under which the people are so tied up together that they find themselves all in the power of a few men, or more often in the power of one single man: a man so perverted by his unnatural position as arbiter of the fate and lives of millions, that he is always in an unhealthy state, and always suffers more or less from a mania of self-aggrandizement, which only his exceptional position conceals from general notice.

Apart from the fact that such men are surrounded from earliest childhood to the grave by the most insensate luxury and an atmosphere of falsehood and flattery which always accompanies them, their whole education and all their occupations are centred on one object: learning about former murders, the best present-day ways of murdering, and the best preparations for future murder. From childhood they learn about killing in all its possible forms. They always carry about with them murderous weapons – swords or sabres; they dress themselves in various uniforms; they attend parades, reviews and manœuvres; they visit one another, presenting one another with Orders and nominating one another to the command of regiments – and not only does no one tell them plainly what they are doing, or say that to busy one's self with preparations for killing is revolting and criminal, but from all sides they hear nothing but approval and enthusiasm for all this activity of theirs. Every time they go out, and at each parade and review, crowds of people flock to greet them with enthusiasm, and it seems to them as if the whole nation approves of their conduct. The only part of the press that reaches them, and that seems to them the expression of the feelings of the whole people, or at least of its best representatives, most slavishly extols their every word and action, however silly or wicked they may be. Those around them, men and women, clergy and laity – all people who do not prize human dignity – vying with one another in refined flattery, agree with them about anything and deceive them about everything, making it impossible for them to see life as it is. Such rulers might live a hundred years without ever seeing one single really independent man or ever hearing the truth spoken. One is sometimes appalled to hear of the words and deeds of these men; but one need only consider their position in order to understand that anyone in their place would act as they do. If a reasonable man found himself in their place, there is only one reasonable action he could perform, and that would be to get away from such a position. Anyone remaining in it would behave as they do.

What, indeed, must go on in the head of some Wilhelm of Germany – a narrow-minded, ill-educated, vain man, with the ideals of a German Junker – when there is nothing he can say so stupid or so horrid that it will not be met by an enthusiastic '*Hoch!*' and be commented on by the press of the entire world as though it were something highly important. When he says that, at his word, soldiers should be ready to kill their own fathers, people shout 'Hurrah!' When he says that the Gospel must be introduced with an iron fist – 'Hurrah!' When he says the army is to take no prisoners in China, but to slaughter everybody, he is not put into a lunatic asylum, but people shout 'Hurrah!' and set sail for China to execute his commands. Or Nicholas II (a man naturally modest) begins his reign by announcing to venerable old men who had expressed a wish to be allowed to discuss their own affairs, that such ideas of self-government were 'insensate dreams' – and the organs of the press he sees, and the people he meets, praise him for it. He proposes a childish, silly and hypocritical project of universal peace, while at the same time ordering an increase in the army – and there are no limits to the laudations of his wisdom and virtue. Without any need, he foolishly and mercilessly insults and oppresses a whole nation, the Finns, and again he hears nothing but praise. Finally, he arranges the Chinese slaughter – terrible in its injustice, cruelty and incompatibility with his peace projects – and, from all sides, people applaud him, both as a victor and as a continuer of his father's peace policy.

What, indeed, must be going on in the heads and hearts of these men?

So it is not the Alexanders and Humberts, nor the Wilhelms, Nicholases and Chamberlains – though they decree these oppressions of the nations and these wars – who are really the most guilty of these sins, but it is rather those who place and support them in the position of arbiters over the lives of their fellow-men. And, therefore, the thing to do is not to kill Alexanders, Nicholases, Wilhelms and Humberts, but to cease to support the arrangement of society of which they are a result. And what supports the present order of society is the selfishness and stupefaction of the people, who sell their freedom and honour for insignificant material advantages.

People who stand on the lowest rung of the ladder – partly as a result of being stupefied by a patriotic and pseudo-religious education, and partly for the sake of personal advantages – cede their freedom and sense of human dignity at the bidding of those who stand above them and offer them material advantages. In the same way – in consequence of stupefaction, and chiefly for the sake of advantages – those who are a little higher up the ladder cede their freedom and manly dignity, and the same thing repeats itself with those standing yet higher, and so on to the topmost rung – to those who, or to him who, standing at the apex of the social cone have nothing more to obtain: for whom the only motives of action are love of power and vanity, and who are generally so perverted and stupefied by the power of life and death which they hold over their fellow-men, and by the consequent servility and flattery of those who surround them, that, without ceasing to do evil, they feel quite assured that they are benefactors to the human race.

It is the people who sacrifice their dignity as men for material profit that produce these men who cannot act otherwise than as they do act, and with whom it is useless to be angry for their stupid and wicked actions. To kill such men is like whipping children whom one has first spoilt.

That nations should not be oppressed, and that there should be none of these useless wars, and that men may not be indignant with those who seem to cause these evils, and may not kill them – it seems that only a very small thing is necessary. It is necessary that men should understand things as they are, should call them by their right names, and should know that an army is an instrument for killing, and that the enrolment and management of an army – the very things which kings, emperors and presidents occupy themselves with so self-confidently – is a preparation for murder.

If only each king, emperor and president understood that his work of directing armies is not an honourable and important duty, as his flatterers persuade him it is, but a bad and shameful act of preparation for murder – and if each private individual understood that the payment of taxes wherewith to hire and equip soldiers, and, above all, army-service itself, are not matters of indifference, but are bad and shameful actions by which he not only permits but participates in murder – then this power of emperors, kings and presidents, which now arouses our indignation, and which causes them to be murdered, would disappear of itself.

So that the Alexanders, Carnots, Humberts and others should not be murdered, but it should be explained to them that they are themselves murderers, and, chiefly, they should not be allowed to kill people: men should refuse to murder at their command.

If people do not yet act in this way, it is only because Governments, to maintain themselves, diligently exercise a hypnotic influence upon the people. And, therefore, we may help to prevent people killing either kings or one another, not by killing – murder only increases the hypnotism – but by arousing people from their hypnotic condition.

And it is this I have tried to do by these remarks.

Prohibited in Russia, an attempt was made to print this article in the Russian language in Germany; but the edition was seized in July 1903, and after a trial in the Provincial Court of Leipzig (August 1903) it was pronounced to be insulting to the German Kaiser, and all copies were ordered to be destroyed. [A. M.]

[Translated by Aylmer Maude]

PATRIOTISM AND GOVERNMENT [1900]

> The time is fast approaching when to call a man a patriot will be the deepest insult you can offer him. Patriotism now means advocating plunder in the interests of the privileged classes of the particular State system into which we have happened to be born.
>
> – E. Belfort Bax

I

I have already several times expressed the thought that in our day the feeling of patriotism is an unnatural, irrational and harmful feeling, and a cause of a great part of the ills from which mankind is suffering; and that, consequently, this feeling should not be cultivated, as is now being done, but should, on the contrary, be suppressed and eradicated by all means available to rational men. Yet, strange to say – though it is undeniable that the universal armaments and destructive wars which are ruining the peoples result from that one feeling – all my arguments showing the backwardness, anachronism and harmfulness of patriotism have been met, and are still met, either by silence, by intentional misinterpretation, or by a strange unvarying reply to the effect that only bad patriotism (Jingoism, or Chauvinism) is evil, but that real good patriotism is a very elevated moral feeling, to condemn which is not only irrational but wicked.

What this real, good patriotism consists in, we are never told; or, if anything is said about it, instead of explanation we get declamatory, inflated phrases, or, finally, some other conception is substituted for patriotism – something which has nothing in common with the patriotism we all know, and from the results of which we all suffer so severely.

It is generally said that the real, good patriotism consists in desiring for one's own people or State such real benefits as do not infringe the well-being of other nations.

Talking recently to an Englishman about the present war,* I said to him that the real cause of the war was not avarice, as people generally say, but patriotism, as is evident from the temper of the whole of English society. The Englishman did not agree with me, and said that even were the case so, it resulted from the fact that the patriotism at present inspiring Englishmen is a bad patriotism; but that good patriotism, such as he was imbued with, would cause Englishmen, his compatriots, to act well.

'Then do you wish only Englishmen to act well?' I asked.

'I wish all men to do so,' said he; indicating clearly by that reply the characteristic of true benefits – whether moral, scientific or even material and practical – which is that they spread out to all men. But, evidently, to wish such benefits to everyone, not only is not patriotic, but is the reverse of patriotic.

Neither do the peculiarities of each people constitute patriotism, though these things are purposely substituted for the conception of patriotism by its defenders. They say that the peculiarities of each people are an essential condition of human progress, and that patriotism, which seeks to maintain those peculiarities, is, therefore, a good and useful feeling. But is it not quite evident that if, once upon a time, these peculiarities of each people – these customs, creeds, languages – were conditions necessary for the life of humanity, in our time these same peculiarities form the chief obstacle to what is already recognized as an ideal – the brotherly union of the peoples? And therefore the maintenance and defence of any nationality – Russian, German, French or Anglo-Saxon, provoking the corresponding maintenance and defence not only of Hungarian, Polish and Irish nationalities, but also of Basque, Provençal,

* That is, the South African War of 1899–1902. [A. M.]

Mordva,* Tchouvash and many other nationalities – serves not to harmonize and unite men, but to estrange and divide them more and more from one another.

So that not the imaginary but the real patriotism, which we all know, by which most people today are swayed and from which humanity suffers so severely, is not the wish for spiritual benefits for one's own people (it is impossible to desire spiritual benefits for one's own people only), but is a very definite feeling of preference for one's own people or State above all other peoples and States, and a consequent wish to get for that people or State the greatest advantages and power that can be got – things which are obtainable only at the expense of the advantages and power of other peoples or States.

It would, therefore, seem obvious that patriotism as a feeling is bad and harmful, and as a doctrine is stupid. For it is clear that if each people and each State considers itself the best of peoples and States, they all live in a gross and harmful delusion.

II

One would expect the harmfulness and irrationality of patriotism to be evident to everybody. But the surprising fact is that cultured and learned men not only do not themselves notice the harm and stupidity of patriotism, but they resist every exposure of it with the greatest obstinacy and ardour (though without any rational grounds), and continue to belaud it as beneficent and elevating.

What does this mean?

Only one explanation of this amazing fact presents itself to me.

All human history, from the earliest times to our own day, may be considered as a movement of the consciousness, both of individuals and of homogeneous groups, from lower ideas to higher ones.

* The Mordva (or Mordvinian) and Tchouvash tribes are of Finnish origin, and inhabit chiefly the governments of the Middle Volga. [A. M.]

The whole path travelled both by individuals and by homogeneous groups may be represented as a consecutive flight of steps from the lowest, on the level of animal life, to the highest attained by the consciousness of man at a given moment of history.

Each man, like each separate homogeneous group, nation or State, always moved and moves up this ladder of ideas. Some portions of humanity are in front, others lag far behind, others, again – the majority – move somewhere between the most advanced and the most backward. But all, whatever stage they may have reached, are inevitably and irresistibly moving from lower to higher ideas. And always, at any given moment, both the individuals and the separate groups of people – advanced, middle or backward – stand in three different relations to the three stages of ideas amid which they move.

Always, both for the individual and for the separate groups of people, there are the ideas of the past, which are worn out and have become strange to them, and to which they cannot revert: as, for instance, in our Christian world, the ideas of cannibalism, universal plunder, the rape of wives, and other customs of which only a record remains.

And there are the ideas of the present, instilled into men's minds by education, by example and by the general activity of all around them; ideas under the power of which they live at a given time: for instance, in our own day, the ideas of property, State organization, trade, utilization of domestic animals, etc.

And there are the ideas of the future, of which some are already approaching realization and are obliging people to change their way of life and to struggle against the former ways: such ideas in our world as those of freeing the labourers, of giving equality to women, of disusing flesh food, etc.; while others, though already recognized, have not yet come into practical conflict with the old forms of life: such in our times are the ideas (which we call ideals) of the extermination of violence, the arrangement of a communal system of property, of a universal religion and of a general brotherhood of men.

And, therefore, every man and every homogeneous group of men, on whatever level they may stand, having behind them the worn-out remembrances of the past, and before them the ideals of the future, are always in a state of struggle between the moribund ideas of the present and the ideas of the future that are coming to life. It usually happens that when an idea which has been useful and even necessary in the past becomes superfluous, that idea, after a more or less prolonged struggle, yields its place to a new idea which was till then an ideal, but which thus becomes a present idea.

But it does occur that an antiquated idea, already replaced in people's consciousness by a higher one, is of such a kind that its maintenance is profitable to those people who have the greatest influence in their society. And then it happens that this antiquated idea, though it is in sharp contradiction to the whole surrounding form of life, which has been altering in other respects, continues to influence people and to sway their actions. Such retention of antiquated ideas always has occurred, and still does occur, in the region of religion. The cause is, that the priests, whose profitable positions are bound up with the antiquated religious idea, purposely use their power to hold people to this antiquated idea.

The same thing occurs, and for similar reasons, in the political sphere, with reference to the patriotic idea, on which all arbitrary power is based. People to whom it is profitable to do so, maintain that idea by artificial means, though it now lacks both sense and utility. And as these people possess the most powerful means of influencing others, they are able to achieve their object.

In this, it seems to me, lies the explanation of the strange contrast between the antiquated patriotic idea, and that whole drift of ideas making in a contrary direction, which have already entered into the consciousness of the Christian world.

III

Patriotism, as a feeling of exclusive love for one's own people, and as a doctrine of the virtue of sacrificing one's tranquillity, one's property, and even one's life, in defence of one's own people from slaughter and outrage by their enemies, was the highest idea of the period when each nation considered it feasible and just, for its own advantage, to subject to slaughter and outrage the people of other nations.

But, already some 2,000 years ago, humanity, in the person of the highest representatives of its wisdom, began to recognize the higher idea of a brotherhood of man; and that idea, penetrating man's consciousness more and more, has in our time attained most varied forms of realization. Thanks to improved means of communication, and to the unity of industry, of trade, of the arts and of science, men are today so bound one to another that the danger of conquest, massacre or outrage by a neighbouring people, has quite disappeared, and all peoples (the peoples, but not the Governments) live together in peaceful, mutually advantageous and friendly commercial, industrial, artistic and scientific relations, which they have no need and no desire to disturb. One would think, therefore, that the antiquated feeling of patriotism – being superfluous and incompatible with the consciousness we have reached of the existence of brotherhood among men of different nationalities – should dwindle more and more until it completely disappears. Yet the very opposite of this occurs: this harmful and antiquated feeling not only continues to exist, but burns more and more fiercely.

The peoples, without any reasonable ground, and contrary alike to their conception of right and to their own advantage, not only sympathize with Governments in their attacks on other nations, in their seizures of foreign possessions, and in defending by force what they have already stolen, but even themselves demand such attacks, seizures and defences: are glad of them, and take pride in them. The small oppressed nationalities which have fallen under the power of the great States – the Poles, Irish, Bohemians, Finns or Armenians – resenting the patriotism of their conquerors, which is the cause of their oppression, catch from them the infection of this feeling of patriotism – which has ceased to be necessary, and is now obsolete, unmeaning and harmful – and catch it to such a degree that all their activity is concentrated upon it, and they, themselves suffering from the patriotism of the stronger nations, are ready, for the sake of patriotism, to perpetrate on other peoples the very same deeds that their oppressors have perpetrated and are perpetrating on them.

This occurs because the ruling classes (including not only the actual rulers with their officials, but all the classes who enjoy an exceptionally advantageous position: the capitalists, journalists, and most of the artists and scientists) can retain their position – exceptionally advantageous in comparison with that of the labouring masses – thanks only to the Government organization, which rests on patriotism. They have in their hands all the most powerful means of influencing the people, and always sedulously support patriotic feelings in themselves and in others, more especially as those feelings which uphold the Government's power are those that are always best rewarded by that power.

Every official prospers the more in his career, the more patriotic he is; so also the army man gets promotion in time of war – the war is produced by patriotism.

Patriotism and its result – wars – give an enormous revenue to the newspaper trade, and profits to many other trades. Every writer, teacher and professor is more secure in his place the more he preaches patriotism. Every emperor and king obtains the more fame the more he is addicted to patriotism.

The ruling classes have in their hands the army, money, the schools, the churches and the press. In the schools they kindle patriotism in the children by means of histories describing their own people as the best of all peoples and always in the right. Among adults they kindle it by spectacles, jubilees, monuments, and by a lying patriotic press. Above all, they inflame patriotism in this way: perpetrating every kind of injustice and harshness against other nations, they provoke in them enmity towards their own people, and then in turn exploit that enmity to embitter their people against the foreigner.

The intensification of this terrible feeling of patriotism has gone on among the European peoples in a rapidly increasing progression, and in our time has reached the utmost limits, beyond which there is no room for it to extend.

IV

Within the memory of people not yet old, an occurrence took place showing most obviously the amazing intoxication caused by patriotism among the people of Christendom.

The ruling classes of Germany excited the patriotism of the masses of their people to such a degree that, in the second half of the nineteenth century, a law was proposed in accordance with which all the men had to become soldiers: all the sons, husbands, fathers, learned men and godly men had to learn to murder, to become submissive slaves of those above them in military rank, and be absolutely ready to kill whomsoever they were ordered to kill; to kill men of oppressed nationalities, and their own working-men standing up for their rights, and even their own fathers and brothers – as was publicly proclaimed by that most impudent of potentates, Wilhelm II.

That horrible measure, outraging all man's best feelings in the grossest manner, was, under the influence of patriotism, acquiesced in without murmur by the people of Germany. It resulted in their victory over the French. That victory yet further excited the patriotism of Germany, and, by reaction, that of France, Russia and the other Powers; and the men of the European countries unresistingly submitted to the introduction of general military service – i.e., to a state of slavery involving a degree of humiliation and submission incomparably worse than any slavery of the ancient world. After this servile submission of the masses to the calls of patriotism, the audacity, cruelty and insanity of the Governments knew no bounds. A competition in the usurpation of other peoples' lands in Asia, Africa and America began – evoked partly by whim, partly by vanity, and partly by covetousness – and was accompanied by ever greater and greater distrust and enmity between the Governments.

The destruction of the inhabitants on the lands seized was accepted as a quite natural proceeding. The only question was, who should be first in seizing other peoples' land and destroying the inhabitants? All the Governments not only most evidently infringed, and are infringing, the elementary demands of justice in relation to the conquered peoples, and in relation to one another, but they were guilty, and continue to be guilty, of every kind of cheating, swindling, bribing, fraud, spying, robbery and murder; and the peoples not only sympathized, and still sympathize, with them in all this, but they rejoice when it is their own Government and not another Government that commits such crimes.

The mutual enmity between the different peoples and States has reached latterly such amazing dimensions that, notwithstanding the fact that there is no reason why one State should attack another, everyone knows that all the Governments stand with their claws out and showing their teeth, and only waiting for someone to be in trouble, or become weak, in order to tear him to pieces with as little risk as possible.

All the peoples of the so-called Christian world have been reduced by patriotism to such a state of brutality, that not only those who are obliged to kill or be killed desire slaughter and rejoice in murder, but all the people of Europe and America, living peaceably in their homes exposed to no danger, are, at each war – thanks to easy means of communication and to the press – in the position of the spectators in a Roman circus, and, like them, delight in the slaughter, and raise the bloodthirsty cry, '*Pollice verso*.'*

Not adults only, but also children, pure, wise children, rejoice, according to their nationality, when they hear that the number killed and lacerated by lyddite or other shells on some particular day was not 700 but 1,000 Englishmen or Boers.

And parents (I know such cases) encourage their children in such brutality.

But that is not all. Every increase in the army of one nation (and each nation, being in danger, seeks to increase its army for patriotic reasons) obliges its neighbours to increase their armies, also from patriotism, and this evokes a fresh increase by the first nation.

And the same thing occurs with fortifications and navies: one

* *Pollice verso* ('thumb down') was the sign given in the Roman amphitheatres by the spectators who wished a defeated gladiator to be slain. [A. M.]

State has built ten ironclads, a neighbour builds eleven; then the first builds twelve, and so on to infinity.

'I'll pinch you.' 'And I'll punch your head.' 'And I'll stab you with a dagger.' 'And I'll bludgeon you.' 'And I'll shoot you' . . . Only bad children, drunken men or animals quarrel or fight so, but yet it is just what is going on among the highest representatives of the most enlightened Governments, the very men who undertake to direct the education and the morality of their subjects.

V

The position is becoming worse and worse, and there is no stopping this descent towards evident perdition.

The one way of escape believed in by credulous people has now been closed by recent events. I refer to the Hague Conference, and to the war between England and the Transvaal which immediately followed it.

If people who think little, or but superficially, were able to comfort themselves with the idea that international courts of arbitration would supersede wars and ever-increasing armaments, the Hague Conference and the war that followed it demonstrated in the most palpable manner the impossibility of finding a solution of the difficulty in that way. After the Hague Conference, it became obvious that as long as Governments with armies exist, the termination of armaments and of wars is impossible. That an agreement should become possible, it is necessary that the parties to it should *trust* each other. And in order that the Powers should trust each other, they must lay down their arms, as is done by the bearers of a flag of truce when they meet for a conference.

So long as Governments, distrusting one another, not only do not disband or decrease their armies, but always increase them in correspondence with augmentations made by their neighbours, and by means of spies watch every movement of troops, knowing that each of the Powers will attack its neighbour as soon as it sees its way to do so, no agreement is possible, and every conference is either a stupidity, or a pastime, or a fraud, or an impertinence, or all of these together.

It was particularly becoming for the Russian rather than any other Government to be the *enfant terrible* of the Hague Conference. No one at home being allowed to reply to all its evidently mendacious manifestations and rescripts, the Russian Government is so spoilt, that – having without the least scruple ruined its own people with armaments, strangled Poland, plundered Turkestan and China, and being specially engaged in suffocating Finland – it proposed disarmament to the Governments, in full assurance that it would be trusted!

But strange, unexpected and indecent as such a proposal was – especially at the very time when orders were being given to increase its army – the words publicly uttered in the hearing of the people were such, that for the sake of appearances the Governments of the other Powers could not decline the comical and evidently insincere consultation; and so the delegates met – knowing in advance that nothing would come of it – and for several weeks (during which they drew good salaries), though they were laughing in their sleeves, they all conscientiously pretended to be much occupied in arranging peace among the nations.

The Hague Conference, followed up as it was by the terrible bloodshed of the Transvaal War, which no one attempted, or is now attempting, to stop, was, nevertheless, of some use, though not at all in the way expected of it – it was useful because it showed in the most obvious manner that the evils from which the peoples are suffering cannot be cured by Governments. That Governments, even if they wished to, can terminate neither armaments nor wars.

Governments, to have a reason for existing, must defend their people from other people's attack. But not one people wishes to attack, or does attack, another. And therefore Governments, far from wishing for peace, carefully excite the anger of other nations against themselves. And having excited other people's anger against themselves, and stirred up the patriotism of their own people, each Government then assures its people that it is in danger and must be defended.

And having the power in their hands, the Governments can both irritate other nations and excite patriotism at home, and they carefully do both the one and the other; nor can they act otherwise, for their existence depends on thus acting.

If, in former times, Governments were necessary to defend their people from other people's attacks, now, on the contrary, Governments artificially disturb the peace that exists between the nations, and provoke enmity among them.

When it was necessary to plough in order to sow, ploughing was wise; but evidently it is absurd and harmful to go on ploughing after the seed has been sown. But this is just what the Governments are obliging their people to do: to infringe the unity which exists, and which nothing would infringe if it were not for the Governments.

VI

In reality what are these Governments, without which people think they could not exist?

There may have been a time when such Governments were necessary, and when the evil of supporting a Government was less than that of being defenceless against organized neighbours; but now such Governments have become unnecessary, and are a far greater evil than all the dangers with which they frighten their subjects.

Not only military Governments, but Governments in general, could be, I will not say useful, but at least harmless, only if they consisted of immaculate, holy people, as is theoretically the case among the Chinese. But then Governments, by the nature of their activity, which consists in committing acts of violence,* are always composed of elements the most contrary to holiness – of the most audacious, unscrupulous and perverted people.

* The word *government* is frequently used in an indefinite sense as almost equivalent to management or direction; but in the sense in which the word is used in the present article, the characteristic feature of a Government is that it claims a moral right to inflict physical penalties, and by its decree to make murder a good action. [A. M.]

A Government, therefore, and especially a Government entrusted with military power, is the most dangerous organization possible.

The Government, in the widest sense, including capitalists and the press, is nothing else than an organization which places the greater part of the people in the power of a smaller part, who dominate them; that smaller part is subject to a yet smaller part, and that again to a yet smaller, and so on, reaching at last a few people, or one single man, who by means of military force has power over all the rest. So that all this organization resembles a cone, of which all the parts are completely in the power of those people, or of that one person, who happen to be at the apex.

The apex of the cone is seized by those who are more cunning, audacious and unscrupulous than the rest, or by someone who happens to be the heir of those who were audacious and unscrupulous.

Today it may be Borís Godunof,* and tomorrow Gregory Otrepyef.† Today the licentious Catherine, who with her paramours has murdered her husband; tomorrow Pougatchef;‡ then Paul the madman, Nicholas I or Alexander III.

Today it may be Napoleon, tomorrow a Bourbon or an Orléans, a Boulanger or a Panama Company; today it may be Gladstone, tomorrow Salisbury, Chamberlain or Rhodes.

And to such Governments is allowed full power, not only over property and lives, but even over the spiritual and moral development, the education and the religious guidance of everybody.

People construct such a terrible machine of power, they allow any one to seize it who can (and the chances always are that it will be seized by the most morally worthless) – they slavishly submit to him, and are then surprised that evil comes of it.

* Boris Godunof, brother-in-law of the weak Tsar Fyodor Ivanovitch, succeeded in becoming Tsar, and reigned in Moscow from 1598 to 1605. [A. M.]

† Gregory Otrepyef was a pretender who, passing himself off as Dimitry, son of Ivan the Terrible, reigned in Moscow in 1605 and 1606. [A. M.]

‡ Pougatchef was the leader of a most formidable insurrection in 1773–75, and was executed in Moscow in 1775. [A. M.]

They are afraid of Anarchists' bombs, and are not afraid of this terrible organization which is always threatening them with the greatest calamities.

People found it useful to tie themselves together in order to resist their enemies, as the Circassians* did when resisting attacks. But the danger is quite past, and yet people go on tying themselves together.

They carefully tie themselves up so that one man can have them all at his mercy; then they throw away the end of the rope that ties them, and leave it trailing for some rascal or fool to seize and to do them whatever harm he likes.

Really, what are people doing but just that – when they set up, submit to, and maintain an organized and military Government?

VII

To deliver men from the terrible and ever-increasing evils of armaments and wars, we want neither congresses nor conferences, nor treaties, nor courts of arbitration, but the destruction of those instruments of violence which are called Governments, and from which humanity's greatest evils flow.

To destroy Governmental *violence*, only one thing is needed: it is that people should understand that the feeling of patriotism, which alone supports that instrument of violence, is a rude, harmful, disgraceful and bad feeling, and, above all, is immoral. It is a rude feeling, because it is one natural only to people standing on the lowest level of morality, and expecting from other nations such outrages as they themselves are ready to inflict; it is a harmful feeling, because it disturbs advantageous and joyous, peaceful relations with other peoples, and above all produces that Governmental organization under which power may fall, and does fall, into the hands of the worst men;

* The Circassians, when surrounded, used to tie themselves together leg to leg, that none might escape, but all die fighting. Instances of this kind occurred when their country was being annexed by Russia. [A. M.]

it is a disgraceful feeling, because it turns man not merely into a slave, but into a fighting cock, a bull or a gladiator, who wastes his strength and his life for objects which are not his own but his Government's; and it is an immoral feeling, because, instead of confessing one's self a son of God (as Christianity teaches us) or even a free man guided by his own reason, each man under the influence of patriotism confesses himself the son of his fatherland and the slave of his Government, and commits actions contrary to his reason and his conscience.

It is only necessary that people should understand this, and the terrible bond, called Government, by which we are chained together, will fall to pieces of itself without struggle; and with it will cease the terrible and useless evils it produces.

And people are already beginning to understand this. This, for instance, is what a citizen of the United States writes:

'We are farmers, mechanics, merchants, manufacturers, teachers, and all we ask is the privilege of attending to our own business. We own our homes, love our friends, are devoted to our families, and do not interfere with our neighbours – we have work to do, and wish to work.

'Leave us alone!

'But they will not – these politicians. They insist on governing us and living off our labour. They tax us, eat our substance, conscript us, draft our boys into their wars. All the myriads of men who live off the Government depend upon the Government to tax us, and, in order to tax us successfully, standing armies are maintained. The plea that the army is needed for the protection of the country is pure fraud and pretence. The French Government affrights the people by telling them that the Germans are ready and anxious to fall upon them; the Russians fear the British; the British fear everybody; and now in America we are told we must increase our navy and add to our army because Europe may at any moment combine against us.

'This is fraud and untruth. The plain people in France, Germany, England and America are opposed to war. We only wish to be let alone. Men with wives, children, sweethearts, homes, aged parents, do not want to go off and fight someone. We are peaceable and we fear war; we hate it.

'We would like to obey the Golden Rule.

'War is the sure result of the existence of armed men. That country which maintains a large standing army will sooner or later have a war on hand. The man who prides himself on fisticuffs is going some day to meet a man who considers himself the better man, and they will fight. Germany and France have no issue save a desire to see which is the better man. They have fought many times – and they will fight again. Not that the people want to fight, but the Superior Class fan fright into fury, and make men think they must fight to protect their homes.

'So the people who wish to follow the teachings of Christ are not allowed to do so, but are taxed, outraged, deceived by Governments.

'Christ taught humility, meekness, the forgiveness of one's enemies, and that to kill was wrong. The Bible teaches men not to swear; but the Superior Class swear us on the Bible in which they do not believe.

'The question is, How are we to relieve ourselves of these scavengers who toil not, but who are clothed in broadcloth and blue, with brass buttons and many costly accoutrements; who feed upon our substance, and for whom we delve and dig?

'Shall we fight them?

'No, we do not believe in bloodshed; and besides that, they have the guns and the money, and they can hold out longer than we.

'But who composes this army that they would order to fire upon us?

'Why, our neighbours and brothers – deceived into the idea that they are doing God's service by protecting their country from its enemies. When the fact is, our country has no enemies save the Superior Class, that pretends to look out for our interests if we will only obey and consent to be taxed.

'Thus do they siphon our resources and turn our true brothers upon us to subdue and humiliate us. You cannot send a telegram to your wife, nor an express package to your friend, nor draw a cheque for your grocer, until you first pay the tax to maintain armed men, who can quickly be used to kill you; and who surely will imprison you if you do not pay.

'The only relief lies in education. Educate men that it is wrong to kill. Teach them the Golden Rule, and yet again teach them the Golden Rule. Silently defy this Superior Class by refusing to bow down to their fetish of bullets. Cease supporting the preachers who cry for war and spout patriotism for a consideration. Let them go to work as we do. We believe in Christ – they do not. Christ spoke what he thought; they speak what they think will please the men in power – the Superior Class.

'We will not enlist. We will not shoot on their order. We will not "charge bayonet" upon a mild and gentle people. We will not fire upon shepherds and farmers, fighting for their firesides, upon a suggestion of Cecil Rhodes. Your false cry of "Wolf! wolf!" shall not alarm us. We pay your taxes only because we have to, and we will pay no longer than we have to. We will pay no pew-rents, no tithes to your sham charities, and we will speak our minds upon occasion.

'We will educate men.

'And all the time our silent influence will be going out, and even the men who are conscripted will be half-hearted and refuse to fight. We will educate men into the thought that Christ's Life of Peace and Good-will is better than the Life of Strife, Bloodshed and War.

' "Peace on earth!" – it can only come when men do away with armies, and are willing to do unto other men as they would be done by.'

So writes a citizen of the United States; and from various sides, in various forms, such voices are sounding.

This is what a German soldier writes:

'I went through two campaigns with the Prussian Guards (in 1866 and 1870), and I hate war from the bottom of my soul, for it has made me inexpressibly unfortunate. We wounded soldiers generally receive such a miserable recompense that we have indeed to be ashamed of having once been patriots. I, for instance, get ninepence a day for my right arm, which was shot through at the attack on St Privat, 18 August 1870. Some hunting dogs have more allowed for their keep. And I have suffered for years from my twice wounded arm. Already in 1866 I took part in the war against Austria, and fought at Trautenau and Königgrätz, and saw horrors enough. In 1870, being in the reserve I was called out again; and, as I have already said, I was wounded in the attack at St Privat: my right arm was twice shot through lengthwise. I had to leave a good place in a brewery, and was unable afterwards to regain it. Since then I have never been able to get on my feet again. The intoxication soon passed, and there was nothing left for the wounded invalid but to keep himself alive on a beggarly pittance eked out by charity . . .

'In a world in which people run round like trained animals, and are not capable of any other idea than that of overreaching one another for the sake of mammon – in such a world let people think me a crank; but, for all that, I feel in myself the divine idea of peace, which is so beautifully expressed in the Sermon on the Mount. My deepest conviction is that war is only trade on a larger scale – the ambitious and powerful trade with the happiness of the peoples.

'And what horrors do we not suffer from it! Never shall I forget the pitiful groans that pierced one to the marrow!

'People who never did each other any harm begin to slaughter one another like wild animals, and petty, slavish souls, thus implicating their good Lord, making Him their co-conspirator in such deeds.

'My neighbour in the ranks had his jaw broken by a bullet. The poor wretch went wild with pain. He ran like a madman, and in the scorching summer heat could not even get water to cool his horrible wound. Our commander, the Crown Prince (who was afterwards the noble Emperor Frederick), wrote in his diary: "War – is an irony on the Gospels" . . .'

People are beginning to understand the fraud of patriotism, in which all the Governments take such pains to keep them involved.

VIII

'But,' it is usually asked, 'what will there be instead of Governments?'

There will be nothing. Something that has long been useless, and therefore superfluous and bad, will be abolished. An organ that, being unnecessary, has become harmful, will be abolished.

'But,' people generally say, 'if there is no Government, people will violate and kill each other.'

Why? Why should the abolition of the organization which arose in consequence of violence, and which has been handed down from generation to generation to do violence – why should the abolition of such an organization, now devoid of use, cause people to outrage and kill one another? On the contrary, the presumption is that the abolition of the organ of violence would result in people ceasing to violate and kill one another.

Now, some men are specially educated and trained to kill and to do violence to other people – there are men who are supposed to have a right to use violence, and who make use of an organization which exists for that purpose. Such deeds of violence and such killing are considered good and worthy deeds.

But then, people will not be so brought up, and no one will have a right to use violence to others, and there will be no organization to do violence, and – as is natural to people of our time – violence and murder will always be considered bad actions, no matter who commits them.

But should acts of violence continue to be committed even after the abolition of the Governments, such acts will certainly be fewer than are committed now, when an organization exists specially devised to commit acts of violence, and a state of things exists in which acts of violence and murders are considered good and useful deeds.

The abolition of Governments will merely rid us of an unnecessary organization which we have inherited from the past, an organization for the commission of violence and for its justification.

'But there will then be no laws, no property, no courts of justice, no police, no popular education,' say people who intentionally confuse the use of violence by Governments with various social activities.

The abolition of the organization of Government formed to do violence, does not at all involve the abolition of what is reasonable and good, and therefore not based on violence, in laws or law courts, or in property, or in police regulations, or in financial arrangements, or in popular education. On the contrary, the absence of the brutal power of Government, which is needed only for its own support, will facilitate a juster and more reasonable social organization, needing no violence. Courts of justice, and public affairs, and popular education, will all exist to the extent to which they are really needed by the people, but in a shape which will not involve the evils contained in the present form of Government. Only that will be destroyed which was evil and hindered the free expression of the people's will.

But even if we assume that with the absence of Governments there would be disturbances and civil strife, even then the position of the people would be better than it is at present. The position now is such that it is difficult to imagine anything worse. The people are ruined, and their ruin is becoming more and more complete. The men are all converted into war-slaves, and have from day to day to expect orders to go to kill and to be killed. What more? Are the ruined peoples to die of hunger? Even that is already beginning in Russia, in Italy and in India. Or are the women as well as the men to go to be soldiers? In the Transvaal even that has begun.

So that even if the absence of Government really meant Anarchy in the negative, disorderly sense of that word – which is far from being the case – even then no anarchical disorder could be worse than the position to which Governments have already led their peoples, and to which they are leading them.

And therefore emancipation from patriotism, and the destruction of the despotism of Government that rests upon it, cannot but be beneficial to mankind.

IX

Men, recollect yourselves! For the sake of your well-being, physical and spiritual, for the sake of your brothers and sisters, pause, consider, and think of what you are doing!

Reflect, and you will understand that your foes are not the Boers, or the English, or the French, or the Germans, or the Finns, or the Russians, but that your foes – your only foes – are you yourselves, who by your patriotism maintain the Governments that oppress you and make you unhappy.

They have undertaken to protect you from danger, and they have brought that pseudo-protection to such a point that you have all become soldiers – slaves, and are all ruined, or are being ruined more and more, and at any moment may and should expect that the tight-stretched cord will snap, and a horrible slaughter of you and your children will commence.

And however great that slaughter may be, and however that conflict may end, the same state of things will continue. In the same way, and with yet greater intensity, the Governments will arm, and ruin, and pervert you and your children, and no one will help you to stop it or to prevent it, if you do not help yourselves.

And there is only one kind of help possible – it lies in the abolition of that terrible linking up into a cone of violence, which enables the person or persons who succeed in seizing the apex to have power over all the rest, and to hold that power the more firmly the more cruel and inhuman they are, as we see by the cases of the Napoleons, Nicholas I, Bismarck, Chamberlain, Rhodes and our Russian Dictators who rule the people in the Tsar's name.

And there is only one way to destroy this binding together – it is by shaking off the hypnotism of patriotism.

Understand that all the evils from which you suffer, you yourselves cause by yielding to the suggestions by which emperors, kings, members of parliament, governors, officers, capitalists, priests, authors, artists, and all who need this fraud of patriotism in order to live upon your labour, deceive you!

Whoever you may be – Frenchman, Russian, Pole, Englishman, Irishman or Bohemian – understand that all your real human interests, whatever they may be – agricultural, industrial, commercial, artistic or scientific – as well as your pleasures and joys, in no way run counter to the interests of other peoples or States; and that you are united, by mutual co-operation, by interchange of services, by the joy of wide brotherly intercourse, and by the interchange not merely of goods but also of thoughts and feelings, with the folk of other lands.

Understand that the question as to who manages to seize Wei-hai-wei, Port Arthur or Cuba – your Government or another – does not affect you, or, rather, that every such seizure made by your Government injures you, by inevitably bringing in its train all sorts of pressure on you by your Government to force you to take part in the robbery and violence by which alone such seizures are made, or can be retained when made. Understand that your life can in no way be bettered by Alsace becoming German or French, and Ireland or Poland being free or enslaved – whoever holds them, you are free to live where you will, if even you be an Alsatian, an Irishman or a Pole. Understand, too, that by stirring up patriotism you will only make the case worse, for the subjection in which your people are kept has resulted simply from the struggle between patriotisms, and every manifestation of patriotism in one nation provokes a corresponding reaction in another. Understand that salvation from your woes is only possible when you free yourself from the obsolete idea of patriotism and from the obedience to Governments that is based upon it, and when you boldly enter into the region of that higher idea, the brotherly union of the peoples, which has long since come to life, and from all sides, is calling you to itself.

If people would but understand that they are not the sons of some fatherland or other, nor of Governments, but are sons of God, and can therefore neither be slaves nor enemies one to another – those insane, unnecessary, worn-out, pernicious organizations called Governments, and all the sufferings, violations, humiliations and crimes which they occasion, would cease.

[Translated by Aylmer Maude]

A REPLY TO THE SYNOD'S EDICT OF EXCOMMUNICATION, AND TO LETTERS RECEIVED BY ME CONCERNING IT [1901]

> He who begins by loving Christianity better than truth, will proceed by loving his own sect or church better than Christianity, and end in loving himself better than all. – Coleridge

At first I did not wish to reply to the Synod's Edict about me but it has called forth very many letters in which correspondents unknown to me write – some of them scolding me for rejecting things I never rejected; others exhorting me to believe in things I have always believed in; others, again, expressing an agreement with me which probably does not really exist, and a sympathy to which I am hardly entitled. So I have decided to reply both to the Edict itself – indicating what is unjust in it – and to the communications of my unknown correspondents.

The Edict of the Synod has, in general, many defects. It is either illegal, or else intentionally equivocal; it is arbitrary, unfounded, untruthful, and is also libellous and incites to evil feelings and deeds.

It is illegal or intentionally equivocal; for if it is intended as an Excommunication from the Church, it fails to conform to the Church regulations subject to which Excommunications can be pronounced; while if it is merely an announcement of the fact that one who does not believe in the Church and its dogmas does not belong to the Church – that is self-evident, and the announcement can have no purpose other than to pass for an Excommunication without really being one; as happened, in fact, for that is how the Edict has been understood.

It is arbitrary, for it accuses only me of disbelief in all the points enumerated in the Edict; whereas many, in fact almost all educated people, share that disbelief and have constantly expressed and still express it both in conversations, in lectures, in pamphlets and in books.

It is unfounded because it gives as a chief cause of its publication the great circulation of the false teaching wherewith I pervert the people – whereas I am well assured that hardly a hundred people can be found who share my views, and the circulation of my writings on religion, thanks to the Censor, is so insignificant that the majority of those who have read the Synod's Edict have not the least notion of what I may have written about religion – as is shown by the letters I have received.

It contains an obvious falsehood, for it says that efforts have been made by the Church to show me my errors, but that these efforts have been unsuccessful. Nothing of the kind ever took place.

It constitutes what in legal terminology is called a libel, for it contains assertions known to be false and tending to my hurt.

It is, finally, an incentive to evil feelings and deeds, for, as was to be expected, it evoked, in unenlightened and unreasoning people, anger and hatred against me, culminating in threats of murder expressed in letters I received. One writes: 'Now thou hast been anathematized, and after death wilt go to everlasting torments, and wilt perish like a dog . . . anathema upon thee, old devil . . . be damned.' Another blames the Government for not having, as yet, shut me up in a monastery, and fills his letter with abuse. A third writes: 'If the Government does not get rid of you, we will ourselves make you shut your mouth', and the letter ends with curses. 'May you be destroyed – you blackguard!' writes a fourth; 'I shall find means to do it . . .' and then follows indecent abuse. After the publication of the Synod's

Edict I also noticed indications of anger of this kind in some of the people I met. On the very day (25 February) when the Edict was made public, while crossing a public square I heard the words: 'See! there goes the devil in human form', and had the crowd been composed of other elements I should very likely have been beaten to death, as happened some years ago to a man at the Panteleymon Chapel.

So that, altogether, the Synod's Edict is very bad; and the statement, at the end, that those who sign it pray that I may become such as they are, does not make it any better.

That relates to the Edict as a whole; as to details, it is wrong in the following particulars. It is said in the Edict: 'A writer well known to the world, Russian by birth, Orthodox by baptism and education – Count Tolstoy – under the seduction of his intellectual pride has insolently risen against the Lord and against his Christ and against his holy heritage, and has publicly, in the sight of all men, renounced the Orthodox Mother Church which has reared him and educated him.'

That I have renounced the Church which calls itself Orthodox is perfectly correct.

But I renounced it not because I had risen against the Lord, but, on the contrary, only because with all the strength of my soul I wished to serve Him. Before renouncing the Church, and fellowship with the people which was inexpressibly dear to me, I – having seen some reasons to doubt the Church's integrity – devoted several years to the investigation of its theoretic and practical teachings. For the theory, I read all I could about Church doctrine, and studied and critically analysed dogmatic theology; while as to practice, for more than a year I followed strictly all the injunctions of the Church, observing all the fasts and all the services. And I became convinced that Church doctrine is theoretically a crafty and harmful lie, and practically a collection of the grossest superstitions and sorcery, which completely conceals the whole meaning of Christ's teaching.*

* One need only read the Prayer-Book, and follow the ritual which is continually performed by the Orthodox priests, and which is considered a Christian worship of God, to see that all these ceremonies are nothing but different kinds of sorcery, adapted to all the incidents of life. That a child in case of death

And I really repudiated the Church, ceased to observe its ceremonies, and wrote a will instructing those near me that when I die they should not allow any servants of the Church to have access to me, but should put away my dead body as quickly as possible – without having any incantations or prayers over it – just as one puts away any objectionable and useless object, that it may not be an inconvenience to the living.

As to the statements made about me, that I devote the 'literary activity and the talent given to him by God, to disseminating among the people teachings contrary to Christ and to the Church', and that, 'in his works and in letters issued by him and by his disciples in great quantities, over the whole world, but particularly within the limits of our dear fatherland, he preaches with the zeal of a fanatic the overthrow of all the dogmas of the Orthodox Church and the very essence of the Christian faith' – this is not true. I never troubled myself about the propagation of my teaching. It is true that for myself I have expressed in writings my understanding of Christ's teaching, and have not hidden these works from those who wished to become acquainted with them, but I never published them myself. Only when they have asked me about it have I told people how I understand Christ's teaching. To those that asked, I said what I thought, and (when I had them) gave them my books.

Then it is said that 'he denies God worshipped in the Holy Trinity, the Creator and Protector of the universe; denies our Lord Jesus Christ, God-man, Redeemer and Saviour of the world, who suffered for us men and for our salvation, and was raised from the dead; denies the immaculate conception of the Lord Christ as man, and the virginity before His birth and

should go to Paradise, one has to know how to oil him and how to immerse him while pronouncing certain words; in order that after child-birth a mother may cease to be unclean, certain incantations have to be pronounced; to be successful in one's affairs, to live comfortably in a new house, that corn may grow well, that a drought may cease, to recover from sickness, to ease the condition in the next world of one who is dying – for all these and a thousand other incidents there are certain incantations which, at a certain place, for a certain consideration, are pronounced by the priest. [L. T.]

after His birth of the Most Pure Mother of God.' That I deny the incomprehensible Trinity; the fable, which is altogether meaningless in our time, of the fall of the first man; the blasphemous story of a God born of a virgin to redeem the human race – is perfectly true. But God, a Spirit; God, Love; the only God – the Source of all – I not only do not deny, but I attribute real existence to God alone, and I see the whole meaning of life only in fulfilling His will, which is expressed in the Christian teaching.

It is also said: 'He does not acknowledge a life and retribution beyond the grave.' If one is to understand, by life beyond the grave, the Second Advent, a hell with eternal torments, devils, and a Paradise of perpetual happiness – it is perfectly true that I do not acknowledge such a life beyond the grave; but eternal life and retribution here and everywhere, now and for ever, I acknowledge to such an extent that, standing now, at my age, on the verge of my grave, I often have to make an effort to restrain myself from desiring the death of this body – that is, birth to a new life; and I believe every good action increases the true welfare of my eternal life, and every evil action decreases it.

It is also stated that I reject all the Sacraments. That is quite true. I consider all the Sacraments to be coarse, degrading sorcery, incompatible with the idea of God or with the Christian teaching, and also as infringements of very plain injunctions in the Gospels. In the Baptism of Infants I see a palpable perversion of the whole meaning which might be attached to the baptism of adults who consciously accepted Christianity; in the performance of the Sacrament of Marriage over those who are known to have had other sexual unions, in the permission of divorce, and in the consecration of the marriages of divorced people, I see a direct infringement both of the meaning and of the words of the Gospel teaching.

In the periodical absolution of sins at Confession I see a harmful deception, which only encourages immorality and causes men not to fear to sin.

Both in Extreme Unction and in Anointing I see methods of gross sorcery – as in the worship of icons and relics, and as in all the rites, prayers and exorcisms which fill the Prayer-Book.

In the Sacrament I see a deification of the flesh, and a perversion of Christian teaching. In Ordination I see (beside an obvious preparation for deception) a direct infringement of the words of Jesus, which plainly forbid anyone to be called teacher, father or master.*

It is stated, finally, as the last and greatest of my sins, that, 'reviling the most sacred objects of the faith of the Orthodox people, he has not shrunk from subjecting to derision the greatest of Sacraments, the Holy Eucharist.'† That I did not shrink from describing simply and objectively what the priest does when preparing this so-called Sacrament is perfectly true; but that this so-called Sacrament is anything holy, and that to describe it simply, just as it is performed, is blasphemy, is quite untrue. Blasphemy does not consist in calling a partition a partition, and not an iconostasis,‡ and a cup a cup, and not a chalice, etc.; but it is a most terrible, continual and revolting blasphemy that men (using all possible means of deception and hypnotization) assure children and simple-minded folk that if bits of bread are cut up in a particular manner while certain words are pronounced over them, and if they are put into wine,§ God will enter into those bits of bread, and any living person named by the priest when he takes out one of these sops will be healthy, and any dead person named by the priest when he takes out one of these sops will be better off in the other world on that account; and that into the man who eats such a sop – God Himself will enter.

* Matthew 23: 8–10: 'But be not ye called Rabbi: for one is your Master, even Christ; and all ye are brethren. And call no man your father upon the earth: for one is your Father, which is in heaven. Neither be ye called masters: for one is your Master, even Christ.' [A. M.]

† See chapter xxxix, book i, of *Resurrection*; but see also, as a probable provocative of Tolstoy's Excommunication, the description of the Head of the Holy Synod in chapter xxvii, book ii, of that work. [A. M.]

‡ The iconostasis in Russo-Greek churches corresponds, somewhat, both to the Western altar-rails and to a rood-screen. [A. M.]

§ In the Greek Church the priest mixes the sacramental bread with the wine before administering it to the communicant. The reader will note in this article allusions to several practices (baptism by immersion, unction, etc.) which do not exist, or are differently carried out, in the Church of England. [A. M.]

Surely that is terrible!

They undertake to teach us to understand the personality of Christ, but His teaching, which destroys evil in the world, and blesses men so simply, easily and undoubtedly, if only they do not pervert it, is all hidden, is all transformed into a gross sorcery of washings, smearing with oil, gestures, exorcisms, eating of bits of bread, etc., so that of the true teaching nothing remains. And if, at any time, someone tries to remind men that Christ's teaching consists not in this sorcery, not in public prayer, liturgies, candles and icons, but in loving one another, in not returning evil for evil, in not judging or killing one another – the anger of those to whom deception is profitable is aroused, and with incomprehensible audacity they publicly declare in churches, and print in books, newspapers and catechisms, that Jesus never forbade oaths (swearing allegiance, or swearing in courts of law), never forbade murder (executions and wars), and that the teaching of non-resistance to evil has with Satanic ingenuity been invented by the enemies of Christ.*

What is most terrible is that people to whom it is profitable not only deceive adults, but (having power to do so) deceive children also – those very children concerning whom Jesus pronounced woe on him who deceives them. It is terrible that these people for such petty advantages do such fearful harm, by hiding from men the truth that was revealed by Jesus, and that gives blessings such as are not counterbalanced even to the extent of a one-thousandth part by the advantages these men secure for themselves. They behave like a robber who killed a whole family of five or six people to carry off an old coat and ten pence in money. They would willingly have given him all their clothes and all their money not to be killed; but he could not act otherwise.

So it is with the religious deceivers. It would be worth while keeping them ten times better, and letting them live in the greatest luxury, if only they would refrain from ruining men with their deceptions. But they cannot act differently. That is what is awful. And, therefore, we not only may, but should,

* Speech by Ambrosius, Bishop of Kharkof. [L. T.]

unmask their deceptions. If there be a sacred thing, it is surely not what they call Sacraments, but just this very duty of unmasking their religious deceptions when one detects them.

When a Tchouvash smears his idol with sour cream, or beats it, I can refrain from insulting his faith, and can pass by with equanimity, for he does these things in the name of a superstition of his own, foreign to me, and he does not interfere with what to me is holy. But when, with their barbarous superstitions, men (however numerous, however ancient their superstitions, and however powerful they may be) in the name of the God by whom I live, and of that teaching of Christ's which has given life to me and is capable of giving life to all men, preach gross sorcery, I cannot endure it passively. And if I call what they are doing by its name, I only do my duty and what I cannot refrain from doing because I believe in God and in the Christian teaching. If they call the exposure of their imposture 'blasphemy', that only shows the strength of their deception, and should increase the efforts to destroy this deception, made by those who believe in God and in Christ's teaching, and who see that this deception hides the true God from men's sight.

They should say of Christ – who drove bulls and sheep and dealers from the temple – that He blasphemed. Were He to come now, and see what is done in His name in church, He would surely, with yet greater and most just anger, throw out all these horrible altar-cloths,* lances, crosses and cups and candles and icons and all the things wherewith the priests – carrying on their sorcery – hide God and His truth from mankind.

So that is what is true and what is untrue in the Synod's Edict about me. I certainly do not believe in what they say they believe in. But I believe in much they wish to persuade people that I disbelieve in.

I believe in this: I believe in God, whom I understand as Spirit, as Love, as the Source of all. I believe that He is in me

* The altar-cloths referred to are those containing fragments of holy relics, on which alone Mass can be celebrated. The 'lances' are diminutive ones with which the priest cuts bits out of the holy bread, in remembrance of the lance that pierced Christ's side. [A. M.]

and I in Him. I believe that the will of God is most clearly and intelligibly expressed in the teaching of the man Jesus, whom to consider as God, and pray to, I esteem the greatest blasphemy. I believe that man's true welfare lies in fulfilling God's will, and His will is that men should love one another, and should consequently do to others as they wish others to do to them – of which it is said in the Gospels that in this is the law and the prophets. I believe, therefore, that the meaning of the life of every man is to be found only in increasing the love that is in him; that this increase of love leads man, even in this life, to ever greater and greater blessedness, and after death gives him the more blessedness the more love he has, and helps more than anything else towards the establishment of the Kingdom of God on earth: that is, to the establishment of an order of life in which the discord, deception and violence that now rule will be replaced by free accord, by truth, and by the brotherly love of one for another. I believe that to obtain progress in love there is only one means: prayer – not public prayer in churches, plainly forbidden by Jesus,* but private prayer, like the sample given them by Jesus, consisting of the renewing and strengthening, in their consciousness, of the meaning of life and of their dependence solely on the will of God.

Whether these beliefs of mine offend, grieve, or prove a stumbling-block to anyone, or hinder anything, or give displeasure to anybody, or not, I can as little change them as I can change my body. I must myself live my own life, and I must myself alone meet death (and that very soon), and therefore I cannot believe otherwise than as I – preparing to go to that God from whom I came – do believe. I do not believe my faith

* 'And when thou prayest, thou shalt not be as the hypocrites are: for they love to pray standing in the synagogues and in the corners of the streets, that they may be seen of men. Verily I say unto you, They have their reward. But thou, when thou prayest, enter into thy closet, and when thou hast shut thy door, pray to thy Father which is in secret, and thy Father which seeth in secret shall reward thee openly. But when ye pray, use not vain repetitions, as the heathen do: for they think that they shall be heard for their much speaking. Be ye not therefore like unto them: for your Father knoweth what things ye have need of, before ye ask him. After this manner therefore pray ye: Our Father,' etc. – Matthew 6: 5–13. [A. M.]

to be the one indubitable truth for all time, but I see no other that is plainer, clearer, or answers better to all the demands of my reason and my heart; should I find such a one, I shall at once accept it; for God requires nothing but the truth. But I can no more return to that from which, with such suffering, I have escaped, than a flying bird can re-enter the eggshell from which it has emerged.

'He who begins by loving Christianity better than truth, will proceed by loving his own sect or church better than Christianity, and end in loving himself [his own peace] better than all,' said Coleridge.

I travelled the contrary way. I began by loving my Orthodox faith more than my peace, then I loved Christianity more than my Church, and now I love truth more than anything in the world. And up to now, truth, for me, corresponds with Christianity as I understand it. And I hold to this Christianity; and to the degree in which I hold to it I live peacefully and happily, and peacefully and happily approach death.

[Translated by Aylmer Maude]

FROM *WHAT IS RELIGION, AND WHEREIN LIES ITS ESSENCE?* [1902]

I

In all human societies, at certain periods of their existence, a time has come when religion has first swerved from its original purpose, then, diverging more and more, it has lost sight of that purpose, and has finally petrified into fixed forms, so that its influence on men's lives has become ever less and less.

At such times the educated minority cease to believe in the established religious teaching, and only pretend to hold it because they think it necessary to do so in order to keep the mass of the people to the established order of life; but the mass of the people, though by inertia they keep to the established forms of religion, no longer guide their lives by its demands, but guide them only by custom and by the State laws.

That is what has repeatedly occurred in various human societies. But what is now happening in our Christian society has never happened before. It never before happened that the rich, ruling and more educated minority, which has the most influence on the masses, not only disbelieved the existing religion, but was convinced that no religion at all is any longer needed, and, instead of influencing those who are doubtful of the truth of the generally professed religion to accept some religious teaching more rational and clear than the prevalent one, influenced them to regard religion in general as a thing that has outlived its day, and is now not merely a useless, but even a harmful, social organ, like the vermiform appendix in the human body.

Religion is regarded by such men, not as something known to us by inward experience, but as an external phenomenon – a disease, as it were, which overtakes certain people, and which we can only investigate by its external symptoms.

Religion, in the opinion of some of these men, arose from attributing a spirit to various aspects of Nature (animism); in the opinion of others, it arose from the supposed possibility of communicating with deceased ancestors; in the opinion of others, again, it arose from fear of the forces of Nature. But, say the learned men of our day, since science has now proved that trees and stones cannot be endowed with a spirit; that dead ancestors do not know what is done by the living; and that the aspects of Nature are explainable by natural causes – it follows that the need for religion has passed, as well as the need for all those restrictions with which (in consequence of religious beliefs) people have hitherto hampered themselves. In the opinion of these learned men there was a period of ignorance: the religious period. That has long been outlived by humanity, though some occasional atavistic indications of it still remain. Then came the metaphysical period, which is now also outlived. But we, enlightened people, are living in a scientific period: a period of positive science which replaces religion and will bring humanity to a height of development it could never have reached while subject to the superstitious teachings of religion.

Early in 1901 the distinguished French savant Berthelot delivered a speech* in which he told his hearers that the day of religion has passed and religion must now be replaced by science. I refer to this speech because it is the first to my hand, and because it was delivered in the metropolis of the educated world by a universally recognized savant. But the same thought is continually and ubiquitously expressed in every form, from philosophic treatises down to newspaper feuilletons.

M. Berthelot says in that speech, that there were formerly two motors moving humanity: Force and Religion; but that

* See the *Revue de Paris*, January 1901. [L. T.]

these motors have now become superfluous, for in their place we have *science*. By *science* M. Berthelot (like all devotees of science) evidently means a science embracing the whole range of things man knows, harmoniously united, co-ordinated, and in command of such methods that the data it obtains are unquestionably true. But as no such science really exists – and what is now called science consists of a collection of haphazard, disconnected scraps of knowledge, many of them quite useless, and such as, instead of supplying undoubted truth, very frequently supply the grossest delusions, exhibited as truth today, but refuted tomorrow – it is evident that the thing M. Berthelot thinks must replace religion is something non-existent. Consequently the assertion made by M. Berthelot and by those who agree with him, to the effect that science will replace religion, is quite arbitrary, and rests on a quite unjustifiable faith in the infallibility of science – a faith similar to the belief in an infallible Church.

Yet men who are said to be, and who consider themselves to be, educated, are quite convinced that a science already exists which should and can replace religion, and which even has already replaced it.

'Religion is obsolete: belief in anything but science is ignorance. Science will arrange all that is needful, and one must be guided in life by science alone.' This is what is thought and said both by scientists themselves and also by those men of the crowd who, though far from scientific, believe in the scientists and join them in asserting that religion is an obsolete superstition, and that we must be guided in life by science only: that is, in reality, by nothing at all; for science, by reason of its very aim (which is to study all that exists), can afford no guidance for the life of man.

II

The learned men of our times have decided that religion is not wanted, and that science will replace it, or has already done so; but the fact remains that, now as formerly, no human society and no rational man has existed or can exist without a religion. I use the term *rational* man because an irrational man may live, as the beasts do, without a religion. But a rational man cannot live without one; for only religion gives a rational man the guidance he needs, telling him what he should do, and what first and what next. A rational man cannot live without religion, precisely because reason is characteristic of his nature. Every animal is guided in its actions (apart from those to which it is impelled by the need to satisfy its immediate desires) by a consideration of the direct results of its actions. Having considered those results by such means of comprehension as it possesses, an animal makes its actions conform to those consequences, and it always unhesitatingly acts in one and the same way, in accord with those considerations. A bee, for instance, flies for honey and stores it in the hive because in winter it will need food for itself and for the young, and beyond these considerations it knows, and can know, nothing. So also a bird is influenced when it builds its nest, or migrates from the north to the south and back again. Every animal acts in a like way when it does anything not resulting from direct, immediate necessity, but prompted by considerations of anticipated results. With man, however, it is not so. The difference between a man and an animal lies in the fact that the perceptive capacities possessed by an animal are limited to what we call instinct, whereas man's fundamental perceptive capacity is reason. A bee, collecting honey, can have no doubts as to whether it is good or bad to collect honey; but a man gathering in his corn or fruit cannot but consider whether he is diminishing the prospects of obtaining future harvests, and whether he is not depriving his neighbour of food. Nor can he help wondering what the children whom he now feeds will become like – and much else. The most important questions of conduct in life cannot be solved conclusively by a reasonable man, just because there is such a superabundance of possible consequences which he cannot but be aware of. Every rational man knows, or at least feels, that in the most important questions of life he can guide himself neither by personal impulses, nor by considerations of the immediate consequences of his activity – for the consequences he foresees are too numerous and too various, and are often contradictory one to another, being as likely to prove harmful as beneficial to himself and to other people. There is a legend which tells of an angel who descended to earth and, entering a devout family, slew a child in its cradle; when asked why he did so, he explained that the child would have become the greatest of malefactors, and would have destroyed the happiness of the family. But it is thus not only with the question, Which human lives are useful, useless or harmful? None of the most important questions of life can a reasonable man decide by considerations of their immediate results and consequences. A reasonable man cannot be satisfied with the considerations that guide the actions of an animal. A man may regard himself as an animal among animals – living for the passing day; or he may consider himself as a member of a family, a society or a nation, living for centuries; or he may, and even must necessarily (for reason irresistibly prompts him to this) consider himself as part of the whole infinite universe existing eternally. And therefore reasonable men should do, and always have done, in reference to the infinitely small affairs of life affecting their actions, what in mathematics is called *integrate*: that is to say, they must set up, besides their relation to the immediate facts of life, a relation to the whole immense Infinite in time and space, conceived as one whole. And such establishment of man's relation to that whole of which he feels himself to be a part, from which he draws guidance for his actions, is what has been called, and is called, Religion. And therefore religion always has been, and cannot cease to be, a necessary and an indispensable condition of the life of a reasonable man and of all reasonable humanity.

XIV

'But is there any true religion? Religions are endlessly various, and we have no right to call one of them true, just because it most nearly suits our own taste' – is what people say who look at the external forms of religion as at some disease from which they feel themselves free, but from which other people still suffer. But this is a mistake; religions differ in their external forms, but they are all alike in their fundamental principles. And it is these principles, that are fundamental to all religions, that form the true religion which alone at the present time is suitable for us all, and the adoption of which alone can save men from their ills.

Mankind has lived long, and just as it has produced and improved its practical inventions through successive generations, so also it could not fail to produce and improve those spiritual principles which have formed the bases of its life, as well as the rules of conduct that resulted from those principles. If blind men do not see these, that does not prove that they do not exist.

This religion of our times, common to all men, exists – not as some sect with all its peculiarities and perversions, but as a religion consisting of those principles which are alike in all the widespread religions known to us, and professed by more than nine-tenths of the human race; and that men are not yet completely brutalized is due to the fact that the best men of all nations hold to this religion and profess it, even if unconsciously, and only the hypnotic deception practised on men by the aid of the priests and scientists now hinders men from consciously adopting it.

The principles of this true religion are so natural to men, that as soon as they are put before them they are accepted as something quite familiar and self-evident. For us the true religion is Christianity in those of its principles in which it agrees, not with the external forms, but with the basic principles of Brahmanism, Confucianism, Taoism, Hebraism, Buddhism, and even Mohammedanism. And just in the same way, for those who profess Brahmanism, Confucianism, etc. – true religion is that of which the basic principles agree with those of all other religions. And these principles are very simple, intelligible and clear.

These principles are: that there is a God, the origin of all things; that in man dwells a spark from that Divine Origin, which man, by his way of living, can increase or decrease in himself; that to increase this divine spark man must suppress his passions and increase love in himself; and that the practical means to attain this result is to do to others as you would they should do to you. All these principles are common to Brahmanism, Hebraism, Confucianism and Mohammedanism. (If Buddhism supplies no definition of God, it nevertheless acknowledges That with which man commingles, and into Which he is absorbed when he attains to Nirvana. So, That with which man commingles, or into Which he is absorbed in Nirvana, is the same Origin that is called God in Hebraism, Christianity and Mohammedanism.)

'But that is not religion,' is what men of today will say, who are accustomed to consider that the supernatural, i.e., the unmeaning, is the chief sign of religion. 'That is anything you like: philosophy, ethics, ratiocination – but not religion.' Religion, according to them, must be absurd and unintelligible (*Credo quia absurdum*). Yet it was only from these very principles, or rather in consequence of their being preached as religious doctrines, that – by a long process of perversion – all those absurd miracles and supernatural occurrences were elaborated, which are now considered to be the fundamental signs of every religion. To assert that the supernatural and irrational form the essential characteristic of religion is like observing only rotten apples, and then asserting that a flabby bitterness and a harmful effect on the stomach are the prime characteristics of the fruit called Apple.

Religion is the definition of man's relation to the Source of all things, and of man's purpose in life which results from that relation; and it supplies rules of conduct resulting from that purpose. And the universal religion, whose first principles are alike in all the faiths, fully meets the demands of this understanding of religion. It defines the relation of man to God, as being that of a part to the whole; from this relation it deduces man's purpose, which is to increase the divine element in himself; and this purpose involves practical demands on man, in accord with the rule: Do to others as you wish them to do to you.

People often doubt, and I myself at one time doubted,

whether such an abstract rule as, Do to others as you wish them to do to you, can be as obligatory a rule and guide for action as the simpler rules: to fast, pray and take communion, etc. But an irrefutable reply to that doubt is supplied, for instance, by the spiritual condition of a Russian peasant who would rather die than spit out the Sacrament on to a manure-heap, but who yet, at the command of men, is ready to kill his brothers.

Why should demands flowing from the rule of doing to others as you wish them to do to you – such, for instance, as: not killing one's brother man, not reviling, not committing adultery, not revenging one's self, not taking advantage of the need of one's brethren to satisfy one's own caprice, and many others – why should not they be instilled as forcibly, and become as binding and inviolable, as the belief in the sanctity of the Sacraments, or of images, etc., now is to men whose faith is founded more on credulity than on any clear inward consciousness.

XV

The truths of the religion common to all men of our time are so simple, so intelligible, and so near the heart of each man, that it would seem only necessary for parents, rulers and teachers to instil into children and adults – instead of the obsolete and absurd doctrines, in which they themselves often do not believe: about Trinities, virgin-mothers, redemptions, Indras, Trimurti, and about Buddhas and Mohammeds who fly away into the sky – those clear and simple truths, the metaphysical essence of which is that the spirit of God dwells in man; and the practical rule of which is that man should do to others as he wishes them to do to him – for the whole life of humanity to change. If only – in the same way that the belief is now instilled into children and confirmed in adults, that God sent His son to redeem Adam's sin, and that He established His Church which must be obeyed; as well as rules deduced from these beliefs: telling when and where to pray and make offerings, when to refrain from such and such food, and on what days to abstain from work – if only it were instilled and confirmed that God is a spirit whose manifestation is present in us, the strength of which we can increase by our lives: if only this and all that naturally flows from this, were instilled in the same way that quite useless stories of impossible occurrences, and rules of meaningless ceremonies deduced from those stories, are now instilled – then, instead of purposeless strife and discord, we should very soon (without the aid of diplomatists, international law, peace-congresses, political economists and Socialists in all their various subdivisions) see humanity living a peaceful, united and happy life guided by the one religion.

But nothing of the kind is done: not only is the deception of false religion not destroyed, and the true one not preached, but, on the contrary, men depart farther and farther away from the possibility of accepting the truth.

The chief cause of people not doing what is so natural, necessary and possible is that men today, in consequence of having lived long without religion, are so accustomed to establish and defend their existence by violence, by bayonets, bullets, prisons and gallows, that it seems to them as if such an arrangement of life were not only normal, but were the only one possible. Not only do those who profit by the existing order think so, but those even who suffer from it are so stupefied by the hypnotism exercised upon them, that they also consider violence to be the only means of securing good order in human society. Yet it is just this arrangement and maintenance of the commonweal by violence that does most to hinder people from comprehending the causes of their sufferings, and consequently from being able to establish a true order.

The results of it are such as might be produced by a bad or malicious doctor who should drive a malignant eruption inwards, thereby cheating the sick man, and making the disease worse and its cure impossible.

To people of the ruling classes, who enslave the masses and think and say: '*Après nous le déluge*',* it seems very convenient by means of the army, the priesthood, the soldiers and the

* Madame de Pompadour's remark, 'After me (us) the deluge.' [A. M.]

police, as well as by threats of bayonets, bullets, prisons, work-houses and gallows, to compel the enslaved people to remain in stupefaction and enslavement, and not to hinder the rulers from exploiting them. And the ruling men do this, calling it the maintenance of good order, but there is nothing that so hinders the establishment of a good social order as this does. In reality, far from being the establishment of good order, it is the establishment of evil.

If men of our Christian nations, still possessing some remnants of those religious principles which in spite of everything yet live in the people, had not before them the continual example of crime committed by those who have assumed the duty of guarding order and morality among men – the wars, executions, prisons, taxation, sale of intoxicants and of opium – they would never have thought of committing one one-hundredth of the evil deeds – the frauds, violence and murders – which they now commit in full confidence that such deeds are good and natural for men to commit.

The law of human life is such, that the only way to improve it, whether for the individual or for a society of men, is by means of inward, moral growth towards perfection. All attempts of men to better their lives by external action – by violence – serve as the most efficacious propaganda and example of evil, and therefore not only do not improve life, but, on the contrary, increase the evil which, like a snowball, grows larger and larger, and removes men more and more from the only possible way of truly bettering their lives.

In proportion as the practice of violence and crime, committed in the name of the law by the guardians of order and morality, becomes more and more frequent and cruel, and is more and more justified by the hypnotism of falsehood presented as religion, men will be more and more confirmed in the belief that the law of their life is not one of love and service to their fellows, but is one demanding that they should strive with, and devour, one another.

And the more they are confirmed in that thought, which degrades them to the plane of the beasts, the harder will it be to shake off the hypnotic trance in which they are living, and to accept as the basis of their life the true religion of our time, common to all humanity.

A vicious circle has been established: the absence of religion makes possible an animal life based on violence; an animal life based on violence makes emancipation from hypnotism and an adoption of true religion more and more impossible. And, therefore, men do not do what is natural, possible and necessary in our times: do not destroy the deception and simulacrum of religion, and do not assimilate and preach the true religion.

XVI

Is any issue from this enchanted circle possible, and if so, what is it?

At first it seems as if the Governments, which have taken on themselves the duty of guiding the life of the people for their benefit, should lead us out of this circle. That is what men who have tried to alter the arrangements of life founded on violence, and to replace them by a reasonable arrangement based on mutual service and love, have always supposed. So thought the Christian reformers, and the founders of various theories of European Communism, and so also thought the celebrated Chinese reformer Mo Tî,* who for the welfare of the people proposed to the Government not to teach school-children military sciences and exercises, and not to give rewards to adults for military achievements, but to teach children and adults the rules of esteem and love, and give rewards and encouragement for feats of love. So also thought, and think, many religious peasant-reformers, of whom I have known and now know several, beginning with Soutayef and ending with an old man who has now five times presented a petition to the Emperor, asking him to decree the abrogation of false religion, and to order that true Christianity be preached.

* Mo Tî (or Mih Teih) lived a little before Mencius (about 372–289 BC), who wrote against the former's doctrine of universal love. [A. M.]

It seems to men natural that the Government – which justifies its existence on the score of its care for the welfare of the people – must, to secure that welfare, wish to use the only means which can never do people any harm, and can only produce the most fruitful results. Government, however, has not only never taken upon itself this duty, but, on the contrary, has always and everywhere maintained with the greatest jealousy any false, effete religion prevalent at the period, and has in every way persecuted those who have tried to inform the people of the principles of true religion. In reality this cannot be otherwise; for Governments to expose the falsity of the present religions, and to preach the true one, would be as if a man were to cut down the branch on which he is sitting.

But if Government will not do this work, it would seem certain that those learned men – who, having freed themselves from the deception of false religion, say they wish to serve the common people whose labour has provided for their education and support – are bound to do it. But these men, like the Government, do not do it: first, because they consider it inexpedient to risk unpleasantness and to suffer the danger of persecution at the hands of the ruling classes for exposing a fraud which Government protects, and which, in their opinion, will disappear of itself; secondly, because, considering all religion to be an effete error, they have nothing to offer the people in place of the deception they are expected to destroy.

There remain those great masses of unlearned men who are under the hypnotic influence of Church and Government deception, and who therefore believe that the simulacrum of religion which has been instilled into them is the one true religion, and that there is and can be no other. These masses are under a constant and intense hypnotic influence. Generation after generation they are born and live and die in the stupefied condition in which they are kept by the clergy and the Government; and if they free themselves from that influence, they are sure to fall into the school of the scientists who deny religion – when their influence becomes as useless and harmful as the influence of their teachers.

So that for some men the work is unprofitable, while for others it is impossible.

XVII

It looks as if no issue were possible.

And indeed for irreligious men there is not, and cannot be, any issue from this position; those who belong to the higher, governing classes, even if they pretend to be concerned for the welfare of the masses, will never seriously attempt (guided by worldly aims, they cannot do it) to destroy the stupefaction and servitude in which these masses live, and which make it possible for the upper classes to rule over them. In the same way, men belonging to the enslaved masses cannot, while guided by worldly motives, wish to make their own hard position harder by entering on a struggle against the upper classes, to expose a false teaching and to preach a true one. Neither of these sets of men has any motive to do this, and if they are intelligent they will never attempt it.

But it is otherwise for religious people: men such as those who – however perverted a society may be – are always to be found guarding with their lives the sacred fire of religion, without which human life could not exist. There are times (and our time is such) when these men are unnoticed, when – as among us in Russia – despised and derided by all, their lives pass unrecorded – in exile, in prisons and in penal battalions – yet they live, and on them depends the rational life of humanity. And it is just these religious men – however few they may be – who alone can and will rend asunder that enchanted circle which keeps men bound. They can do it, because all the disadvantages and dangers which hinder a worldly man from opposing the existing order of society, not only do not impede a religious man, but rather increase his zeal in the struggle against falsehood, and impel him to confess by word and deed what he holds to be divine truth. If he belongs to the ruling classes he will not only not wish to hide the truth out of regard for his own advantageous position, but, on the contrary, having come to hate such advantages, he will exert his whole strength to free himself from them, and to preach the truth, for he will no longer have any other aim in life than to serve God. If he belongs to the enslaved, then in the same way, unbiased by the wish, common among those of his position, to improve the conditions of his physical life, such a man will have no aim but to fulfil the will of God by exposing falsehood and confessing truth; and no sufferings or threats will make him cease to live in accord with that purpose which he has recognized in his life. They will both act thus, as naturally as a worldly man exerts himself and puts up with privations to obtain riches, or to please a ruler from whom he expects to receive advantages. Every religious man acts thus, because a human soul enlightened by religion no longer lives merely by the life of this world, as irreligious people do, but lives an eternal, infinite life, for which suffering and death in this life are as insignificant as are blisters on his hands, or weariness of limbs, to a ploughman when he is ploughing a field.

These are the men who will rend asunder the enchanted circle in which people are now confined. However few such men there may be, however humble their social position, however poor in education or ability, as surely as fire lights the dry steppe, so surely will these people set the whole world aflame, and kindle all the hearts of men, withered by long lack of religion, and now thirsting for a renewal of life.

Religion is not a belief, settled once for all, in certain supernatural occurrences supposed to have taken place once upon a time, nor in the necessity for certain prayers and ceremonies; nor is it, as the scientists suppose, a survival of the superstitions of ancient ignorance, which in our time has no meaning or application to life; but religion is a certain relation of man to eternal life and to God, a relation accordant with reason and contemporary knowledge, and it is the one thing that alone moves humanity forward towards its destined aim.

A wise Hebrew proverb says, 'The soul of man is the lamp of God.' Man is a weak and miserable animal until the light of God burns in his soul. But when that light burns (and it burns only in souls enlightened by religion) man becomes the most powerful being in the world. Nor can this be otherwise, for what then acts in him is no longer *his* strength, but is the strength of God.

So this is what religion is, and in what its essence consists.

[Translated by Aylmer Maude]

LETTER ON EDUCATION*
[1902]

Dear S.,

I was very glad to have a serious conversation with X. about the education of children. What he and I quite agree about, but what is only negative, is that children should be taught *as little as possible*.† That children should grow up without having learnt certain subjects is not nearly so bad as what happens to nearly all children, especially those whose education is directed by mothers who do not know the subjects their children learn – viz., they get educational *indigestion* and come to detest education. A child, or a man, can learn when he has an appetite for what he studies. Without appetite, instruction is an evil – a terrible evil causing people to become mentally crippled. For Heaven's sake, dear S., if you do not quite agree with me, take my word for it, that were it not a matter of such enormous importance I would not write to you about it. Above all, believe your husband, who sees the thing quite reasonably.

But then comes the customary reply: If children are not taught, how are they to be occupied? Are they to play knuckle-bones with the village children, and learn all sorts of stupidities and nastiness? With our squirely way of life, this reply has

* This letter was written to a near relation, belonging to the upper class of Russian society, in which the children are generally sent to the high schools (gymnasia), where they are crammed with much knowledge, chiefly in order to pass examinations and to obtain certain privileges (e.g. diminution of military service). The 'X.' mentioned is the husband of the lady addressed. [A. M.]

† This is meant to be taken comparatively and not absolutely. Elsewhere Tolstoy has expressed the opinion that a child may reasonably do lessons for eight hours a day; though he should not be compelled to learn what he does not wish to learn. [A. M.]

some reasonable ground. But is it really necessary to accustom children to a squirely way of life, and to make them feel that all their requirements are satisfied by someone, somehow, without their having to take any part in the work? I think the first condition of a good education is that the child should know that all he uses does not fall from heaven ready-made, but is produced by other people's labour. To understand that all he lives on comes from the labour of other people who neither know nor love him is too much for a child (God grant he may understand it when he is grown up); but to understand that the chamber-pot he uses is emptied and wiped, without any pleasure, by a nurse or a housemaid, and that the boots and goloshes he always puts on clean are cleaned in the same way – not out of love for him, but for some other reason quite unintelligible to him – is something he can and should understand, and of which he should be ashamed. If he is not ashamed and if he continues to use them, that is the very worst commencement of an education, and leaves the deepest traces for his whole life. To avoid that, however, is very simple, and is just what (to use poetic language), standing on the threshold of the grave, I beseech you to do for your children. Let them do all they can for themselves: carry out their own slops, fill their own jugs, wash up, arrange their rooms, clean their boots and clothes, lay the table, etc. Believe me that, unimportant as these things may seem, they are a hundred times more important for your children's happiness than a knowledge of French, or of history, etc. It is true that here the chief difficulty crops up: children do willingly only what their parents do, and therefore I beg of you, do these things. This will effect two objects at once: it makes it possible to learn less, by filling the time in the most useful and natural way, and it trains the children to simplicity, to work and to self-dependence. Please do this. You will be gratified from the first month, and the children yet more so. If to this you can add work on the land, if it be but a kitchen-garden, that will be well; though it too often becomes a mere pastime. The necessity of attending to one's own needs and carrying out one's own slops is admitted by all the best schools, where the director of the school himself takes a share in such work. Believe me, that without that condition there is no possibility of a moral education, a Christian education, or a consciousness of the fact that all men are brothers and equals. A child may yet understand that a grown-up man, his father – a banker or turner, an artist or an overseer, who by his work feeds the whole family – may free himself from occupations which prevent his giving all his time to his profitable work. But how can a child – as yet untried and unable to do anything – explain to himself that others do for him what he naturally should do for himself?

The only explanation for him is that people are divided into two classes – masters and slaves; and however much we may talk to him in words about equality and the brotherhood of man, all the conditions of his life, from his getting up, to his evening meal, show him the contrary.

Not only does he cease to believe what his elders tell him about morality, he sees in the depth of his soul that all these teachings are mendacious, and he ceases to believe his parents and teachers, and ceases even to believe in the need for any kind of morality whatever.

Yet one more consideration. If it is not possible to do all that I have mentioned, at least one must set children to do things the disadvantage of not doing which would be at once felt by them – e.g. if one's clothes and boots for going out in are not cleaned, one must not go out; if water has not been fetched and the crockery washed up, there is nothing to drink. Above all, in this matter do not be afraid of *ridicule*. Nine-tenths of all the bad things in the world are done because not to do them would be held ridiculous.

[Translated by Aylmer Maude]

AN APPEAL TO THE CLERGY [1902]

I

Whoever you may be: popes, cardinals, bishops, superintendents, priests or pastors, of whatever Church, forgo for a while your assurance that you – you in particular – are the only true disciples of the God Christ, appointed to preach His only true teaching; and remember that before being popes, cardinals, bishops or superintendents, etc., you are first of all men: that is, according to your own teaching, beings sent into this world by God to fulfil His will; remember this, and ask yourselves what you are doing. Your whole life is devoted to preaching, maintaining and spreading among men a teaching which you say was revealed to you by God Himself, and is, therefore, the only one that is true and brings redemption.

In what, then, does this one true and redeeming doctrine that you preach, consist? To whichever one of the so-called Christian Churches – Roman Catholic, Russo-Greek, Lutheran or Anglican – you may belong, you acknowledge that your teaching is quite accurately expressed in the articles of belief formulated at the Council of Nicaea 1,600 years ago. Those articles of belief are as follows:

First: There is a God the father (the first person of a Trinity), who has created the sky and the earth, and all the angels who live in the sky.

Second: There is an only son of God the father, not created, but born (the second person of the Trinity). Through this son the world was made.

Third: This son, to save people from sin and death (by which they were all punished for the disobedience of their forefather Adam), came down to the earth, was made flesh by the Holy Ghost and the virgin Mary, and became a man.

Fourth: This son was crucified for the sins of men.

Fifth: He suffered and was buried, and rose on the third day, as had been foretold in Hebrew books.

Sixth: Having gone up into the sky, this son seated himself at his father's right side.

Seventh: This son of God will, in due time, come again to the earth to judge the living and the dead.

Eighth: There is a Holy Ghost (the third person of the Trinity), who is equal to the father, and who spoke through the prophets.

Ninth (held by some of the largest Churches): There is one holy, infallible Church (or, more exactly, the Church to which he who makes the confession belongs is held to be unique, holy and infallible). This Church consists of all who believe in it, living or dead.

Tenth (also for some of the largest Churches): There exists a Sacrament of Baptism, by means of which the power of the Holy Ghost is communicated to those who are baptized.

Eleventh: At the second coming of Christ, the souls of the dead will re-enter their bodies, and these bodies will be immortal; and

Twelfth: After the second coming, the just will have eternal life in paradise on a new earth under a new sky, and sinners will have eternal life in the torments of hell.

Not to speak of things taught by some of your largest Churches (the Roman Catholic and Russo-Greek Orthodox) – such as the belief in saints, and in the good effects of bowing to their bodily remains, and to representations of them as well as of Jesus and the mother of God – the above twelve points embrace the fundamental positions of that truth which you say has been revealed to you by God Himself for the redemption of man. Some of you preach these doctrines simply as they are expressed; others try to give them an allegorical meaning more or less in accord with present-day knowledge and common sense; but you all alike are bound to confess, and do confess, these statements to be the exact expression of that unique truth which God Himself has revealed to you, and which you preach to men for their salvation.

II

Very well. You have had the one truth capable of saving mankind revealed to you by God Himself. It is natural for men to strive towards truth, and when it is clearly presented to them they are always glad to accept it, and to be guided by it.

And, therefore, to impart this saving truth revealed to you by God Himself, it would seem sufficient, plainly and simply, verbally and through the press, to communicate it with reasonable persuasion to those capable of receiving it.

But how have you preached this truth?

From the time a society calling itself the Church was formed, your predecessors taught this truth chiefly by violence. They laid down the truth, and punished those who did not accept it. (Millions and millions of people have been tortured, killed and burnt for not wishing to accept it.) This method of persecution, which was evidently not suited to its purpose, came in course of time to be less and less employed, and is now, of all the Christian Churches, used, I think, only in Russia.

Another means was through external action on people's feelings – by solemnity of setting: with pictures, statues, singing, music, even dramatic performances and oratorical art. In time this method, also, began to be less and less used. In Protestant countries – except the orator's art – it is now but little used (though the Salvation Army, which has devised new methods of external action on the feelings, supplies an exception).

But all the strength of the clergy is now directed to a third and most powerful method, which has always been used, and is now with special jealousy retained by the clergy in their own hands. This method is that of instilling Church doctrine into people who are not in a position to judge of what is given them:

for instance, into quite uneducated working people who have no time for thought, and chiefly into children, who accept indiscriminately what is imparted to them and on whose minds it remains permanently impressed.

III

So that in our day your chief method of imparting to men the truth God has revealed to you, consists in teaching this truth to uneducated adults, and to children who do not reason, but accept everything.

This teaching generally begins with what is called Scripture History: that is to say, with selected passages from the Bible: the Hebrew books of the Old Testament; which according to your teaching are the work of the Holy Ghost, and are therefore not only unquestionably true, but also holy. From this history your pupil draws his first notions of the world, of the life of man, of good and evil, and of God.

This Scripture History begins with a description of how God, the ever-living, created the sky and the earth 6,000 years ago out of nothing; how He afterwards created beasts, fishes, plants, and finally man: Adam, and Adam's wife, who was made of one of Adam's ribs. Then it describes how, fearing lest the man and his wife should eat an apple which had the magic quality of giving knowledge, He forbade them to eat that apple; how, notwithstanding this prohibition, the first people ate the apple, and were therefore expelled from Paradise; and how all their descendants were therefore cursed, and the earth was cursed also, so that since then it has grown weeds. Then the life of Adam's descendants is described: how they became so perverted that God not only drowned them all, but drowned all the animals with them, and left alive only Noah and his family and the animals he took into the ark. Then it describes how God chose Abraham alone of all people, and made an agreement with him; which agreement was that Abraham was to consider God to be God, and, as a sign of this, was to be circumcised. On His side God undertook to give Abraham a numerous progeny, and to patronize him and all his offspring. Then it tells how God, patronizing Abraham and his descendants, performed on their behalf most unnatural actions called miracles, and most terrible cruelties. So that the whole of this history – excepting certain stories, which are sometimes naïve (as the visit of God with two angels to Abraham, the marriage of Isaac, and others), and are sometimes innocent, but are often immoral (as the swindles of God's favourite, Jacob, the cruelties of Samson, and the cunning of Joseph) – the whole of this history, from the plagues Moses called down upon the Egyptians, and the murder by an angel of all their firstborn, to the fire that destroyed 250 conspirators, the tumbling into the ground of Korah, Dathan and Abiram, and the destruction of 14,700 men in a few minutes, and on to the sawing of enemies with saws,* and the execution of the priests who did not agree with him by Elijah (who rode up into the sky), and to the story of Elisha, who cursed the boys that laughed at him, so that they were torn in pieces and eaten by two bears – all this history is a series of miraculous occurrences and of terrible crimes, committed by the Hebrew people, by their leaders, and by God Himself.

But your teaching of the history you call sacred is not limited to that. Besides the history of the Old Testament, you also impart the New Testament to children and to ignorant people, in a way that makes the importance of the New Testament consist not in its moral teaching, not in the Sermon on the Mount, but in the conformity of the Gospels with the stories of the Old Testament, in the fulfilment of prophecies, and in miracles, the movement of a star, songs from the sky, talks with the devil, the turning of water into wine, walking on the water, healings, calling people back to life, and, finally, the resurrection of Jesus himself, and his flying up into the sky.

If all these stories, both from the Old and New Testaments, were taught as a series of fairy tales, even then hardly any

* Father John of Kronstadt having published an article in which he says that this passage shows Tolstoy's ignorance of the Bible, it may be well here to quote 1 Chron. 20: 3: 'And he brought out the people that were in it, and cut them with saws, and with harrows of iron, and with axes. Even so dealt David with all the cities of the children of Ammon.' [A. M.]

teacher would decide to tell them to children and adults he desired to enlighten. But these tales are imparted to people unable to reason, as though they were the most trustworthy description of the world and its laws, as if they gave the truest information about the lives of those who lived in former times, of what should be considered good and evil, of the existence and nature of God, and of the duties of man.

People talk of harmful books! But is there in Christendom a book that has done more harm to mankind than this terrible book, called 'Scripture History from the Old and New Testaments'?* And all the men and women of Christendom have to pass through a course of this Scripture History during their childhood, and this same history is also taught to ignorant adults as the first and most essential foundation of knowledge – as the one, eternal, truth of God.

IV

You cannot introduce a foreign substance into a living organism without the organism suffering, and sometimes perishing, from its efforts to rid itself of this foreign substance. What terrible evil to a man's mind must, then, result from this rendering of the teaching of the Old and New Testaments – foreign alike to present-day knowledge, and to common sense, and to moral feeling – and instilled into him at a time when he is unable to judge, but accepts all that is given him!

For a man – into whose mind has been introduced as sacred truths a belief in the creation of the world out of nothing 6,000 years ago; in the flood, and Noah's ark which accommodated all the animals; in a Trinity; in Adam's fall; in an immaculate conception; in Christ's miracles, and in salvation for men by the sacrifice of his death – for such a man the demands of reason are no longer obligatory, and such a man cannot be sure of any

* The reference here is not to the Old and New Testaments in their entirety (the extreme value of many parts of which Tolstoy does not question), but to a compilation for school use, which is largely used in place of the Bible. [A. M.]

truth. If the Trinity, and an immaculate conception, and the salvation of mankind by the blood of Jesus, are possible – then anything is possible, and the demands of reason are not obligatory.

Drive a wedge between the floor-boards of a granary, and no matter how much grain you may pour into the granary, it will not stay there. Just so a head into which the wedge has been driven of a Trinity, or of a God who became man and redeemed the human race by His sufferings and then flew up into the sky, can no longer grasp any reasonable or firm understanding of life.

However much you may put into the granary which has cracks in its floor, all will run out. Whatever you may put into a mind which has accepted nonsense as a matter of faith, nothing will remain in it.

Such a man, if he values his beliefs, will inevitably, all his life long, either be on his guard (as against something harmful) against all that might enlighten him and destroy his superstitions; or – having once for all assumed (and the preachers of Church doctrine will always encourage him in this) that reason is the source of error – he will repudiate the only light given to man to enable him to find his path of life; or, most terrible of all, he will, by cunning argumentation, try to demonstrate the reasonableness of what is unreasonable, and, worst of all, will discard, together with the superstitions that were instilled into him, all consciousness of the necessity for any faith whatever.

In each of these three cases, a man into whom, during childhood, meaningless and contradictory assertions have been instilled as religious truth – unless with much effort and suffering he free himself from them – is a man mentally diseased. Such a man, seeing around him the constantly moving and changing facts of life, cannot without a feeling of desperation watch this movement destroying his conception of life, and cannot but experience (openly or secretly) an unkindly feeling towards those who co-operate in this reasonable progress. Nor can he help being a conscious partisan of obscurity and lies against light and truth.

And such the majority of people in Christendom – by the inculcation of nonsensical beliefs deprived from childhood of the capacity to think clearly and firmly – actually are.

V

Such is the evil done to man's mind by having it impregnated with Church doctrines. But much worse than this is the moral perversion which that impregnation produces in man's soul. Every man comes into the world with a consciousness of his dependence on a mysterious, all-powerful Source which has given him life, and consciousness of his equality with all men, the equality of all men with one another, a desire to love and be loved, and a consciousness of the need of striving towards perfection. But what do you instil into him?

Instead of the mysterious Source of which he thinks with reverence, you tell him of an angry, unjust God, who executes and torments people.

Instead of the equality of all men, which the child and the simple man recognize with all their being, you tell them that not only people, but nations, are unequal; that some of them are loved, and others are not loved, by God; and that some people are called by God to rule, others to submit.

Instead of that wish to love and to be loved, which forms the strongest desire in the soul of every unperverted man, you teach him that the relations between men can only be based on violence, on threats, on executions; and you tell him that judicial and military murders are committed not only with the sanction but at the command of God.

In place of the need of self-improvement, you tell him that man's salvation lies in belief in the Redemption, and that by improving himself by his own powers, without the aid of prayers, sacraments and belief in the Redemption, man is guilty of sinful pride, and that for his salvation man must trust, not to his own reason but to the commands of the Church, and must do what she decrees.

It is terrible to think of the perversion of thought and feeling produced in the soul of a child or an ignorant adult by such teaching.

VI

Only to think of the things I know of that have been done in Russia during the sixty years of my conscious life, and that are still being done!

In the theological colleges, and among the bishops, learned monks and missionaries, hair-splitting discussions of intricate theological problems are carried on – they talk of reconciling moral and dogmatic teaching, they dispute about the development or immutability of dogmas, and discuss similar religious subtleties. But to the hundred million populace all that is preached is a belief in Iberian or Kazan icons of the Mother of God, a belief in relics, in devils, in the redemptive efficacy of having bread blessed and placing candles, and having prayers for the dead, etc.; and not only is this all preached and practised, but the inviolability of these popular superstitions is guarded with particular jealousy from any infringement. A peasant has but to omit to observe the name's day of the local saint, or to omit to invite to his house a wonder-working icon when it makes the round of his village, or he has only to work on the Friday before St Elias's day – and he will be denounced, and prosecuted and exiled. Not to speak of sectarians being punished for not observing the ceremonies of the Church, they are tried for even meeting together to read the Gospels, and are punished for that. And the result of all this activity is that tens of millions of people, including nearly all the peasant women, are not only ignorant of Jesus, but have never even heard who he was, or that he existed. This is hard to believe, but it is a fact which anyone can easily verify for himself.

Listen to what is said by the bishops and academicians at their conferences, read their magazines, and you would think that the Russian priesthood preaches a faith which, even if it be backward, is still a Christian faith, in which the Gospel truths find a place and are taught to the people. But watch the activity of the clergy among the people, and you will see that what *is* preached, and energetically inculcated, is simply idolatry: the elevation of icons, blessing of water, the carrying from house to house of miracle-working icons, the glorification of relics, the wearing of crosses, and so forth; while every attempt to understand the real meaning of Christianity is energetically persecuted.

Within my recollection the Russian labouring classes have, in a great measure, lost the traits of true Christianity which they formerly possessed, but which are now carefully banished by the clergy.

Among the people there formerly existed (but now only in out-of-the-way districts) Christian legends and proverbs, verbally handed down from generation to generation, and these legends – such as the legend of Christ wandering in the guise of a beggar, of the angel who doubted God's mercy, of the crazy man who danced at a drum-shop; and such sayings as: 'Without God one can't reach the threshold', 'God is not in might, but in right', 'Live till eve, live for ever', etc. – these legends and proverbs formed the spiritual food of the people.

Besides these, there were Christian customs: to have pity on a criminal or a wanderer, to give of one's last resources to a beggar, and to ask forgiveness of a man one has offended.

All this is now forgotten and discarded. It is now all replaced by learning by rote the Catechism, the triune composition of the Trinity, prayers before lessons, and prayers for teachers and for the Tsar, etc. So, within my recollection, the people have grown religiously ever coarser and more coarse.

Some – most of the women – remain as superstitious as they were 600 years ago, but without that Christian spirit which formerly permeated their lives; the others, who know the Catechism by heart, are absolute atheists. And all this is consciously brought about by the clergy.

'But that applies to Russia,' is what Western Europeans – Catholics and Protestants – will say. But I think that the same, if not worse, is happening in Catholicism, with its prohibition of the Gospels and its Notre-Dames; and in Protestantism, with its holy idleness on the Sabbath day, and its bibliolatry –

that is, its blind belief in the letter of the Bible. I think, in one form or another, it is the same throughout the quasi-Christian world.

In proof of this, it is sufficient to remember the age-old fraud of the flame that kindles in Jerusalem on the day of the Resurrection, and which no one of the Church people exposes; or the faith in the Redemption, which is preached with peculiar energy in the very latest phases of Christian Protestantism.

VII

But not only is the Church teaching harmful by its irrationality and immorality, it is specially harmful because people professing this teaching, while living without any moral demands to restrain them, feel quite convinced they are living a really Christian life.

People live in insensate luxury, obtaining their wealth by the labour of the humble poor, and defending themselves and their riches by policemen, law-courts and executions – and the clergy, in the name of Christ, approve, sanctify and bless this way of life, merely advising the rich to allot a small part of what they have stolen to the service of those from whom they continue to steal. (When slavery existed, the clergy always and everywhere justified it, and did not consider it inconsistent with Christianity.)

People strive by force of arms, by murder, to attain their covetous aims, personal or public, and the clergy approve, and in Christ's name bless preparations for war, and war itself, and not only approve, but often encourage these things; holding war – that is, murder – not to be contrary to Christianity.

People who believe in such teaching are not merely led by it into an evil way of life, but are fully persuaded that their evil life is a good one, which there is no need for them to alter.

Nor is that all: the chief evil of this teaching is that it is so skilfully interwoven with the external forms of Christianity that, while professing it, people think your doctrine is the one true Christianity, and that there is no other! It is not only that you have diverted from men the spring of living water – were that all, people might still find it – but you have poisoned it with your teachings, so that people cannot find any Christianity but this one poisoned by your interpretations.

The Christianity preached by you is an inoculation of false Christianity, resembling the inoculation for smallpox or diphtheria, and has the effect of making those who are inoculated immune to true Christianity.

People having for many generations built their lives on foundations irreconcilable with true Christianity, feel fully persuaded that they are living Christian lives, and thus they are unable to return to true Christianity.

VIII

Thus it is with those who profess your doctrines; but there are others, who have emancipated themselves from those doctrines: the so-called unbelievers.

They (though in most cases more moral in their lives than the majority of those who profess Church doctrines), as a result of the spiritual taint to which they were exposed in their childhood, have an influence on their neighbours which is worse even than that of those who profess your teachings. They are specially harmful because, having in childhood shared the misfortune of the rest of the inhabitants of Christendom and been trained in the Church frauds, they have so identified Church teachings with Christianity in their own perception, that they now cannot distinguish the one from the other, and in rejecting the false Church teaching throw away with it that true Christian teaching which it has hidden.

These people, detesting the fraud that has caused them so much suffering, preach not only the uselessness but the harmfulness of Christianity, and not of Christianity only, but of any religion whatever.

Religion, in their perception, is a remnant of superstition, which may have been of use to people once, but now is simply harmful. And so their doctrine is, that the quicker and more completely people free themselves from every trace of religious consciousness, the better it will be.

And preaching this emancipation from all religion, they – including among them most educated and learned men, who, therefore, have the greatest authority with people searching for the truth – consciously or unconsciously become most harmful preachers of moral laxity.

By suggesting to people that the most important mental characteristic of rational creatures – that of ascertaining their relation to the Source of all things, from which alone any firm moral laws can be deduced – is something man has outlived, the deniers of religion involuntarily postulate as the basis of human activity simply self-love, and the bodily appetites that flow therefrom.

And among these people sprang up that teaching of egotism, evil and hatred, which (though it was always present in hidden, latent form in the life-conception of the materialists) at first showed itself timidly, but has latterly been so vividly and deliberately expressed in the doctrines of Nietzsche, and is now spreading so rapidly, evoking the most coarsely animal and cruel instincts in mankind.

So that, on the one hand, the so-called believers find complete approval of their evil way of life in your teaching, which recognizes as compatible with Christianity those actions and conditions which are most contrary to it; while, on the other hand, unbelievers – arriving at the denial of all religion, as a consequence of your teaching – wipe out all distinction between good and evil, preach a doctrine of inequality among men, of egotism, of strife, and of the oppression of the weak by the strong – and preach this as the highest truth attainable by man.

IX

You, and none but you, by your teaching forcibly instilled into people, are the cause of this dreadful evil from which they suffer so cruelly.

Most terrible of all is the fact that, while causing this evil, you do not believe the teaching you preach; not only do not believe all the assertions of which it is composed, but often do not believe a single one of them.

I know that, repeating the celebrated *credo quia absurdum*, many of you think that, in spite of everything, you do believe all that you preach. But the fact that you *say* you believe that God is a Trinity, or that the heavens opened and the voice of God spoke from up there, or that Jesus rose up into the heavens and will come from there to judge all mankind in their bodies, does not prove that you really believe that the things mentioned have occurred, or will occur. You believe you ought to say that you believe these things happened. But you do not believe them; for the assertions that God is One and Three; that Jesus flew up into the sky and will come back from there to judge those who will rise in their bodies – have, for you, no meaning. One may utter words that have no sense, but one cannot *believe* what has no sense. It is possible to believe that the souls of the dead will pass into other forms of life, pass into animals, or that the annihilation of the passions, or the attainment of love, is the destiny of man; or it is possible to believe simply that God has forbidden us to kill men, or even that He forbids us to eat – and many other things may be believed that do not involve self-contradiction: but one cannot believe that God is, at the same time, both One and also Three, or that the sky – which for us is no longer a thing that exists – opened, etc.

The people of former ages, who framed these dogmas, could believe in them, but you can no longer do so. If you say you have faith in them, you say so only because you use the word 'faith' in one sense, while you apply to it another. One meaning of the word 'faith' refers to a relation adopted by man towards God, which enables him to define the meaning of his whole life, and guides all his conscious actions. Another meaning of the word 'faith' is the credulous acceptance of assertions made by a certain person or persons.

In the first sense, the objects of faith – though the definition of man's relation to God and to the world is generally accepted as framed by those who lived previously – are verified and accepted by reason.

But in the second sense, the objects of faith are not only accepted independently of reason, but are accepted on the absolute condition that reason is not to be allowed to question what is asserted.

On this double meaning of the word 'faith' is founded that misunderstanding which enables people to say they believe, or have 'faith', in propositions devoid of sense or involving a contradiction in terms. And the fact that you are blindly credulous towards your teachers is no proof that you have faith in what – being senseless and, therefore, supplying no meaning either to your imagination or your reason – cannot be an object of faith.

The well-known preacher, Père Didon, in the introduction to his *Vie de Jésus-Christ*, announces that he believes, not in some allegorical sense but plainly, without explanations, that Christ, having risen, was carried up into the sky, and sits there at the right hand of his father.

An illiterate Samara peasant of my acquaintance, in reply to the question whether he believed in God, simply and firmly replied, as his priest told me: 'No, sinner that I am, I don't believe.' His disbelief in God the peasant explained by saying that one could not live as he was living if one believed in God: 'One scolds, and grudges help to a beggar, and envies, and over-eats, and drinks strong drinks. Could one do such things if one believed in God?'

Père Didon affirms that he has faith both in God and in the ascension of Jesus, while the Samara peasant says he does not believe in God, since he does not obey His commandments.

Evidently Père Didon does not even know what faith is, and only says he believes: while the Samara peasant knows what faith is, and, though he says he does not believe in God, really believes in Him in the very way that is true faith.

X

But I know that arguments addressed to the intellect do not persuade – only feeling persuades, and therefore, leaving arguments aside, I appeal to you – whoever you may be: popes, bishops, archdeacons, priests, or what not – I appeal to your feelings and to your conscience.

For you know that what you teach about the creation of the world, about the inspiration of the Bible by God, and much else, is not true; how then can you teach it to little children and to ignorant adults, who look to you for true enlightenment?

Ask yourself, with your hand on your heart, do you believe what you preach? If you really ask yourself that question, not before men but before God, remembering the approaching hour of death, you cannot but answer, 'No, I do not believe it.' You do not believe in the inspiration by God of the whole of those writings which you call sacred: you do not believe all the horrors and wonders of the Old Testament, you do not believe in hell, you do not believe in an immaculate conception, in the resurrection and ascension of Christ, you do not believe in the physical resurrection of the dead, and in the triune personality of God – not only do you not believe all the articles of the creed which expresses the essence of your faith, but many of you do not even believe a single one of them.

Disbelief, if but in a single dogma, involves disbelief in the infallibility of the Church which has set up the dogma you do not believe. But if you have not faith in the Church, you will not believe in the dogmas she set up.

If you do not believe, if even you have any doubts, think what you are doing in preaching as divine, unquestionable truth – what you do not yourselves believe: and in preaching it by methods which are exceptional and unfair: methods such as you employ. And do not say you cannot take on yourselves the responsibility of depriving people of intimate union with the great or small number of your co-religionists. That is not fair. By instilling into them your special faith, you are doing just what you say you do not wish to do: you are depriving people of their natural union with all mankind, and are confining them within the narrow limits of your single sect, thereby involuntarily and inevitably placing them, if not in a hostile, at least in an alien attitude towards everyone else.

I know that you do not consciously do this terrible thing. I know that you yourselves, for the most part, are entangled, hypnotized, and often so situated that for you to confess the truth would mean to condemn all your former activity, the activity sometimes of several decades. I know how difficult, just for you, with the training you have had, and especially with the assurance common among you, that you are the infallible successors of the God-Christ – I know how difficult it will be for you to face sober realities and to confess yourselves wandering sinners, engaged in one of the worst activities a man can possibly pursue.

I know all the difficulties of your position; but remembering the words of the Gospels you acknowledge as divine – that God rejoices more over one sinner that repenteth than over a hundred righteous persons – I think that for each one of you, whatever his position may be, it should be easier to repent, and to cease to take part in what you are doing, than, not believing, to continue to do it.

Whoever you may be: popes, cardinals, metropolitans, archbishops, bishops, superintendents, priests or pastors – think of this.

If you belong to those of the clergy – of whom there are unfortunately in our days very many (and continually more and more) – who see clearly how obsolete, irrational and immoral is the Church teaching, but who, without believing in it, still from personal motives (for their salaries as priests or bishops) continue to preach it, do not console yourself with the supposition that your activity is justified by any utility it has for the masses of the people, who do not yet understand what you understand.

Falsehood cannot be useful to anyone. What you know – that falsehoods are falsehoods – could be known equally by the common man whom you have indoctrinated, and are indoctrinating, with them, and he might be free from them. Not only might he, but for you, free himself from these falsehoods – he might find the truth which Christ has shown, and which by your doctrines you – standing between the common man and his God – have hidden away. What you are doing, you are doing not to serve man, but only from ambition or covetousness.

Therefore, however magnificent may be the palaces in which you live, the churches in which you officiate and preach, and the vestments in which you adorn yourselves, your occupation is not made better by these things. 'That which is highly esteemed among men is an abomination in the sight of God.'

So it is with those who, not believing, continue to preach what is false, and to strengthen men in it.

But there are among you those also – and their number is continually increasing – who, though they see the bankrupt position of the Church creeds in our day, cannot make up their minds to examine them critically. Belief has been so instilled into them in childhood, and is so strongly supported by their environment and by the influence of the crowd, that they (without even trying to free themselves from it) devote all the strength of their minds and education to justify, by cunning allegories and false and confused reasonings, the incompatibilities and contradictions of the creed they profess.

If you belong to this class of clergy, which though less guilty is even more harmful than the class previously mentioned, do not imagine that your reasonings will quiet your conscience or justify you before God. In the depth of your soul you cannot but know that all you can devise and invent will not make the immoral stories of Scripture history – which are nowadays in opposition to man's knowledge and understanding – or the archaic affirmations of the Nicene Creed, either moral, reasonable, clear or accordant with contemporary knowledge and common sense.

You know that you cannot by your arguments convince anyone of the truth of your faith, and that no fresh, grown-up, educated man, not trained from childhood to your belief, can believe you; but that such a man will either laugh, or will suppose you to be mentally afflicted, when he hears your account of the commencement of the world, of the first man, of Adam's sin, and of the redemption of man by the death of the son of God.

All you can effect by your false, pseudo-scientific argumentations, and (what counts for more) by your authority, will be temporarily to retain in hypnotic submission to a false faith, those who are awakening from its influence and preparing to free themselves from it.

That is what you are doing; and it is a very evil work. Instead of employing your mental powers to free yourselves and others from the fraud you and they are involved in, and which causes you and them to suffer, you use your powers yet further to entangle yourselves and them.

You, the clergy of this class, should not entangle yourselves and others by obscure argumentation, should not try to demonstrate that truth is what you call truth; but, on the contrary, making an effort, you should try to verify the beliefs you have accepted as truth – by comparing them with what you and everyone else accept as sure knowledge, and also by the simple demands of common sense. You need only sincerely set yourselves that task, and you will at once awake from the hypnotic sleep in which you now are – and the terrible delusion in which you have lived will become clear to you.

So it is with this second class, the philosophizing clergy, who in our day are very numerous and most harmful.

But there is also a third, most numerous, class of simple-minded clergy who have never doubted the truth of the faith they profess and preach. These men have either never thought about the sense and meaning of the affirmations taught them in their childhood as sacred divine truth; or, if they have thought, were so unaccustomed to independent thinking that they did not see the incompatibilities and contradictions involved in those affirmations, or, seeing them, were yet so overpowered by the authority of the Church tradition that they have not dared to think otherwise than as former and present ecclesiastics have thought. These men generally console themselves with the thought that Church doctrine probably has some satisfactory explanation of the incompatibilities which (as they suppose) only appear incompatibilities to them owing to their own deficiency in theological erudition.

If you belong to that class of men – sincerely and naïvely believing, or who, though they do not believe are yet willing to believe, and are oblivious of the obstacles to so doing – whether you are an already ordained priest, or a young man only preparing for the priesthood, pause for a while in your activity or in your preparations for that activity, and consider what you are doing or are about to do.

You are preaching, or are preparing to preach, a teaching which will define for men the meaning of their life, will define its aim, will indicate the features of good and evil, and will give direction to all their activity. And this teaching you preach not as any other human doctrine – imperfect and open to question – but as a teaching revealed by God Himself, and therefore not to be questioned; and you preach it not in a book or ordinary conversation, but either to children – at an age when they cannot understand the meaning of what is conveyed to them, but when it all stamps itself indelibly on their consciousness – or you preach it to ignorant adults unable to weigh the instruction you give them.

Such is your activity, or for such activity you are preparing.

But what if this that you teach, or are preparing to teach, be untrue?

Is it possible that this cannot be, or must not be, considered? If you consider it and compare this teaching with other teachings claiming to be equally unique and infallible, and compare it with what you yourselves know, and with common sense; if, in a word, you consider it, not in a spirit of blind credulity, but freely – you cannot fail to see that what has been given to you as sacred truth, is not only not sacred truth, but is simply an obsolete and superstitious belief, which, like other similar beliefs, is maintained and preached by men not for the benefit of their brother-men but for some other object. And as soon as you have understood that, all those of you who look on life seriously and attend to the voice of conscience will be unable to continue to preach this doctrine, or to prepare to preach it.

XI

But I hear the usual reply: 'What will become of men if they cease to believe the Church doctrines? Won't things be worse than they now are?'

What will happen if the people of Christendom cease to believe in Church doctrine? The result will be – that not the Hebrew legends alone, but the religious wisdom of the whole world, will become accessible and intelligible to them. People will grow up and develop with unperverted understandings and feelings. Having discarded a teaching accepted credulously, people will order their relation towards God reasonably, in conformity with their knowledge; and will recognize the moral obligations flowing from that relation.

'But will not the results be worse?'

If the Church doctrine is not true – how can it be worse for men not to have falsehood preached to them as truth, especially in a way so unfair as is now adopted for the purpose?

'But,' some people say, 'the common folk are coarse and uneducated; and what we, educated people, do not require may yet be useful and even indispensable for the masses.'

If all men are made alike, then all must travel one and the same path from darkness to light, from ignorance to knowledge, from falsehood to truth. You have travelled that road and have attained consciousness of the unreliability of the belief in which you were trained. By what right, then, will you check others from making the same advance?

You say, that though you do not need such food, it is needed by the masses. But no wise man undertakes to decide the physical food another must eat; how, then, can it be decided – and who can decide – what spiritual food the masses of the people must have?

The fact that you notice among the people a demand for this doctrine, in no way proves that the demand ought to be supplied. There exists a demand for intoxicants and tobacco – and other yet worse demands. And the fact is that you yourselves, by complex methods of hypnotization, evoke this very demand, by the existence of which you try to justify your own occupation. Only cease to evoke the demand, and it will not exist; for, as in your own case so with everyone else, there can be no demand for lies, but all men have moved and still move from darkness to light; and you, who stand nearer to the light, should try to make it accessible to others, and not to hide it from them.

'But,' I hear a last objection, 'will the result not be worse if we – educated, moral men, who desire to do good to the people – abandon our posts because of the doubts that have arisen in our souls, and let our places be taken by coarse, immoral men, indifferent to the people's good?'

Undoubtedly the abandonment of the clerical profession by the best men will have the effect that the ecclesiastical business passing into coarse, immoral hands will more and more disintegrate, and expose its own falseness and harmfulness. But the result will not be worse, for the disintegration of ecclesiastical establishments is now going on, and is one of the means by which people are being liberated from the fraud in which they have been held. And, therefore, the quicker this emancipation is accomplished, by enlightened and good men abandoning the clerical profession, the better it will be. And so, the greater the number of enlightened and good men who leave the clerical profession, the better.

So from whichever side you look at your activity, that activity remains harmful, and therefore all those among you who still fear God and have not quite stifled the voice of conscience, cannot do otherwise than exert all your strength to release yourselves from the false position in which you are placed.

I know that many of you are encumbered with families, or are dependent on parents who require you to follow the course you have begun; I know how difficult it is to abandon a post that brings honour or wealth, or even gives a competence and enables you and your families to continue a life to which you are accustomed, and I know how painful it is to go against relations one loves. But anything is better than to do what destroys your own soul and injures your fellow men.

Therefore, the sooner and more definitely you repent of your sin and cease your activity, the better it will be not only for others, but for yourselves.

That is what I – standing now on the brink of my grave, and clearly seeing the chief source of human ills – wished to say to you; and to say, not in order to expose or condemn you (I know how imperceptibly you were yourselves led into the snare which has made you what you are), but I wished to say it in order to co-operate in the emancipation of men from the terrible evil which the preaching of your doctrine produces by obscuring the truth: and at the same time I wished to help you to rouse yourselves from the hypnotic sleep in which now you often fail to understand all the wickedness of your own actions.

May God, who sees your hearts, help you in the effort.

[Translated by Aylmer Maude]

WORK, DEATH AND SICKNESS

[1903]

A Legend

This is a legend current among the South American Indians.

God, say they, at first made men so that they had no need to work: they needed neither houses, nor clothes, nor food, and they all lived till they were a hundred, and did not know what illness was.

When, after some time, God looked to see how people were living, He saw that instead of being happy in their life, they had quarrelled with one another, and, each caring for himself, had brought matters to such a pass that far from enjoying life, they cursed it.

Then God said to Himself: 'This comes of their living separately, each for himself.' And to change this state of things, God so arranged matters that it became impossible for people to live without working. To avoid suffering from cold and hunger, they were now obliged to build dwellings, and to dig the ground, and to grow and gather fruits and grain.

'Work will bring them together,' thought God. 'They cannot make their tools, prepare and transport their timber, build their houses, sow and gather their harvests, spin and weave, and make their clothes, each one alone by himself.

'It will make them understand that the more heartily they work together, the more they will have and the better they will live; and this will unite them.'

Time passed on, and again God came to see how men were living, and whether they were now happy.

But He found them living worse than before. They worked together (that they could not help doing), but not all together, being broken up into little groups. And each group tried to snatch work from other groups, and they hindered one another, wasting time and strength in their struggles, so that things went ill with them all.

Having seen that this, too, was not well, God decided so as to arrange things that man should not know the time of his death, but might die at any moment; and He announced this to them.

'Knowing that each of them may die at any moment,' thought God, 'they will not, by grasping at gains that may last so short a time, spoil the hours of life allotted to them.'

But it turned out otherwise. When God returned to see how people were living, He saw that their life was as bad as ever.

Those who were strongest, availing themselves of the fact that men might die at any time, subdued those who were weaker, killing some and threatening others with death. And it came about that the strongest and their descendants did no work, and suffered from the weariness of idleness, while those who were weaker had to work beyond their strength, and suffered from lack of rest. Each set of men feared and hated the other. And the life of man became yet more unhappy.

Having seen all this, God, to mend matters, decided to make use of one last means; He sent all kinds of sickness among men. God thought that when all men were exposed to sickness they would understand that those who are well should have pity on those who are sick, and should help them, that when they themselves fall ill, those who are well might in turn help them.

And again God went away; but when He came back to see how men lived now that they were subject to sicknesses, He saw that their life was worse even than before. The very sickness that in God's purpose should have united men, had divided them more than ever. Those men who were strong enough to make others work, forced them also to wait on them in times of sickness; but they did not, in their turn, look after others who were ill. And those who were forced to work for others, and to look after them when sick, were so worn with work that they had no time to look after their own sick, but left them without attendance. That the sight of sick folk might not disturb the pleasures of the wealthy, houses were arranged in which these poor people suffered and died, far from those whose sympathy might have cheered them, and in the arms of hired people who nursed them without compassion, or even with disgust. Moreover, people considered many of the illnesses infectious, and, fearing to catch them, not only avoided the sick, but even separated themselves from those who attended the sick.

Then God said to Himself: 'If even this means will not bring men to understand wherein their happiness lies, let them be taught by suffering.' And God left men to themselves.

And, left to themselves, men lived long before they understood that they all ought to, and might be, happy. Only in the very latest times have a few of them begun to understand that work ought not to be a bugbear to some and like galley-slavery for others, but should be a common and happy occupation, uniting all men. They have begun to understand that with death constantly threatening each of us, the only reasonable business of every man is to spend the years, months, hours and minutes allotted him – in unity and love. They have begun to understand that sickness, far from dividing men, should, on the contrary, give opportunity for loving union with one another.

[Translated by Aylmer Maude]

THREE QUESTIONS
[1903]

It once occurred to a certain King, that if he always knew the right time to begin everything; if he knew who were the right people to listen to, and whom to avoid; and, above all, if he always knew what was the most important thing to do, he would never fail in anything he might undertake.

And this thought having occurred to him, he had it proclaimed throughout his kingdom that he would give a great reward to anyone who would teach him what was the right time for every action, and who were the most necessary people, and how he might know what was the most important thing to do.

And learned men came to the King, but they all answered his questions differently.

In reply to the first question, some said that to know the right time for every action, one must draw up in advance a table of days, months and years, and must live strictly according to it. Only thus, said they, could everything be done at its proper time. Others declared that it was impossible to decide beforehand the right time for every action; but that, not letting oneself be absorbed in idle pastimes, one should always attend to all that was going on, and then do what was most needful. Others, again, said that however attentive the King might be to what was going on, it was impossible for one man to decide correctly the right time for every action, but that he should have a Council of wise men, who would help him to fix the proper time for everything.

But then again others said there were some things which could not wait to be laid before a Council, but about which one had at once to decide whether to undertake them or not.

But in order to decide that, one must know beforehand what was going to happen. It is only magicians who know that; and, therefore, in order to know the right time for every action, one must consult magicians.

Equally various were the answers to the second question. Some said the people the King most needed were his councillors; others, the priests; others, the doctors; while some said the warriors were the most necessary.

To the third question, as to what was the most important occupation: some replied that the most important thing in the world was science. Others said it was skill in warfare; and others, again, that it was religious worship.

All the answers being different, the King agreed with none of them, and gave the reward to none. But still wishing to find the right answers to his questions, he decided to consult a hermit, widely renowned for his wisdom.

The hermit lived in a wood which he never quitted, and he received none but common folk. So the King put on simple clothes, and before reaching the hermit's cell dismounted from his horse, and, leaving his bodyguard behind, went on alone.

When the King approached, the hermit was digging the ground in front of his hut. Seeing the King, he greeted him and went on digging. The hermit was frail and weak, and each time he stuck his spade into the ground and turned a little earth, he breathed heavily.

The King went up to him and said: 'I have come to you, wise hermit, to ask you to answer three questions: How can I learn to do the right thing at the right time? Who are the people I most need, and to whom should I, therefore, pay more attention than to the rest? And, what affairs are the most important, and need my first attention?'

The hermit listened to the King, but answered nothing. He just spat on his hand and recommenced digging.

'You are tired,' said the King, 'let me take the spade and work a while for you.'

'Thanks!' said the hermit, and, giving the spade to the King, he sat down on the ground.

When he had dug two beds, the King stopped and repeated

his questions. The hermit again gave no answer, but rose, stretched out his hand for the spade, and said:

'Now rest a while – and let me work a bit.'

But the King did not give him the spade, and continued to dig. One hour passed, and another. The sun began to sink behind the trees, and the King at last stuck the spade into the ground, and said:

'I came to you, wise man, for an answer to my questions. If you can give me none, tell me so, and I will return home.'

'Here comes someone running,' said the hermit, 'let us see who it is.'

The King turned round, and saw a bearded man come running out of the wood. The man held his hands pressed against his stomach, and blood was flowing from under them. When he reached the King, he fell fainting on the ground moaning feebly. The King and the hermit unfastened the man's clothing. There was a large wound in his stomach. The King washed it as best he could, and bandaged it with his handkerchief and with a towel the hermit had. But the blood would not stop flowing, and the King again and again removed the bandage soaked with warm blood, and washed and rebandaged the wound. When at last the blood ceased flowing, the man revived and asked for something to drink. The King brought fresh water and gave it to him. Meanwhile the sun had set, and it had become cool. So the King, with the hermit's help, carried the wounded man into the hut and laid him on the bed. Lying on the bed the man closed his eyes and was quiet; but the King was so tired with his walk and with the work he had done, that he crouched down on the threshold, and also fell asleep – so soundly that he slept all through the short summer night. When he awoke in the morning, it was long before he could remember where he was, or who was the strange bearded man lying on the bed and gazing intently at him with shining eyes.

'Forgive me!' said the bearded man in a weak voice, when he saw that the King was awake and was looking at him.

'I do not know you, and have nothing to forgive you for,' said the King.

'You do not know me, but I know you. I am that enemy of

yours who swore to revenge himself on you, because you executed his brother and seized his property. I knew you had gone alone to see the hermit, and I resolved to kill you on your way back. But the day passed and you did not return. So I came out from my ambush to find you, and I came upon your bodyguard, and they recognized me, and wounded me. I escaped from them, but should have bled to death had you not dressed my wound. I wished to kill you, and you have saved my life. Now, if I live, and if you wish it, I will serve you as your most faithful slave, and will bid my sons do the same. Forgive me!'

The King was very glad to have made peace with his enemy so easily, and to have gained him for a friend, and he not only forgave him, but said he would send his servants and his own physician to attend him, and promised to restore his property.

Having taken leave of the wounded man, the King went out into the porch and looked around for the hermit. Before going away he wished once more to beg an answer to the questions he had put. The hermit was outside, on his knees, sowing seeds in the beds that had been dug the day before.

The King approached him, and said:

'For the last time, I pray you to answer my questions, wise man.'

'You have already been answered!' said the hermit still crouching on his thin legs, and looking up at the King, who stood before him.

'How answered? What do you mean?' asked the King.

'Do you not see,' replied the hermit. 'If you had not pitied my weakness yesterday, and had not dug these beds for me, but had gone your way, that man would have attacked you, and you would have repented of not having stayed with me. So the most important time was when you were digging the beds; and I was the most important man; and to do me good was your most important business. Afterwards, when that man ran to us, the most important time was when you were attending to him, for if you had not bound up his wounds he would have died without having made peace with you. So he was the most important man, and what you did for him was your most important business. Remember then: there is only one time that is important – Now! It is the most important time because it is the only time when we have any power. The most necessary man is he with whom you are, for no man knows whether he will ever have dealings with anyone else: and the most important affair is, to do him good, because for that purpose alone was man sent into this life!'

[Translated by Aylmer Maude]

ALYOSHA GORSHOK OR ALYOSHA-THE-POT [1905]

Alyoshka was the younger brother. He'd been nicknamed Gorshok, or 'the pot', because once his mother sent him to take a pot of milk to the deacon's wife, and he stumbled and broke it. His mother gave him a beating; the other children started to tease him by calling him 'the pot'. Alyosha Gorshok, Alyosha-the-Pot – that's how he got his name.*

Alyoshka was a skinny, lop-eared lad (his ears stuck out like wings), and he had a large nose. Children would tease him, saying: 'Alyoshka's nose looks like a mutt on a mound.' There was a school in the village but he just couldn't learn how to read and write; besides, he had no time to study. His older brother lived with a merchant in town; since childhood Alyoshka had been helping his father. When he was only six, he and his little sister would tend the cows and sheep in the pasture; when he got a little older, he'd tend the horses night and day. By the age of twelve he'd already begun to plough the field and drive the cart. He wasn't very strong, but he had the knack. He was always cheerful. Whenever other children laughed at him, he would either laugh or keep silent. When his father scolded him, he would keep silent and listen. And, as soon as the scolding stopped, he'd smile and set about doing whatever task needed to be done.

Alyosha was nineteen when his brother was drafted into the army. His father sent him to replace his brother and become

* The full form of the hero's name is Aleksei, but he's most often referred to by the two diminutive forms, Alyósha or Alyoshka. The heroine's name is Ustínya, also called Ustyusha.

the merchant's yard-keeper. They gave Alyosha his brother's old boots, his father's cap and long coat, and then took him into town. Alyosha couldn't get his fill of admiring his new clothes, but the merchant didn't like the way he looked.

'I thought you'd send me a real replacement for Semyon,' the merchant said, looking Alyosha over. 'But you've brought me a little snot-nosed kid. What good is he?'

'He can do everything – harness the horses, go where you send him, and work like a fiend; he only looks as thin as a rail. But he's really wiry.'

'Well, we'll see about that.'

'And most of all – he's humble. Very eager to work.'

'Well, what can I do? Leave him here.'

And so, Alyosha began to work at the merchant's house.

The merchant's family wasn't large: his wife, her old mother, an older married son who'd had only a primary education and now worked with his father; another son – educated, who'd finished high school, gone off to university, been expelled, and now lived at home; and a daughter who was still a pupil at the high school.

At first they didn't much like Alyoshka – he behaved like a peasant and was dressed poorly; he didn't have any manners, addressed everyone informally; but they soon got used to him. He worked even harder than his brother. He really was humble: whatever they sent him to do, he did willingly and quickly, moving from one task to another without stopping. And, just as at home, so too at the merchant's house, all sorts of tasks were piled upon him. The more he did, the more they gave him to do. The wife, and her mother, and her daughter, and her son, and the shop assistant, and the cook – all sent him here and there, asking him to do this and that. All you could hear was: 'Go fetch this, Alyosha,' or 'Fix that, brother.' 'Hey, what's wrong? Did you forget, Alyosha?' 'Take care and don't forget, Alyosha.' And Alyosha fetched, and fixed, and took care, and didn't forget; he managed to do everything, smiling all the while.

He soon wore out his brother's boots and the merchant berated him for going around with holes in his boots and his toes sticking out, and ordered him to buy some new boots at the market. Alyosha bought some new boots and was delighted with them, but his feet were the same old feet, and by evening they were aching from all his running around, and he got angry at them. Alyosha was afraid that when his father came to collect his salary, he'd be angry that the merchant had deducted the cost of the boots.

During the winter Alyosha would get up before dawn, chop the firewood, sweep the courtyard, feed the cow and horses, and give them water. Then he'd stoke the stove, brush the clothes and boots, then clean and prepare the samovars; following that, either the shop assistant would call him to unpack the goods or the cook would tell him to knead the dough and scrub the saucepans. Then they'd send him into town, either with a note to deliver, to take their daughter to school, or to buy oil for the old woman's icon lamps. 'Where are you off to, damn you,' one or another would say. 'Why go yourself? Alyosha will fetch it. Alyoshka! Hey, Alyoshka!' And Alyosha ran and fetched.

He'd eat breakfast on the run and rarely was he on time to have dinner with the others. The cook would scold him for not joining everyone, but she felt sorry for him and would save him leftovers for his dinner and supper. There was an even greater amount of work to be done around the holidays. Alyosha enjoyed the holidays especially because he would receive some tips; even though it amounted to very little, only about sixty kopecks in all, it was still his own money. He could spend it however he chose. As for his salary, he never got to see that. His father would arrive, collect it from the merchant, and merely rebuke Alyosha for having worn out his boots so quickly.

When he'd saved up two roubles from his tips, he bought, on the cook's advice, a red knitted jacket; when he put it on, he couldn't keep from smacking his lips with satisfaction.

He said little and, when he did speak, it was always abrupt and brief. Whenever anyone ordered him to do something or asked if he could do such and such, he always replied without the least hesitation: 'Of course, I can,' and he immediately rushed off to do it and he did it.

He didn't know any prayers; he forgot those that his mother had taught him; nevertheless, he prayed both morning and evening – with his hands, crossing himself.

Thus Alyosha lived for a year and half; in the second half of the second year there occurred the most unusual event in his entire life. This event was as follows: much to his own surprise, he discovered that, in addition to relations between people deriving from their mutual need for one another, there also exist very special relations: not that a person has to clean someone's boots, or carry a purchase, or harness a horse, but rather that a person just like that, not for any special reason, could be needed by another; that it was necessary to serve that other person and be kind to him; and that he, Alyosha, was none other than that very person. He discovered this all through Ustinya. Ustyusha was an orphan, young, and just as hard-working as Alyosha. She began to feel sorry for him; and, for the first time, Alyosha felt that he, he himself, and not his services, but he himself, was important to another person. When his mother felt sorry for him, he didn't even notice it; that seemed to be the way it was supposed to be, just as if he was feeling sorry for himself. But now, all of a sudden, he saw that Ustinya, a complete stranger, felt sorry for him. She left him some kasha and milk in the pot, and, while he ate, she'd rest her chin on her bare arms and watch him. He'd glance up at her and she'd start to laugh; then he'd start to laugh, too.

It was all so new and strange that at first Alyosha was frightened. He felt that it interfered with his work. Still he was glad and, when he looked at his trousers that she'd mended, he shook his head and smiled. Often while working or on the go, he'd think about Ustinya and say to himself, 'Oh, that Ustinya!' She helped him when she could, and he helped her. She told him about her plight, how she'd been orphaned, how her aunt had taken her away, how she'd been sent into town, how the merchant's son had tried to talk her into some foolishness, and how she'd put him in his place.

She loved to talk and he found it pleasant to listen to her. He heard about what often happens in towns: how hired servants up and marry cooks. Once she even asked if he was going to be married off soon. He replied that he didn't know and wasn't eager to take a wife from the village.

'Well, and have you picked someone?' she asked.

'I'd pick you,' he said. 'Would you have me, or not?'

'Oh, *gorshok*, *gorshok*! You put it so cunningly,' she said, snapping her hand towel across his back. 'And why shouldn't I have you?'

At Shrovetide his father came to town to collect his salary. The merchant's wife had learned that Aleksei had taken it into his head to marry Ustinya, and she didn't like the idea. 'She'll get pregnant, and then what use will she be with a child?' she said to her husband.

The merchant paid the money to Aleksei's father.

'So, how's he doing, my boy?' asked the peasant. 'I told you he was humble.'

'Humble he may be, but he's come up with a foolish idea,' said the merchant. 'He's taken it into his head to marry our cook. I don't keep married servants. That doesn't suit us at all.'

'Simple he may be, but what an idea,' said the father. 'Don't worry. I'll tell him to drop the whole thing.'

Upon entering the kitchen, the father sat down at the table to wait for his son. Alyosha was running around doing several tasks and came in all out of breath.

'Here I thought you were a sensible lad,' said his father. 'What have you come up with now?'

'Nothing much.'

'What do you mean, "nothing much"? You've decided to get married. I'll marry you off when the time comes and to the person I choose, not to some slut from town.'

The father said quite a bit. Alyosha stood there and sighed. When the father finished, Alyosha smiled.

'Well then, I can give it up.'

'That's better.'

When the father had gone and Alyosha was left alone with Ustinya, he said to her (she'd been standing behind the door, listening while the father was talking with his son):

'Things aren't so good for us; it didn't work out. Do you hear? He's angry and won't allow it.'

She wept silently into her apron.

Alyosha clicked his tongue.

'But I have to obey him. It seems we have to give it up.'

In the evening when the merchant's wife called for him to close the shutters, she said:

'Well, did you hear what your father said? Have you given up that foolish idea?'

'Yes, I did,' said Alyosha, and began laughing, and then immediately started crying.

From then on Alyosha didn't mention marriage to Ustinya and resumed his former life.

One day the shop assistant sent him to clean the snow off the roof. He climbed up the ladder, cleaned off all the snow, and began to scrape the ice from the gutters; his feet slipped and he fell with his shovel. Unfortunately, he didn't fall into the snow, but on to the iron roof over the exit. Ustinya came running up to him, as did the merchant's daughter.

'Did you hurt yourself, Alyosha?' she asked.

'Hurt myself? It's nothing.'

He tried to stand, but he couldn't, and began to smile. They carried him into the yard-keeper's lodge. The doctor's assistant arrived. He examined him and asked where it hurt.

'It hurts all over,' he said. 'But it's nothing. The master will be angry. We have to let my father know.'

Alyosha lay there for two days and two nights, and on the third day they sent for the priest.

'Well, are you really going to die?' asked Ustinya.

'What of it?' said Alyosha, hastily as always. 'Do you think we get to live for ever? You have to die some time. Thanks, Ustinya, for feeling sorry for me. See, it was better they didn't let us get married, because nothing would've come of it. Now, it's all for the best.'

He prayed with the priest only with his hands and with his heart. And in his heart it seemed that just as it was good here if you obeyed and didn't offend, it would also be good there.

He said little. He merely asked for something to drink, and felt a growing sense of wonder.

Suddenly he was overcome with wonder, stretched out, and died.

NOTE

Tolstoy wrote 'Alyosha Gorshok' (literally, 'Alyosha-the-Pot') in 1905. The only mention of the story in his diary is an entry for 28 February: 'Have been writing Alyosha. Quite bad. Gave it up.' The story was published posthumously in 1911 with several other works of his late, post-conversion period. Prince Dmitry Mirsky, in his pioneering survey *The History of Russian Literature* (1949), regarded the story as a masterpiece. 'Concentrated into its six pages . . . [it] is one of [Tolstoy's] most perfect creations, and one of the few which make one forget the bedrock Luciferianism and pride of the author.'

[Translated by Michael R. Katz]

SHAKESPEARE AND THE DRAMA
[1906]

I

An article by Ernest Howard Crosby* on Shakespeare's attitude towards the people has suggested to me the idea of expressing the opinion I formed long ago about Shakespeare's works, an opinion quite contrary to that established throughout the European world. Recalling the struggle with doubts, the pretences, and the efforts to attune myself to Shakespeare that I went through owing to my complete disagreement with the general adulation, and supposing that many people have experienced and are experiencing the same perplexity, I think it may be of some use definitely and frankly to express this disagreement of mine with the opinion held by the majority, especially as the conclusions I came to on examining the causes of my disagreement are it seems to me not devoid of interest and significance.

My disagreement with the established opinion about Shakespeare is not the result of a casual mood or of a light-hearted attitude towards the subject, but it is the result of repeated and strenuous efforts extending over many years to harmonize my

* E. H. Crosby was for some time a member of the New York State Legislature; subsequently he went to Egypt as a Judge in the Mixed Tribunals. While there he began reading the works of Tolstoy, which influenced him strongly. He visited Tolstoy, and afterwards co-operated with him in various ways. In an essay on 'Shakespeare and the Working Classes' he drew attention to the anti-democratic tendency of that poet's plays, and Tolstoy began his own essay intending it as a preface to Crosby's. [A. M.]

views with the opinions about Shakespeare accepted throughout the whole educated Christian world.

I remember the astonishment I felt when I first read Shakespeare. I had expected to receive a great aesthetic pleasure, but on reading one after another the works regarded as his best, *King Lear*, *Romeo and Juliet*, *Hamlet* and *Macbeth*, not only did I not experience pleasure but I felt an insuperable repulsion and tedium, and a doubt as to whether I lacked sense – since I considered as insignificant, or even simply bad, works which are regarded as the summit of perfection by the whole educated world – or whether the importance attributed to Shakespeare's works by that educated world lacks sense. My perplexity was increased by the fact that I have always keenly felt the beauties of poetry in all its forms: why then did Shakespeare's works, recognized by the whole world as works of artistic genius, not only fail to please me but even seem detestable? For a long time I distrusted my judgement, and to check my conclusions I have repeatedly, during the past fifty years, set to work to read Shakespeare in all possible forms – in Russian, in English, and in German in Schlegel's translation, as I was advised to. I read the tragedies, comedies and historical plays several times over, and I invariably experienced the same feelings – repulsion, weariness and bewilderment. Now, before writing this article as an old man of seventy-five,* wishing once more to check my conclusions, I have again read the whole of Shakespeare, including the historical plays, the *Henrys*, *Troilus and Cressida*, *The Tempest* and *Cymbeline*, etc., and have experienced the same feeling still more strongly, no longer with perplexity but with a firm and unshakable conviction that the undisputed fame Shakespeare enjoys as a great genius – which makes writers of our time imitate him, and readers and spectators, distorting their aesthetic and ethical sense, seek non-existent qualities in him – is a great evil, as every falsehood is.

Although I know that the majority of people have such faith in Shakespeare's greatness that on reading this opinion of mine

* Tolstoy was born in 1828. This essay appeared in 1906, so that he began his re-reading of Shakespeare three years before this article was published. [A. M.]

they will not even admit the possibility of its being correct and will not pay any attention to it, I shall nevertheless try as best I can to show why I think Shakespeare cannot be admitted to be either a writer of great genius or even an average one.

For this purpose I will take one of the most admired of Shakespeare's dramas – *King Lear*, in enthusiastic praise of which most of the critics agree.

'The tragedy of Lear is deservedly celebrated among the dramas of Shakespeare,' says Dr Johnson. 'There is perhaps no play which keeps the attention so strongly fixed, which so much agitates our passions and interests our curiosity.'

'We wish that we could pass this play over and say nothing about it,' says Hazlitt. 'All that we can say must fall far short of the subject, or even of what we ourselves conceive of it. To attempt to give a description of the play itself or of its effect upon the mind is mere impertinence; yet we must say something. It is then the best of Shakespeare's plays, for it is the one in which he was most in earnest.'

'If the originality of invention did not so much stamp almost every play of Shakespeare that to name one as the most original seems a disparagement to others,' says Hallam, 'we might say that this great prerogative of genius was exercised above all in *Lear*. It diverges more from the model of regular tragedy than *Macbeth* or *Othello*, or even more than *Hamlet*, but the fable is better constructed than in the last of these and it displays full as much of the almost superhuman inspiration of the poet as the other two.'

'*King Lear* may be recognized as the perfect model of the dramatic art of the whole world,' says Shelley.

'I am not minded to say much of Shakespeare's Arthur,' says Swinburne. 'There are one or two figures in the world of his work of which there are no words that would be fit or good to say. Another of these is Cordelia. The place they have in our lives and thoughts is not one for talk. The niche set apart for them to inhabit in our secret hearts is not penetrable by the lights and noises of common day. There are chapels in the cathedral of man's highest art, as in that of his inmost life, not made to be set open to the eyes and feet of the world. Love and

Death and Memory keep charge for us in silence of some beloved names. It is the crowning glory of genius, the final miracle and transcendent gift of poetry that it can add to the number of these and engrave on the very heart of our remembrance fresh names and memories of its own creation.'

'*Lear*, c'est l'occasion de Cordelia,' says Victor Hugo. 'La maternité de la fille sur le père; sujet profonde; la maternité vénérable entre toutes, si admirablement traduite par la légende de cette romaine, nourrice, au fond d'un cachot, de son père vieillard. La jeune mamelle près de la barbe blanche, il n'est point de spectacle plus sacré. Cette mamelle filiale c'est Cordelia.

'Une fois cette figure rêvée et trouvée Shakespeare a créé son drame . . . Shakespeare, portant Cordelia dans sa pensée, a créé cette tragédie comme un dieu, qui ayant une aurore à placer, ferait tout exprès un monde pour l'y mettre.'*

'In *Lear* Shakespeare's vision sounded the abyss of horror to its very depths, and his spirit showed neither fear, nor giddiness, nor faintness at the sight,' says Brandes. 'On the threshold of this work a feeling of awe comes over one as on the threshold of the Sistine Chapel with its ceiling-frescoes by Michael Angelo, only that the suffering here is far more intense, the wail wilder, the harmonies of beauty more definitely shattered by the discords of despair.'

Such are the judgements of the critics on this drama, and therefore I think I am justified in choosing it as an example of Shakespeare's best plays.

I will try as impartially as possible to give the contents of the play, and then show why it is not the height of perfection, as it is said to be by the learned critics, but something quite different.

* '*Lear* is Cordelia's play. The maternal feeling of the daughter towards the father – profound subject – a maternity venerable among all other maternities – so admirably set forth in the legend of that Roman girl who nursed her old father in the depths of a prison. There is no spectacle more holy than that of the young breast near the white beard. That filial breast is Cordelia.

'Once this figure was dreamed and found Shakespeare created his drama . . . Shakespeare, carrying Cordelia in his thoughts, created that tragedy like a god who having an aurora to place makes a world expressly for it.' [L. T.]

II

The tragedy of *Lear* begins with a scene in which two courtiers, Kent and Gloucester, are talking. Kent, pointing to a young man who is present, asks Gloucester whether that is his son. Gloucester says that he has often blushed to acknowledge the young man as his son but has now ceased to do so. Kent says: 'I cannot conceive you.' Then Gloucester, in the presence of his son, says: 'Sir, this young fellow's mother could; whereupon she grew round-wombed, and had indeed, sir, a son for her cradle ere she had a husband for her bed . . .' He goes on to say that he had another son who was legitimate, but 'though this knave came somewhat saucily before he was sent for, yet was his mother fair, there was good sport at his making, and the whoreson must be acknowledged.'*

Such is the introduction. Not to speak of the vulgarity of these words of Gloucester, they are also out of place in the mouth of a man whom it is intended to represent as a noble character. It is impossible to agree with the opinion of some critics that these words are put into Gloucester's mouth to indicate the contempt for illegitimacy from which Edmund suffered. Were that so, it would in the first place have been necessary to make the father express the contempt felt by people in general, and secondly Edmund, in his monologue about the injustice of those who despise him for his birth, should have referred to his father's words. But this is not done, and therefore these words of Gloucester's at the very beginning of the piece were merely for the purpose of informing the public in an amusing way of the fact that Gloucester has a legitimate and an illegitimate son.

After this trumpets are blown, King Lear enters with his daughters and sons-in-law, and makes a speech about being aged and wishing to stand aside from affairs and divide his kingdom between his daughters. In order to know how much

* When he cites the original, Tolstoy's quotations, not unlike his plot summaries, are often inaccurate. [J. P.]

he should give to each daughter he announces that to the daughter who tells him she loves him most he will give most. The eldest daughter, Goneril, says that there are no words to express her love, that she loves him 'dearer than eyesight, space, and liberty', and she loves him so much that it 'makes her breath poor'. King Lear immediately allots on the map to this daughter her share, with fields, woods, rivers and meadows, and puts the same question to his second daughter. The second daughter, Regan, says that her sister has correctly expressed her own feelings, but insufficiently. She, Regan, loves her father so that everything is abhorrent to her except his love. The King rewards this daughter also, and asks his youngest, favourite daughter, in whom, according to his expression, 'the wine of France and milk of Burgundy strive to be interess'd' – that is, who is courted by the King of France and the Duke of Burgundy – asks Cordelia how she loves him. Cordelia, who personifies all the virtues as the two elder sisters personify all the vices, says quite inappropriately, as if on purpose to vex her father, that though she loves and honours him and is grateful to him, yet, if she marries, not all her love will belong to him, but she will love her husband also.

On hearing these words the King is beside himself, and immediately curses his favourite daughter with most terrible and strange maledictions, saying, for instance, that he will love a man who eats his own children as much as he now loves her who was once his daughter.

> The barbarous Scythian,
> Or he that makes his generation messes
> To gorge his appetite, shall to my bosom
> Be as well neighbour'd, pitied, and reliev'd,
> As thou, my sometime daughter.

The courtier, Kent, takes Cordelia's part, and wishing to bring the King to reason upbraids him with his injustice and speaks reasonably about the evil of flattery. Lear, without attending to Kent, banishes him under threat of death, and calling to him Cordelia's two suitors, the King of France and the Duke of

Burgundy, proposes to each in turn to take Cordelia without a dowry. The Duke of Burgundy says plainly that he will not take Cordelia without a dowry, but the King of France takes her without dowry and leads her away. After this the elder sisters, there and then conversing with one another, prepare to offend their father who had endowed them. So ends the first scene.

Not to mention the inflated, characterless style in which King Lear – like all Shakespeare's kings – talks, the reader or spectator cannot believe that a king, however old and stupid, could believe the words of the wicked daughters with whom he had lived all their lives, and not trust his favourite daughter, but curse and banish her; therefore the reader or spectator cannot share the feeling of the persons who take part in this unnatural scene.

Scene ii begins with Edmund, Gloucester's illegitimate son, soliloquizing on the injustice of men who concede rights and respect to a legitimate son but deny them to an illegitimate son, and he determines to ruin Edgar and usurp his place. For this purpose he forges a letter to himself, as from Edgar, in which the latter is made to appear to wish to kill his father. Having waited till Gloucester appears, Edmund, as if against his own desire, shows him this letter, and the father immediately believes that his son Edgar, whom he tenderly loves, wishes to kill him. The father goes away, Edgar enters, and Edmund suggests to him that his father for some reason wishes to kill him. Edgar also at once believes him, and flees from his father.

The relations between Gloucester and his two sons, and the feelings of these characters, are as unnatural as Lear's relation to his daughters, if not more so; and therefore it is even more difficult for the spectator to put himself into the mental condition of Gloucester and his sons and to sympathize with them, than it was in regard to Lear and his daughters.

In Scene iv the banished Kent, disguised so that Lear does not recognize him, presents himself to the King who is now staying with Goneril. Lear asks who he is, to which Kent, one does not know why, replies in a jocular tone quite inappropriate to his position: 'A very honest-hearted fellow and as poor as the King.' 'If thou be'st as poor for a subject as he's for a King, thou art poor enough,' replies Lear. 'How old art thou?' 'Not so young, sir, to love a woman for singing, nor so old as to dote on her for anything,' to which the King replies that if he likes him not worse after dinner he will let him remain in his service.

This talk fits in neither with Lear's position nor with Kent's relation to him, and is evidently put into their mouths only because the author thought it witty and amusing.

Goneril's steward appears and is rude to Lear, for which Kent trips him up. The King, who still does not recognize Kent, gives him money for this and takes him into his service. After this the fool appears, and a talk begins between the fool and the King, quite out of accord with the situation, leading to nothing, prolonged, and intended to be amusing. Thus, for instance, the fool says, 'Give me an egg, and I'll give thee two crowns.' The King asks what crowns they shall be. 'Why, after I have cut the egg i'the middle and eat up the meat, the two crowns of the egg. When thou clovest thy crown i'the middle, and gavest away both parts, thou borest thine ass on thy back o'er the dirt; thou hadst little wit in thy bald crown when thou gavest thy golden one away. If I speak like myself in this, let him be whipped that first finds it so.'

In this manner prolonged conversations go on, producing in the spectator or reader a sense of wearisome discomfort such as one experiences when listening to dull jokes.

This conversation is interrupted by the arrival of Goneril. She demands that her father should diminish his retinue: instead of a hundred courtiers he should be satisfied with fifty. On hearing this proposal Lear is seized with terrible, unnatural rage, and asks:

> Does any here know me? This is not Lear!
> Does Lear walk thus? Speak thus? Where are his eyes?
> Either his notion weakens, his discernings
> Are lethargied. Ha! Waking? 'tis not so,
> Who is it that can tell me who I am?

and so forth.

Meanwhile the fool unceasingly interpolates his humourless jokes. Goneril's husband appears and wishes to appease Lear, but Lear curses Goneril, invoking sterility upon her, or the birth of such a child as would repay with ridicule and contempt her maternal cares, and would thereby show her all the horror and suffering caused by a child's ingratitude.

These words, which express a genuine feeling, might have been touching had only this been said, but they are lost among long high-flown speeches Lear continually utters quite inappropriately. Now he calls down blasts and fogs on his daughter's head, now desires that curses should 'pierce every sense about thee', or, addressing his own eyes, says that if they weep he will pluck them out and cast them, with the waters that they lose, 'to temper clay'.

After this Lear sends Kent, whom he still does not recognize, to his other daughter and notwithstanding the despair he has just expressed he talks with the fool and incites him to jests. The jests continue to be mirthless, and besides the unpleasant feeling akin to shame that one feels at unsuccessful witticisms, they are so long-drawn-out as to be wearisome. So, for instance, the fool asks the King: 'Canst thou tell why one's nose stands i' the middle of one's face?' Lear says he does not know.

'Why, to keep one's eyes of either side one's nose: that what a man cannot smell out he may spy into.'

'Canst tell how an oyster makes his shell?' the fool asks.

'No.'

'Nor I neither; but I can tell why a snail has a house.'

'Why?'

'Why, to put his head in; not to give it away to his daughters, and leave his horns without a case.'

'Be my horses ready?' asks Lear.

'Thy asses are gone about 'em. The reason why the seven stars are no more than seven is a pretty reason.'

'Because they are not eight?' says Lear.

'Yes, indeed; thou wouldst make a good fool,' says the fool, and so forth.

After this long scene a gentleman comes and announces that the horses are ready. The fool says:

> She that's a maid now and laughs at my departure,
> Shall not be a maid long, unless things be cut shorter,

and goes off.

Scene i of Act II begins with the villain Edmund persuading his brother, when his father enters, to pretend that they are fighting with their swords. Edgar agrees, though it is quite incomprehensible why he should do so. The father finds them fighting. Edgar runs away, and Edmund scratches his own arm to draw blood, and persuades his father that Edgar was using charms to kill his father and had wanted Edmund to help him, but that he had refused to do so and Edgar had then thrown himself upon him and wounded him in the arm. Gloucester believes everything, curses Edgar, and transfers all the rights of his elder and legitimate son to the illegitimate Edmund. The Duke of Cornwall, hearing of this, also rewards Edmund.

In Scene ii, before Gloucester's castle, Lear's new servant Kent, still unrecognized by Lear, begins without any reason to abuse Oswald (Goneril's steward), calling him 'a knave, a rascal, an eater of broken meats; a base, proud, shallow, beggarly, three-suited, hundred-pound, filthy, worsted-stocking knave; . . . the son and heir of a mongrel bitch', and so on. Then, drawing his sword, he demands that Oswald should fight him, saying that he will make of him a 'sop o' the moonshine', words no commentator has been able to explain, and when he is stopped he continues to give vent to the strangest abuse, saying, for instance, that he, Oswald, has been made by a tailor, because 'a stone-cutter, or a painter, could not have made him so ill, though they had been but two hours at the trade'. He also says that if he is allowed he will tread this unbolted villain into mortar, and daub the wall of a privy with him.

And in this way Kent, whom nobody recognizes – though both the King and the Duke of Cornwall, as well as Gloucester who is present, should know him well – continues to brawl in the character of a new servant of Lear's, until he is seized and put in the stocks.

Scene iii takes place on a heath. Edgar, flying from his father's pursuit, hides himself in a tree, and he tells the audience what kinds of lunatics there are, beggars who go about naked, thrust pins and wooden pricks into their bodies, and scream with wild voices and enforce charity, and he says that he intends to play the part of such a lunatic in order to escape from the pursuit. Having told the audience this he goes off.

Scene iv is again before Gloucester's castle. Lear and the fool enter. Lear sees Kent in the stocks and, still not recognizing him, is inflamed with anger against those who have dared so to treat his messenger, and he calls for the Duke and Regan. The fool goes on with his queer sayings. Lear with difficulty restrains his anger. The Duke and Regan enter. Lear complains of Goneril, but Regan justifies her sister. Lear curses Goneril, and when Regan tells him he had better go back to her sister he is indignant and says: 'Ask her forgiveness?' and goes on his knees, showing how improper it would be for him abjectly to beg food and clothing as charity from his own daughter, and he curses Goneril with the most terrible curses, and asks who has dared to put his messenger in the stocks. Before Regan can answer Goneril arrives. Lear becomes yet more angry and again curses Goneril, and when he is told that the Duke had ordered the stocks he says nothing, for at this moment Regan tells him that she cannot receive him now and that he had better return with Goneril, and in a month's time she will herself receive him but with only fifty followers instead of a hundred. Lear again curses Goneril and does not want to go with her, still hoping that Regan will receive him with all his hundred followers, but Regan now says she will only allow him twenty-five, and then Lear decides to go back with Goneril who allows fifty. Then, when Goneril says that even twenty-five are too many, Lear utters a long discourse about the superfluous and sufficient being conditional conceptions, and says that if a man is allowed only as much as is necessary he is no different from a beast. And here Lear, or rather the actor who plays Lear, addresses himself to a finely dressed woman in the audience, and says that she too does not need her finery, which does not keep her warm. After this he falls into a mad rage, says that he will do something terrible to be revenged upon his daughters, but will not weep, and so he departs. The noise of a storm that is commencing is heard.

Such is the second Act, full of unnatural occurrences and still more unnatural speeches not flowing from the speaker's circumstances, and finishing with the scene between Lear and his daughters, which might be powerful if it were not overloaded with speeches most naïvely absurd and unnatural, and quite inappropriate, moreover, put into Lear's mouth. Lear's vacillations between pride, anger, and hope of concessions from his daughters would be exceedingly touching were they not spoilt by these verbose absurdities which he utters about being ready to divorce Regan's dead mother should Regan not be glad to see him, or about evoking 'fensucked fogs' to infect his daughter, or about the heavens being obliged to protect old men as they themselves are old, and much else.

Act III begins with thunder, lightning and storm – a special kind of storm such as there never was before, as one of the characters in the play says. On the heath a gentleman tells Kent that Lear, expelled by his daughters from their houses, is wandering about the heath alone tearing his hair and throwing it to the winds, and that only the fool is with him. Kent tells the gentleman that the Dukes have quarrelled and that a French army has landed at Dover, and having communicated this he dispatches the gentleman to Dover to meet Cordelia.

Scene ii of Act III also takes place on the heath. Lear walks about the heath and utters words intended to express despair: he wishes the winds to blow so hard that they (the winds) should crack their cheeks, and that the rain should drench everything, and that the lightning should singe his white head and thunder strike the earth flat and destroy all the germs 'that make ingrateful man!' The fool keeps uttering yet more senseless words. Kent enters. Lear says that for some reason all criminals shall be discovered and exposed in this storm. Kent, still not recognized by Lear, persuades Lear to take shelter in a hovel. The fool thereupon utters a prophecy quite unrelated to the situation and they all go off.

Scene iii is again transferred to Gloucester's castle. Gloucester tells Edmund that the French king has already landed with an army and intends to help Lear. On learning this Edmund decides to accuse his father of treason in order to supplant him.

Scene iv is again on the heath in front of the hovel. Kent invites Lear to enter the hovel, but Lear replies that he has no reason to shelter himself from the storm, that he does not feel it, as the tempest in his mind aroused by his daughters' ingratitude overpowers all else. This true feeling, if expressed in simple words, might evoke sympathy, but amid his inflated and incessant ravings it is hard to notice it, and it loses its significance.

The hovel to which Lear is led turns out to be the same that Edgar has entered disguised as a madman, that is to say, without clothes. Edgar comes out of the hovel and, though they all know him, nobody recognizes him any more than they recognize Kent; and Edgar, Lear and the fool begin to talk nonsense which continues with intervals for six pages. In the midst of this scene Gloucester enters (who also fails to recognize either Kent or his own son Edgar), and tells them how his son Edgar wished to kill him.

This scene is again interrupted by one in Gloucester's castle, during which Edmund betrays his father and the Duke declares he will be revenged on Gloucester. The scene again shifts to Lear: Kent, Edgar, Gloucester, Lear and the fool are in a farmhouse and are talking. Edgar says, 'Frateretto calls me and tells me, Nero is an angler in the lake of darkness . . .' The fool says: 'Nuncle, tell me, whether a madman be a gentleman, or a yeoman?' Lear, who is out of his mind, says that a madman is a king. The fool says: 'No, he's a yeoman, that has a gentleman to his son; for he's a mad yeoman, that sees his son a gentleman before him.' Lear cries out: 'To have a thousand with red burning spits come hissing in upon them.' And Edgar shrieks that the foul fiend bites his back. Then the fool utters an adage that one cannot trust 'the tameness of a wolf, a horse's health, a boy's love, or a whore's oath'. Then Lear imagines that he is trying his daughters. 'Most learned justicer,' says he, addressing the naked Edgar. 'Thou, sapient sir, sit here. Now, you she foxes!' To this Edgar says:

> Look, where he stands and glares!
> Wantonest thou eyes at trial, madam?
> Come o'er the bourn, Bessy, to me!

and the fool sings:

> Her boat hath a leak,
> And she must not speak
> Why she dares not come over to thee.

Edgar again says something, and Kent begs Lear to lie down, but Lear continues his imaginary trial.

> Bring in the evidence.
> Thou robed man of justice, take thy place; (*to Edgar*)
> And thou, his yoke-fellow of equity, (*to the fool*)
> Bench by his side. You are of the commission, (*to Kent*)
> Sit you too.

'Pur! the cat is grey,' cries Edgar.

'Arraign her first; 'tis Goneril,' says Lear. 'I here take my oath before this honourable assembly, she kicked the poor King her father.'

> *Fool*: Come hither, mistress. Is your name Goneril? (*addressing a joint-stool*)
> *Lear*: And here's another . . . Stop her there!
> Arms, arms, sword, fire! Corruption in the place!
> False justicer, why hast thou let her 'scape?

and so on.

This raving ends by Lear falling asleep and Gloucester persuading Kent, still without recognizing him, to take the King to Dover. Kent and the fool carry Lear off.

The scene changes to Gloucester's castle. Gloucester himself is accused of treason, and is brought in and bound. The Duke of Cornwall tears out one of his eyes and stamps on it. Regan says that one eye is still whole and that this healthy eye is laughing at the other eye, and urges the Duke to crush it too. The Duke is about to do so, but for some reason one of the servants suddenly takes Gloucester's part and wounds the Duke. Regan kills the servant. The servant dies and tells Gloucester that he has still one eye to see that the evil-doer is punished. The Duke says: 'Lest it see more, prevent it: out, vile jelly!' and tears out Gloucester's other eye and throws it on the floor. Here Regan mentions that Edmund has denounced his father, and Gloucester suddenly understands that he has been deceived and that Edgar did not wish to kill him.

This ends the third Act. Act IV is again in the open country. Edgar, still in the guise of a maniac, talks in artificial language about the perversities of fate and the advantages of a humble lot. Then, curiously enough, to the very spot on the open heath where he is, comes his father, blind Gloucester, led by an old man, and he too talks about the perversities of fate in that curious Shakespearian language the chief peculiarity of which is that the thoughts arise either from the sound of the words, or by contrast. He tells the old man who leads him to leave him. The old man says that without eyes one cannot go alone, because one cannot *see* the way. Gloucester says:

'I have no way, and therefore want no *eyes*.'

And he argues that he stumbled when he *saw* and that our defects often save us.

'Ah! dear son Edgar,' adds he,

> The food of thy abused father's wrath.
> Might I but live to *see* thee in my touch,
> I'd say I had eyes again!

Edgar, naked, in the character of a lunatic, hears this, but does not disclose himself; he takes the place of the old man who had acted as guide, and talks with his father who does not recognize his voice and believes him to be a madman. Gloucester takes the opportunity to utter a witticism about 'when madmen lead the blind', and insists on driving away the old man, obviously not from motives which might be natural to him at that moment, but merely to enact an imaginary leap over the cliff when left alone with Edgar. And though he has only just seen his blinded father and learned that he repents of having driven him away, Edgar utters quite unnecessary sayings which Shakespeare might know, having read them in Harsnet's book,* but which Edgar had no means of becoming acquainted with, and which, above all, it is quite unnatural for him to utter in his then condition. He says:

'Five fiends have been in poor Tom at once: of last, as Obidicut; Hobbididence, prince of dumbness; Mahu, of stealing; Modo, of murder; and Flibbertigibbet, of mopping and mowing, who since possesses chamber-maids and waiting-women.'

On hearing these words, Gloucester gives Edgar his purse, saying:

> That I am wretched
> Makes thee the happier. Heavens, deal so still!
> Let the superfluous and lust-dieted man
> That braves your ordinance, that will not see
> Because he doth not feel, feel your power quickly;
> So distribution should undo excess,
> And each man have enough.

Having uttered these strange words, the blind Gloucester demands that Edgar should lead him to a cliff that he does not himself know, but that hangs over the sea, and they depart.

Scene ii of Act IV takes place before the Duke of Albany's palace. Goneril is not only cruel but also dissolute. She despises her husband, and discloses her love to the villain Edmund, who has obtained his father's title of Gloucester. Edmund goes away and a conversation takes place between Goneril and her husband. The Duke of Albany, the only character who shows human feelings, has already grown dissatisfied with his wife's treatment of her father, and now definitely takes Lear's part, but he expresses himself in words which destroy one's belief in his feelings. He says that a bear would lick Lear's reverence, and that if the heavens do not send their visible spirits to tame these vile offences, humanity must prey on itself like monsters, and so forth.

* *A Declaration of egregious popish impostures, etc.*, by Dr Samuel Harsnet, London, 1603, which contains almost all that Edgar says in his feigned madness. [A. M.]

Goneril does not listen to him, and he then begins to denounce her.

He says:

> See thyself, devil!
> Proper deformity seems not in the fiend
> So horrid, as in woman.

'O vain fool!' says Goneril, but the Duke continues:

> Thou changed and self-cover'd thing, for shame,
> Be-monster not thy feature. Were it my fitness
> To let these hands obey my blood,
> They are apt enough to dislocate and tear
> Thy flesh and bones: – Howe'er thou art a fiend,
> A woman's shape doth shield thee.

After this a messenger enters and announces that the Duke of Cornwall, wounded by a servant while he was tearing out Gloucester's eyes, has died. Goneril is glad, but already anticipates with fear that Regan, being now a widow, will snatch Edmund from her. This ends the second scene.

Scene iii of Act IV represents the French camp. From a conversation between Kent and a gentleman, the reader or spectator learns that the King of France is not in the camp, and that Cordelia has received a letter from Kent and is greatly grieved by what she learns about her father. The gentleman says that her face reminded one of sunshine and rain.

> Her smiles and tears
> Were like a better day: Those happy smilets,
> That play'd on her ripe lip, seem'd not to know
> What guests were in her eyes; which parted thence,
> As pearls from diamonds dropp'd,

and so forth. The gentleman says that Cordelia desires to see her father, but Kent says that Lear is ashamed to see the daughter he has treated so badly.

In Scene iv Cordelia, talking with a physician, tells him that Lear has been seen, and that he is quite mad, wearing on his head a wreath of various weeds and roaming about, and that she has sent soldiers to find him, and she adds the wish that all secret medicinal virtues of the earth may spring to him in her tears, and so forth.

She is told that the forces of the Dukes are approaching; but she is only concerned about her father, and goes off.

In Scene v of Act IV, which is in Gloucester's castle, Regan talks with Oswald, Goneril's steward, who is carrying a letter from Goneril to Edmund, and tells him that she also loves Edmund and that as she is a widow it is better for her to marry him than for Goneril to do so, and she asks Oswald to persuade her sister of this. Moreover she tells him that it was very unwise to put out Gloucester's eyes and yet to let him live, and therefore she advises Oswald if he meets Gloucester to kill him, and promises him a great reward if he does so.

In Scene vi Gloucester again appears with his unrecognized son Edgar, who, now dressed as a peasant, is leading his father to the cliff. Gloucester is walking along on level ground, but Edgar assures him that they are with difficulty ascending a steep hill. Gloucester believes this. Edgar tells his father that the noise of the sea is audible; Gloucester believes this also. Edgar stops on a level place and assures his father that he has ascended the cliff and that below him is a terrible abyss, and he leaves him alone. Gloucester, addressing the gods, says that he shakes off his affliction as he could not bear it longer without condemning them, the gods, and having said this he leaps on the level ground and falls, imagining that he has jumped over the cliff. Edgar thereupon utters to himself a yet more confused phrase:

> And yet I know not how conceit may rob
> The treasury of life, when life itself
> Yields to the theft; had he been where he thought,
> By this had thought been past,

and he goes up to Gloucester pretending to be again a different man, and expresses astonishment at the latter not having been killed by his fall from such a dreadful height. Gloucester believes that he has fallen and prepares to die, but he feels that he is alive and begins to doubt having fallen. Then Edgar assures him that he really did jump from a terrible height, and says that the man who was with him at the top was a fiend, for he had eyes like two full moons, and a thousand noses, and wavy horns.

Gloucester believes this, and is persuaded that his despair was caused by the devil, and therefore decides that he will despair no longer but will quietly await death. Just then Lear enters, for some reason all covered with wild flowers. He has gone mad and utters speeches yet more meaningless than before. He talks about coining money, about a bow, calls for a clothier's yard, then he cries out that he sees a mouse which he wishes to entice with a piece of cheese, and then he suddenly asks the password of Edgar, who at once replies with the words, 'Sweet Marjoram'. Lear says, 'Pass!' and the blind Gloucester, who did not recognize his son's or Kent's voice, recognizes the King's.

Then the King, after his disconnected utterances, suddenly begins to speak ironically about flatterers who said 'ay and no' like the theologians and assured him that he could do everything, but when he got into a storm without shelter he saw that this was not true; and then he goes on to say that as all creatures are wanton, and as Gloucester's bastard son was kinder to his father than Lear's daughters had been to theirs (though, according to the course of the play, Lear could know nothing of Edmund's treatment of Gloucester), therefore let copulation thrive, especially as he, a King, lacks soldiers. And thereupon he addresses an imaginary, hypocritically virtuous lady who acts the prude while at the same time, like an animal in heat, she is addicted to lust. All women 'but to the girdle do the gods inherit. Beneath is all the fiend's . . .', and saying this Lear screams and spits with horror. This monologue is evidently meant to be addressed by actor to audience, and probably produces an effect on the stage, but is quite uncalled for in the mouth of Lear – as is his desire to wipe his hand because it 'smells of mortality' when Gloucester wishes to kiss it. Then

Gloucester's blindness is referred to, which gives an opportunity for a play of words on eyes and Cupid's blindness, and for Lear to say that Gloucester has 'no eyes in your head, nor no money in your purse. Your eyes are in a *heavy* case, your purse in a *light*.' Then Lear declaims a monologue on the injustice of legal judgement, which is quite out of place in his mouth, seeing that he is insane. Then a gentleman enters with attendants, sent by Cordelia to fetch her father. Lear continues to behave madly and runs away. The gentleman sent to fetch Lear does not run after him but continues to tell Edgar lengthily about the position of the French and the British armies.

Oswald enters, and seeing Gloucester, and wishing to obtain the reward promised by Regan, attacks him; but Edgar, with his stave, kills Oswald, who when dying gives Edgar (the man who has killed him) Goneril's letter to Edmund, the delivery of which will earn a reward. In this letter Goneril promises to kill her husband and marry Edmund. Edgar drags out Oswald's body by the legs, and then returns and leads his father away.

Scene vii of Act IV takes place in a tent in the French camp. Lear is asleep on a bed. Cordelia enters with Kent, still in disguise. Lear is awakened by music, and seeing Cordelia does not believe she is alive but thinks her an apparition, and does not believe that he is himself alive. Cordelia assures him that she is his daughter and begs him to bless her. He goes on his knees before her, begs forgiveness, admits himself to be old and foolish, and says he is ready to take poison, which he thinks she probably has prepared for him as he is persuaded that she must hate him.

> For your sisters
> Have, as I do remember, done me wrong;
> You have some cause, they have not.

Then little by little he comes to his senses and ceases to rave. His daughter suggests that he should take a little walk. He consents, and says:

You must bear with me:
Pray you now, forget and forgive: I am old and foolish.

They go off. The gentleman and Kent, who remain on the scene, talk in order to explain to the audience that Edmund is at the head of the forces and that a battle must soon begin between Lear's defenders and his enemies. So Act IV ends.

In this fourth Act the scene between Lear and his daughter might have been touching had it not been preceded in three previous acts by the tedious monotonous ravings of Lear, and also had it been the final scene expressing his feelings, but it is not the last.

In Act V Lear's former cold, pompous, artificial ravings are repeated, destroying the impression the preceding scene might have produced.

Scene i of Act V shows us Edmund and Regan (who is jealous of her sister and offers herself to Edmund). Then Goneril comes on with her husband and soldiers. The Duke of Albany, though he pities Lear, considers it his duty to fight against the French who have invaded his country, and so prepares himself for battle.

Then Edgar enters, still disguised, and hands the Duke of Albany the letter, and says that if the Duke wins the battle he should let a herald sound a trumpet, and then (this is 800 years BC) a champion will appear who will prove that the contents of the letter are true.

In Scene ii Edgar enters leading his father, whom he seats by a tree, and himself goes off. The sounds of a battle are heard, Edgar runs back and says that the battle is lost; Lear and Cordelia are prisoners. Gloucester is again in despair. Edgar, still not disclosing himself to his father, tells him that he should not despair, and Gloucester at once agrees with him.

Scene iii opens with a triumphal progress of Edmund the victor. Lear and Cordelia are prisoners. Lear, though he is now no longer insane, still utters the same sort of senseless, inappropriate words, as, for instance, that in prison with Cordelia,

> We two alone will sing like birds i' the cage,
> When thou dost ask me blessing, I'll kneel down,
> And ask of thee forgiveness.

(This kneeling down comes three times over.) He also says that when they are in prison they will wear out poor rogues and 'sects of great ones that ebb and flow by the moon', that he and she are sacrifices upon which 'the gods throw incense', that 'he that parts them shall bring a brand from heaven, and fire us hence like foxes', and that

> The good years shall devour them, flesh and fell,
> Ere they shall make us weep,

and so forth.

Edmund orders Lear and his daughter to be led away to prison, and having ordered a captain to do them some hurt, asks him whether he will fulfil it. The captain replies, 'I cannot draw a cart, nor eat dried oats; but if it be man's work I will do it.' The Duke of Albany, Goneril and Regan enter. The Duke wishes to take Lear's part, but Edmund opposes this. The sisters intervene and begin to abuse each other, being jealous of Edmund. Here everything becomes so confused that it is difficult to follow the action. The Duke of Albany wants to arrest Edmund, and tells Regan that Edmund had long ago entered into guilty relations with his wife and that therefore Regan must give up her claim on Edmund, and if she wishes to marry should marry him, the Duke of Albany.

Having said this, the Duke challenges Edmund and orders the trumpet to be sounded, and if no one appears intends to fight him himself.

At this point Regan, whom Goneril has evidently poisoned, writhes with pain. Trumpets are sounded and Edgar enters with a visor which conceals his face, and without giving his name challenges Edmund. Edgar abuses Edmund; Edmund casts back all the abuse on Edgar's head. They fight and Edmund falls. Goneril is in despair.

The Duke of Albany shows Goneril her letter. Goneril goes off.

Edmund, while dying, recognizes that his opponent is his brother. Edgar raises his visor and moralizes to the effect that for having an illegitimate son, Edmund, his father has paid with the loss of his sight. After this Edgar tells the Duke of Albany of his adventures and that he has only now, just before coming to this combat, disclosed himself to his father, and his father could not bear it and died of excitement. Edmund, who is not yet dead, asks what else happened.

Then Edgar relates that while he was sitting by his father's body a man came, embraced him closely, cried out as if he would burst heaven, threw himself on his father's corpse, and told a most piteous tale about Lear and himself, and having told it 'the strings of life began to crack', but just then the trumpet sounded twice and he, Edgar, left him 'tranced'. And this was Kent. Before Edgar has finished telling this story a gentleman runs in with a bloody knife, shouting, 'Help!' To the question 'Who has been killed?' the gentleman says that Goneril is dead, who had poisoned her sister. She had confessed this. Kent enters, and at this moment the bodies of Regan and Goneril are brought in. Edmund thereupon says that evidently the sisters loved him greatly, as the one had poisoned the other and then killed herself for his sake. At the same time he confesses that he had given orders to kill Lear and hang Cordelia in prison, under the pretence that she had committed suicide; but that he now wishes to prevent this, and, having said so, he dies and is carried out.

After this Lear enters with Cordelia's dead body in his arms (though he is over eighty years of age and ill). And again there begin his terrible ravings which make one feel as ashamed as one does when listening to unsuccessful jokes. Lear demands that they should all howl, and alternately believes that Cordelia is dead and that she is alive. He says:

> Had I your tongues and eyes, I'd use them so
> That heaven's vault should crack.

Then he recounts how he has killed the slave who hanged Cordelia. Next he says that his eyes see badly, and thereupon recognizes Kent whom all along he had not recognized.

The Duke of Albany says that he resigns his power as long as Lear lives, and that he will reward Edgar and Kent and all who have been true to him. At that moment news is brought that Edmund has died; and Lear, continuing his ravings, begs that they will undo one of his buttons, the same request that he made when roaming about the heath. He expresses his thanks for this, tells them all to look somewhere, and with these words he dies.

In conclusion the Duke of Albany, who remains alive, says:

> The weight of this sad time we must obey;
> Speak what we feel, not what we ought to say.
> The oldest hath borne most: we that are young
> Shall never see so much, nor live so long.

All go off to the sound of a dead march. This ends Act V of the play.

III

Such is this celebrated play. Absurd as it may appear in this rendering (which I have tried to make as impartial as possible), I can confidently say that it is yet more absurd in the original. To any man of our time, were he not under the hypnotic influence of the suggestion that this play is the height of perfection, it would be enough to read it to the end, had he patience to do so, to convince himself that far from being the height of perfection it is a very poor, carelessly constructed work, which if it may have been of interest to a certain public of its own day, can evoke nothing but aversion and weariness in us now. And any man of our day free from such suggestion would receive just the same impression from the other much praised dramas of Shakespeare, not to speak of the absurd dramatized tales, *Pericles*, *Twelfth Night*, *The Tempest*, *Cymbeline* and *Troilus and Cressida*.

But such free-minded people not predisposed to Shakespeare worship are no longer to be found in our time and in our

Christian society. The idea that Shakespeare is a poetic and dramatic genius, and that all his works are the height of perfection, has been instilled into every man of our society and time from an early period of his conscious life. And therefore, superfluous as it would seem, I will try to indicate, in the play of *King Lear* which I have chosen, the defects characteristic of all Shakespeare's tragedies and comedies, as a result of which they not only fail to furnish models of dramatic art but fail to satisfy the most elementary and generally recognized demands of art.

According to the laws laid down by those very critics who extol Shakespeare, the conditions of every tragedy are that the persons who appear should, as a result of their own characters, actions, and the natural movement of events, be brought into conditions in which, finding themselves in opposition to the world around them, they should struggle with it and in that struggle display their inherent qualities.

In the tragedy of *King Lear* the persons represented are indeed externally placed in opposition to the surrounding world and struggle against it. But the struggle does not result from a natural course of events and from their own characters, but is quite arbitrarily arranged by the author and therefore cannot produce on the reader that illusion which constitutes the chief condition of art. Lear is under no necessity to resign his power, and has no reason to do so. And having lived with his daughters all their lives he also has no reason to believe the words of the two elder, and not the truthful statement of the youngest; yet on this the whole tragedy of his position is built.

Equally unnatural is the secondary and very similar plot: the relation of Gloucester to his sons. The position of Gloucester and Edgar arises from the fact that Gloucester, like Lear, immediately believes the very grossest deception, and does not even try to ask the son who had been deceived whether the accusation against him is true, but curses him and drives him away.

The fact that the relation of Lear to his daughters is just the same as that of Gloucester to his sons, makes one feel even more strongly that they are both arbitrarily invented and do not flow from the characters or the natural course of events. Equally unnatural and obviously invented is the fact that all through the play Lear fails to recognize his old courtier, Kent; and so the relations of Lear and Kent fail to evoke the sympathy of reader or hearer. This applies in an even greater degree to the position of Edgar, whom nobody recognizes, who acts as guide to his blind father and persuades him that he has leapt from a cliff when he has really jumped on level ground.

These positions in which the characters are quite arbitrarily placed are so unnatural that the reader or spectator is unable either to sympathize with their sufferings or even to be interested in what he reads or hears. That in the first place.

Secondly there is the fact that both in this and in Shakespeare's other dramas all the people live, think, speak and act quite out of accord with the given period and place. The action of *King Lear* takes place 800 years BC, and yet the characters in it are placed in conditions possible only in the Middle Ages: kings, dukes, armies, illegitimate children, gentlemen, courtiers, doctors, farmers, officers, soldiers, knights in armour, and so on, appear in it. Perhaps such anachronisms (of which all Shakespeare's plays are full) did not infringe the possibility of illusion in the sixteenth century and the beginning of the seventeenth, but in our time it is no longer possible to be interested in the development of events that could not have occurred in the conditions the author describes in detail.

The artificiality of the positions, which do not arise from a natural course of events and from the characters of the people engaged, and their incompatibility with the period and the place, is further increased by the coarse embellishments Shakespeare continually makes use of in passages meant to be specially touching. The extraordinary storm during which Lear roams about the heath, the weeds which for some reason he puts on his head, as Ophelia does in *Hamlet*, Edgar's attire – all these effects, far from strengthening the impression, produce a contrary effect. '*Man sieht die Absicht und man wird verstimmt*,* as Goethe says. It often happens – as for instance with

* 'One sees the intention and is put off.' [A. M.]

such obviously intentional effects as the dragging out of half a dozen corpses by the legs, with which Shakespeare often ends his tragedies – that instead of feeling fear and pity one feels the absurdity of the thing.

IV

Not only are the characters in Shakespeare's plays placed in tragic positions which are quite impossible, do not result from the course of events, and are inappropriate to the period and the place, they also behave in a way that is quite arbitrary and not in accord with their own definite characters. It is customary to assert that in Shakespeare's dramas character is particularly well expressed and that with all his vividness his people are as many-sided as real people, and that while exhibiting the nature of a certain given individual they also show the nature of man in general. It is customary to say that Shakespeare's delineation of character is the height of perfection. This is asserted with great confidence and repeated by everyone as an indisputable verity, but much as I have tried to find confirmation of this in Shakespeare's dramas I have always found the reverse.

From the very beginning of reading any of Shakespeare's plays I was at once convinced that it is perfectly evident that he is lacking in the chief, if not the sole, means of portraying character, which is individuality of language – that each person should speak in a way suitable to his own character. That is lacking in Shakespeare. All his characters speak not a language of their own but always one and the same Shakespearian, affected, unnatural language, which not only could they not speak, but which no real people could ever have spoken anywhere.

No real people could speak, or could have spoken, as Lear does – saying that, 'I would divorce me from thy mother's tomb' if Regan did not receive him, or telling the winds to 'crack your cheeks', or bidding 'the wind blow the earth into the sea', or 'swell the curl'd waters 'bove the main', as the gentleman describes what Lear said to the storm, or that it is easier to bear one's griefs and 'the mind much sufferance doth o'erskip, when grief hath mates, and bearing fellowship' ('bearing' meaning suffering), that Lear is 'childed, as I father'd', as Edgar says, and so forth – unnatural expressions such as overload the speeches of the people in all Shakespeare's dramas.

But it is not only that the characters all talk as no real people ever talked or could talk; they are also all afflicted by a common intemperance of language.

In love, preparing for death, fighting or dying, they all talk at great length and unexpectedly about quite irrelevant matters, guided more by the sounds of the words and by puns than by the thoughts.

And they all talk alike. Lear raves just as Edgar does when feigning madness. Kent and the fool both speak alike. The words of one person can be put into the mouth of another, and by the character of the speech it is impossible to know who is speaking. If there is a difference in the speech of Shakespeare's characters, it is only that Shakespeare makes different speeches for his characters, and not that they speak differently.

Thus Shakespeare always speaks for his kings in one and the same inflated, empty language. Similarly all his women who are intended to be poetic, speak the same pseudo-sentimental Shakespearian language: Juliet, Desdemona, Cordelia and Miranda. In just the same way also it is Shakespeare who always speaks for his villains: Richard, Edmund, Iago and Macbeth – expressing for them those malignant feelings which villains never express. And yet more identical is the talk of his madmen, with their terrible words, and the speeches of his fools with their mirthless witticisms.

So that the individual speech of living people – that individual speech which in drama is the chief means of presenting character – is lacking in Shakespeare. (If gesture is also a means of expressing character, as in the ballet, it is only a subsidiary means.) If the characters utter whatever comes to hand and as it comes to hand and all in one and the same way, as in Shakespeare, even the effect of gesture is lost; and therefore whatever blind worshippers of Shakespeare may say, Shakespeare does not show us characters.

Those persons who in his dramas stand out as characters, are characters borrowed by him from earlier works which served as the bases of his plays, and they are chiefly depicted, not in the dramatic manner which consists of making each person speak in his own diction, but in the epic manner, by one person describing the qualities of another.

The excellence of Shakespeare's depiction of character is asserted chiefly on the ground of the characters of Lear, Cordelia, Othello, Desdemona, Falstaff and Hamlet. But these characters, like all the others, instead of belonging to Shakespeare, are taken by him from previous dramas, chronicles and romances. And these characters were not merely not strengthened by him, but for the most part weakened and spoilt. This is very evident in the drama of *King Lear* which we are considering, and which was taken by Shakespeare from the play of *King Leir* by an unknown author. The characters of this drama, such as Lear himself and in particular Cordelia, were not only not created by Shakespeare, but have been strikingly weakened by him and deprived of personality as compared with the older play.

In the older play Leir resigns his power because, having become a widower, he thinks only of saving his soul. He asks his daughters about their love for him in order to keep his youngest and favourite daughter with him on his island by means of a cunning device. The two eldest are betrothed, while the youngest does not wish to contract a loveless marriage with any of the neighbouring suitors Leir offers her, and he is afraid she may marry some distant potentate.

The device he has planned, as he explains to his courtier Perillus (Shakespeare's Kent), is this: that when Cordelia tells him that she loves him more than anyone, or as much as her elder sisters do, he will say that in proof of her love she must marry a prince he will indicate on his island.

All these motives of Lear's conduct are lacking in Shakespeare's play. In the older play, when Leir asks his daughters about their love for him, Cordelia does not reply (as Shakespeare has it) that she will not give her father all her love but will also love her husband if she marries – to say which is quite unnatural – she simply says that she cannot express her love in words but hopes her actions will prove it. Goneril and Regan make remarks to the effect that Cordelia's answer is not an answer and that their father cannot quietly accept such indifference. So that in the older play there is an explanation, lacking in Shakespeare, of Leir's anger at the youngest daughter's reply. Leir is vexed at the non-success of his cunning device, and the venomous words of his elder daughters add to his irritation. After the division of his kingdom between the two elder daughters in the older play comes a scene between Cordelia and the King of Gaul which, instead of the impersonal Shakespearian Cordelia, presents us with a very definite and attractive character in the truthful, tender, self-denying youngest daughter. While Cordelia, not repining at being deprived of a share in the inheritance, sits grieving that she has lost her father's love, and looking forward to earning her bread by her own toil, the King of Gaul enters, who in the disguise of a pilgrim wishes to choose a bride from among Leir's daughters. He asks Cordelia the cause of her grief and she tells him. Having fallen in love with her, he woos her for the King of Gaul in his pilgrim guise, but Cordelia says she will only marry a man she loves. Then the pilgrim offers her his hand and heart, and Cordelia confesses that she loves him and agrees to marry him, notwithstanding the poverty and privation that she thinks await her. Then the pilgrim discloses to her that he is himself the King of Gaul, and Cordelia marries him.

Instead of this scene Lear, according to Shakespeare, proposes to Cordelia's two suitors to take her without dowry, and one cynically refuses, while the other takes her without our knowing why.

After this in the older play, as in Shakespeare, Leir undergoes insults from Goneril to whose house he has gone, but he bears these insults in a very different way from that represented by Shakespeare: he feels that by his conduct to Cordelia he has deserved them and he meekly submits. As in Shakespeare so also in the older play, the courtier, Perillus (Kent), who has taken Cordelia's part and has therefore been punished, comes to Leir; not disguised, but simply as a faithful servant who does not abandon his King in a moment of need, and assures him of his love. Leir says to him what in Shakespeare Lear says to

Cordelia in the last scene – that if his daughters whom he has benefited hate him, surely one to whom he has done evil cannot love him. But Perillus (Kent) assures the King of his love, and Leir, pacified, goes on to Regan. In the older play there are no tempests or tearing out of grey hairs, but there is a weakened old Leir, overpowered by grief and humbled, and driven out by his second daughter also, who even wishes to kill him. Turned out by his elder daughters, Leir in the older play, as a last resource, goes with Perillus to Cordelia. Instead of the unnatural expulsion of Lear during a tempest and his roaming about the heath, in the old play Leir with Perillus during their journey to France very naturally come to the last degree of want. They sell their clothes to pay for the sea-crossing, and exhausted by cold and hunger they approach Cordelia's house in fishermen's garb. Here again, instead of the unnatural conjoint ravings of the fool, Lear and Edgar, as presented by Shakespeare, we have in the older play a natural scene of the meeting between the daughter and father. Cordelia – who notwithstanding her happiness has all the time been grieving about her father and praying God to forgive her sisters who have done him so much wrong – meets him, now in the last stage of want, and wishes immediately to disclose herself to him, but her husband advises her not to do so for fear of agitating the weak old man. She agrees and takes Leir into her house, and without revealing herself to him takes care of him. Leir revives little by little, and then the daughter asks him who he is, and how he lived formerly. If, says Leir,

> . . . from the first I should relate the cause,
> I would make a heart of adamant to weep.
> And thou, poor soul,
> Kind-hearted as thou art,
> Dost weep already ere I do begin.

Cordelia replies:

> For God's love tell it, and when you have done,
> I'll tell the reason why I weep so soon.

And Leir relates all he has suffered from his elder daughters and says that he now wishes to find shelter with the one who would be right should she condemn him to death. 'If, however,' he says, 'she will receive me with love, it will be God's and her work and not my merit!' To this Cordelia replies, 'Oh, I know for certain that thy daughter will lovingly receive thee!' 'How canst thou know this without knowing her?' says Leir. 'I know,' says Cordelia, 'because not far from here, I had a father who acted towards me as badly as thou hast acted towards her, yet if I were only to see his white head, I would creep to meet him on my knees.' 'No, this cannot be,' says Leir, 'for there are no children in the world so cruel as mine.' 'Do not condemn all for the sins of some,' says Cordelia, falling on her knees. 'Look here, dear father,' she says, 'look at me: I am thy loving daughter.' The father recognizes her and says: 'It is not for thee but for me to beg thy pardon on my knees for all my sins towards thee.'

Is there anything approaching this charming scene in Shakespeare's drama?

Strange as the opinion may appear to Shakespeare's devotees, the whole of this older play is in all respects beyond compare better than Shakespeare's adaptation. It is so, first because in it those superfluous characters – the villain Edmund and the unnatural Gloucester and Edgar, who only distract one's attention – do not appear. Secondly, it is free from the perfectly false 'effects' of Lear's roaming about on the heath, his talks with the fool, and all those impossible disguises, non-recognitions and wholesale deaths – above all because in this play there is the simple, natural and deeply touching character of Leir, and the yet more touching and clearly defined character of Cordelia, which are lacking in Shakespeare. And also because in the older drama, instead of Shakespeare's daubed scene of Lear's meeting with Cordelia and her unnecessary murder, there is the exquisite scene of Leir's meeting with Cordelia, which is unequalled by anything in Shakespeare's drama.

The older play also terminates more naturally and more in accord with the spectators' moral demands than does Shakespeare's, namely, by the King of the Gauls conquering the husbands of the elder sisters, and Cordelia not perishing, but replacing Leir in his former position.

This is the position as regards the drama we are examining, borrowed from the old play *King Leir*.

It is the same with *Othello*, which is taken from an Italian story, and it is the same again with the famous *Hamlet*. The same may be said of Antony, Brutus, Cleopatra, Shylock, Richard, and all Shakespeare's characters; they are all taken from antecedent works. Shakespeare, taking the characters already given in previous plays, stories, chronicles, or in Plutarch's *Lives*, not only fails to make them more true to life and more vivid as his adulators assert, but on the contrary always weakens and often destroys them, as in *King Lear*; making his characters commit actions unnatural to them, and making them above all talk in a way natural neither to them nor to any human being. So in *Othello*, though this is – we will not say the best, but the least bad – the least overloaded with pompous verbosity, of all Shakespeare's dramas, the characters of Othello, Iago, Cassio and Emilia are far less natural and alive in Shakespeare than in the Italian romance. In Shakespeare Othello suffers from epilepsy, of which he has an attack on the stage. Afterwards in Shakespeare the murder of Desdemona is preceded by a strange vow uttered by Othello on his knees, and besides this, Othello in Shakespeare's play is a negro and not a Moor. All this is unusual, inflated, unnatural, and infringes the unity of the character. And there is none of all this in the romance. In the romance also the causes of Othello's jealousy are more naturally presented than in Shakespeare. In the romance Cassio, knowing whose the handkerchief is, goes to Desdemona to return it, but when approaching the back door of Desdemona's house he sees Othello coming and runs away from him. Othello perceives Cassio running away, and this it is that chiefly confirms his suspicion. This is omitted in Shakespeare, and yet this casual incident explains Othello's jealousy more than anything else. In Shakespeare this jealousy is based entirely on Iago's machinations, which are always successful, and on his crafty speeches, which Othello blindly believes. Othello's monologue over the sleeping Desdemona, to the effect that he wishes that she when killed should look as she is when alive, and that he will love her when she is dead and now wishes to inhale her 'balmy breath' and so forth, is quite impossible. A man who is preparing to murder someone he loves cannot utter such phrases, and still less after the murder can he say that the sun and the moon ought now to be eclipsed and the globe to yawn, nor can he, whatever kind of a negro he may be, address devils, inviting them to roast him in sulphur, and so forth. And finally, however effective may be his suicide (which does not occur in the romance), it quite destroys the conception of his firm character. If he really suffers from grief and remorse then, when intending to kill himself, he would not utter phrases about his own services, about a pearl, about his eyes dropping tears '*as fast as the Arabian trees their medicinable gum*', and still less could he talk about the way a Turk scolded a Venetian, and how '*thus*' he punished him for it! So that despite the powerful movement of feeling in Othello, when under the influence of Iago's hints jealousy rises in him, and afterwards in his scene with Desdemona, our conception of his character is constantly infringed by false pathos and by the unnatural speeches he utters.

So it is with the chief character – Othello. But notwithstanding the disadvantageous alterations he has undergone in comparison with the character from which he is taken in the romance, Othello still remains a character. But all the other personages have been quite spoilt by Shakespeare.

Iago in Shakespeare's play is a complete villain, a deceiver, a thief, and avaricious; he robs Roderigo, succeeds in all sorts of impossible designs, and is therefore a quite unreal person. In Shakespeare the motive of his villainy is, first, that he is offended at Othello not having given him a place he desired; secondly, that he suspects Othello of an intrigue with his wife; and thirdly that, as he says, he feels a strange sort of love for Desdemona. There are many motives, but they are all vague. In the romance there is one motive, and it is simple and clear: Iago's passionate love for Desdemona, changing into hatred of her and of Othello after she had preferred the Moor to him and had definitely repulsed him. Yet more unnatural is the quite unnecessary figure of Roderigo, whom Iago deceives and robs, promising him Desdemona's love and obliging him to do as he is ordered: make Cassio drunk, provoke him, and then kill him. Emilia, who utters anything it occurs to the author to put into her mouth, bears not even the slightest resemblance to a real person.

'But Falstaff, the wonderful Falstaff!' Shakespeare's eulogists will say. 'It is impossible to assert that he is not a live person, and that, having been taken out of an anonymous comedy, he has been weakened.'

Falstaff, like all Shakespeare's characters, was taken from a play by an unknown author, written about a real person, a Sir John Oldcastle who was the friend of some duke. This Oldcastle had once been accused of heresy and had been saved by his friend the Duke, but was afterwards condemned and burnt at the stake for his religious beliefs, which clashed with Catholicism. To please the Roman Catholic public an unknown author wrote a play about Oldcastle, ridiculing this martyr for his faith and exhibiting him as a worthless man, a boon companion of the Duke, and from this play Shakespeare took not only the character of Falstaff but also his own humorous attitude towards him. In the first plays of Shakespeare in which this character appears he was called Oldcastle; but afterwards, when under Elizabeth Protestantism had again triumphed, it was awkward to mock at this martyr of the struggle with Catholicism and, besides, Oldcastle's relatives had protested, and Shakespeare changed the name from Oldcastle to Falstaff – also an historical character, notorious for having run away at the battle of Agincourt.

Falstaff is really a thoroughly natural and characteristic personage, almost the only natural and characteristic one depicted by Shakespeare. And he is natural and characteristic because, of all Shakespeare's characters, he alone speaks in a way proper to himself. He speaks in a manner proper to himself because he talks just that Shakespearian language, filled with jests that lack humour and unamusing puns, which while unnatural to all Shakespeare's other characters is quite in harmony with the boastful, distorted, perverted character of the drunken Falstaff. That is the only reason why this figure really presents a definite character. Unfortunately the artistic effect of the character is spoilt by the fact that it is so repulsive in its gluttony, drunkenness, debauchery, rascality, mendacity and cowardice, that it is difficult to share the feeling of merry humour Shakespeare adopts towards it. Such is the case with Falstaff.

But in none of Shakespeare's figures is, I will not say his inability, but his complete indifference to giving his people characters so strikingly noticeable as in the case of *Hamlet*, and with no other of Shakespeare's works is the blind worship of Shakespeare so strikingly noticeable – that unreasoning hypnotism which does not even admit the thought that any production of his can be other than a work of genius, or that any leading character in a drama of his can fail to be the expression of a new and profoundly conceived character.

Shakespeare takes the ancient story – not at all bad of its kind – relating: *avec quelle ruse Amlet qui depuis fut Roy de Dannemarch, vengea la mort de son père Horvendille, occis par Fengon, son frère, et autre occurrence de son histoire*,* or a drama that was written on the same theme fifteen years before him; and he writes his play on this subject introducing inappropriately (as he constantly does) into the mouth of the chief character all such thoughts of his own as seem to him worthy of attention. Putting these thoughts into his hero's mouth – about life (the grave-diggers); about death ('To be or not to be'); those he had expressed in his sixty-sixth sonnet about the theatre and about women – he did not at all concern himself as to the circumstances under which these speeches were to be delivered, and it naturally results that the person uttering these various thoughts becomes a mere phonograph of Shakespeare, deprived of any character of his own; and his actions and words do not agree.

In the legend Hamlet's personality is quite intelligible: he is revolted by the conduct of his uncle and his mother, wishes to be revenged on them, but fears that his uncle may kill him as

* With what trick Hamlet who, since he was King of Denmark, avenged the death of his father Horvendille, slain by Fengon, his brother, and other circumstances of his history. [J. P.]

he had killed his father, and therefore pretends to be mad, wishing to wait and observe all that was going on at court. But his uncle and his mother, being afraid of him, wish to find out whether he is feigning or is really mad, and send a girl he loves to him. He keeps up his role and afterwards sees his mother alone, kills a courtier who was eavesdropping, and convicts his mother of her sin. Then he is sent to England. He intercepts letters, returns from England, and revenges himself on his enemies, burning them all.

This is all intelligible and flows from Hamlet's character and position. But Shakespeare, by putting into Hamlet's mouth speeches he wished to publish, and making him perform actions needed to secure effective scenes, destroys all that forms Hamlet's character in the legend. Throughout the whole tragedy Hamlet does not do what he might wish to do, but what is needed for the author's plans: now he is frightened by his father's ghost and now he begins to chaff it, calling it 'old mole'; now he loves Ophelia, now he teases her, and so on. There is no possibility of finding any explanation of Hamlet's actions and speeches, and therefore no possibility of attributing any character to him.

But as it is accepted that Shakespeare, the genius, could write nothing bad, learned men devote all the power of their minds to discovering extraordinary beauties in what is an obvious and glaring defect – particularly obvious in Hamlet – namely, that the chief person in the play has no character at all. And, lo and behold, profound critics announce that in this drama, in the person of Hamlet, a perfectly new and profound character is most powerfully presented: consisting in this, that the person has no character; and that in this absence of character lies an achievement of genius – the creation of a profound character! And having decided this, the learned critics write volumes upon volumes, until the laudations and explanations of the grandeur and importance of depicting the character of a man without a character fill whole libraries. It is true that some critics timidly express the thought that there is something strange about this person, and that Hamlet is an unsolved riddle; but no one ventures to say, as in Hans Andersen's story, that the king is naked; that it is clear as day that Shakespeare was unable, and did not even wish, to give Hamlet any character and did not even understand that this was necessary! And learned critics continue to study and praise this enigmatical production, which reminds one of the famous inscribed stone found by Pickwick at a cottage doorstep – which divided the scientific world into two hostile camps.

So that neither the character of Lear, nor of Othello, nor of Falstaff, and still less of Hamlet, at all confirms the existing opinion that Shakespeare's strength lies in the delineation of character.

If in Shakespeare's plays some figures are met with that have characteristic traits (mostly secondary figures such as Polonius in *Hamlet*, and Portia in *The Merchant of Venice*), these few life-like figures – among the five hundred or more secondary figures, and with the complete absence of character in the principal figures – are far from proving that the excellence of Shakespeare's dramas lies in the presentation of character.

That a great mastery in the presentation of character is attributed to Shakespeare arises from his really possessing a peculiarity which when helped out by the play of good actors may appear to superficial observers to be a capacity to manage scenes in which a movement of feeling is expressed. However arbitrary the positions in which he puts his characters, however unnatural to them the language he makes them speak, however lacking in individuality they may be, the movement of feeling itself, its increase and change and the combination of many contrary feelings, are often expressed correctly and powerfully in some of Shakespeare's scenes. And this when performed by good actors evokes, if but for a while, sympathy for the persons represented.

Shakespeare, himself an actor and a clever man, knew not only by speeches, but by exclamations, gestures and the repetition of words, how to express the state of mind and changes of feeling occurring in the persons represented. So that in many places Shakespeare's characters, instead of speaking, merely exclaim, or weep, or in the midst of a monologue indicate the pain of their position by gesture (as when Lear asks to have a button undone), or at a moment of strong excitement they repeat a question several times and cause a word to be repeated which strikes them, as is done by Othello, Macduff, Cleopatra and others. Similar clever methods of expressing a movement of feeling – giving good actors a chance to show their powers – have often been taken by many critics for the expression of character. But however strongly the play of feeling may be expressed in one scene, a single scene cannot give the character of a person when after the appropriate exclamations or gesture that person begins to talk lengthily not in a natural manner proper to him but according to the author's whim – saying things unnecessary and not in harmony with his character.

V

'Well, but the profound utterances and sayings delivered by Shakespeare's characters?' Shakespeare's eulogists will exclaim. 'Lear's monologue on punishment, Kent's on vengeance, Edgar's on his former life, Gloucester's reflections on the perversity of fate, and in other dramas the famous monologues of Hamlet, Antony and others?'

Thoughts and sayings may be appreciated, I reply, in prose works, in essays, in collections of aphorisms, but not in artistic dramatic works the aim of which is to elicit sympathy with what is represented. And therefore the monologues and sayings of Shakespeare even if they contained many very profound and fresh thoughts, which is not the case, cannot constitute the excellence of an artistic and poetic work. On the contrary, these speeches, uttered in unnatural conditions, can only spoil artistic works.

An artistic poetic work, especially a drama, should first of all evoke in reader or spectator the illusion that what the persons represented are living through and experiencing is being lived through and experienced by himself. And for this purpose it is not more important for the dramatist to know precisely what he should make his acting characters do and say, than it is to know what he should not make them do and say, so as not to infringe the reader's or spectator's illusion. However eloquent and profound they may be, speeches put into the mouths of acting characters, if they are superfluous and do not accord with the situation and the characters, infringe the main condition of dramatic work – the illusion causing the reader or spectator to experience the feelings of the persons represented. One may without infringing the illusion leave much unsaid: the reader or spectator will himself supply what is needed, and sometimes as a result of this his illusion is even increased; but to say what is superfluous is like jerking and scattering a statue made up of small pieces, or taking the lamp out of a magic lantern. The reader's or spectator's attention is distracted, the reader sees the author, the spectator sees the actor, the illusion is lost, and to recreate it is sometimes impossible. And therefore without a sense of proportion there cannot be an artist, especially a dramatist. And Shakespeare is entirely devoid of this feeling.

Shakespeare's characters continually do and say what is not merely unnatural to them but quite unnecessary. I will not cite examples of this, for I think that a man who does not himself perceive this striking defect in all Shakespeare's dramas will not be convinced by any possible examples or proofs. It is sufficient to read *King Lear* alone, with the madness, the murders, the plucking out of eyes, Gloucester's jump, the poisonings and the torrents of abuse – not to mention *Pericles*, *A Winter's Tale* or *The Tempest* – to convince oneself of this. Only a man quite devoid of the sense of proportion and taste could produce the types of *Titus Andronicus* and *Troilus and Cressida*, and so pitilessly distort the old drama of *King Leir*.

Gervinus tries to prove that Shakespeare possessed a feeling of beauty, *Schönheitssinn*, but all Gervinus's proofs only show that he himself, Gervinus, completely lacked it.* In Shakespeare everything is exaggerated: the actions are exaggerated, so are their consequences, the speeches of the characters are exaggerated, and therefore at every step the possibility of artistic impression is infringed.

* Georg Gottfried Gervinus (1805–71) was a German critic and historian whose major study of Shakespeare in four volumes was published posthumously. [J. P.]

Whatever people may say, however they may be enraptured by Shakespeare's works, whatever merits they may attribute to them, it is certain that he was not an artist and that his works are not artistic productions. Without a sense of proportion there never was or could be an artist, just as without a sense of rhythm there cannot be a musician. And Shakespeare may be anything you like – only not an artist.

'But one must not forget the times in which Shakespeare wrote,' say his laudators. 'It was a time of cruel and coarse manners, a time of the then fashionable euphuism, that is, an artificial manner of speech – a time of forms of life strange to us, and therefore to judge Shakespeare one must keep in view the times when he wrote. In Homer, as in Shakespeare, there is much that is strange to us, but this does not prevent our valuing the beauties of Homer,' say the laudators. But when one compares Shakespeare with Homer, as Gervinus does, the infinite distance separating true poetry from its imitation emerges with special vividness. However distant Homer is from us we can without the slightest effort transport ourselves into the life he describes. And we are thus transported chiefly because, however alien to us may be the events Homer describes, he believes in what he says and speaks seriously of what he is describing, and therefore he never exaggerates and the sense of measure never deserts him. And therefore it happens that, not to speak of the wonderfully distinct, lifelike and excellent characters of Achilles, Hector, Priam, Odysseus, and the eternally touching scenes of Hector's farewell, of Priam's embassy, of the return of Odysseus, and so forth, the whole of the *Iliad* and still more the *Odyssey*, is as naturally close to us all as if we had lived and were now living among the gods and heroes. But it is not so with Shakespeare. From his first words exaggeration is seen: exaggeration of events, exaggeration of feeling, and exaggeration of expression. It is at once evident that he does not believe in what he is saying, that he has no need to say it, that he is inventing the occurrences he describes, is indifferent to his characters and has devised them merely for the stage, and therefore makes them do and say what may strike his public; and so we do not believe either in the events or in the actions, or in the sufferings of his characters. Nothing so clearly shows the complete absence of aesthetic feeling in Shakespeare as a comparison between him and Homer. The works which we call the works of Homer are artistic, poetic, original works, lived through by their author or authors.

But Shakespeare's works are compositions devised for a particular purpose, and having absolutely nothing in common with art or poetry.

VI

But perhaps the loftiness of Shakespeare's conception of life is such that, even though he does not satisfy the demands of aesthetics, he discloses to us so new and important a view of life that in consideration of its value all his artistic defects become unnoticeable. This is indeed what some laudators of Shakespeare say. Gervinus plainly says that besides Shakespeare's significance in the sphere of dramatic poetry, in which in his opinion he is the equal of 'Homer in the sphere of the epic; Shakespeare, being the greatest judge of the human soul, is a teacher of most indisputable ethical authority, and the most select leader in the world and in life'.

In what then does this indubitable authority of the most select teacher in the world and in life consist? Gervinus devotes the concluding chapter of his second volume (some fifty pages) to an explanation of this.

The ethical authority of this supreme teacher of life, in the opinion of Gervinus, consists in this: 'Shakespeare's moral view starts from the simple point that man is born with powers of activity,' and therefore, first of all, says Gervinus, Shakespeare regarded it as 'an obligation to use our inherent power of action'. (As if it were possible for man not to act!)*

'*Die tatkräftigen Männer, Fortinbras, Bolingbroke, Alcibi-*

* This and the quotations in English that follow are taken from *Shakespeare's Commentaries*, by Dr G. G. Gervinus, translated by F. G. Bennett, London, 1877. [L. T.]

*ades, Octavius spielen hier die gegensätzlichen Rollen gegen die verschiedenen Tatlosen; nicht ihre Charaktere verdienen ihnen allen ihr Glück und Gedeihen etwa durch eine grosse Ueberlegenheit ihre Natur, sondern trotz ihrer geringern Anlage stellt sich ihre Tatkraft an sich über die Untätigkeit der Anderen hinaus, gleichviel aus wie schöner Quelle diese Passivität, aus wie schlechter jene Tätigkeit fliesse.'**

That is to say, Gervinus informs us, that active people like Fortinbras, Bolingbroke, Alcibiades and Octavius are contrasted by Shakespeare with various characters who do not display energetic activity. And, according to Shakespeare, happiness and success are attained by people who possess this active character, not at all as a result of their superiority of nature. On the contrary, in spite of their inferior talents their energy in itself always gives them the advantage over the inactive people, regardless of whether their inactivity results from excellent impulses, or the activity of the others from base ones. Activity is good, inactivity is evil. Activity transforms evil into good, says Shakespeare, according to Gervinus. 'Shakespeare prefers the principle of Alexander to that of Diogenes,' says Gervinus. In other words, according to him, Shakespeare prefers death and murder from ambition, to self-restraint and wisdom.†

According to Gervinus, Shakespeare considers that humanity should not set itself ideals, but that all that is necessary is healthy activity, and a golden mean in everything. Indeed Shakespeare is so imbued with this wise moderation that, in the words of Gervinus, he even allows himself to deny Christian morality which makes exaggerated demands on human nature. 'How thoroughly penetrated Shakespeare was with this principle of wise moderation,' says Gervinus, 'is shown perhaps most strongly in this, that he ventured even to oppose Christian laws which demand an overstraining of human nature; for he did not approve of the limits of duty being extended beyond

* *Shakespeare*, by G. G. Gervinus, Leipzig, 1872, vol. ii, pp. 550–51. [L. T.]
† Tolstoy's essay *Non-Acting* deals with a controversy that occurred in 1893 between Zola and Dumas. In it Tolstoy controverts the opinion that activity in itself, lacking moral guidance, is beneficial. [A. M.]

the intention of nature. He taught therefore the wise and human medium between the Christian and heathen precepts' – a reasonable mean, natural to man, between Christian and pagan injunctions – on the one hand love of one's enemies, and on the other hatred of them!

'That it is possible to do too much in good things is an express doctrine of Shakespeare, both in word and example . . . Thus excessive liberality ruins Timon, while moderate generosity keeps Antonio in honour; the genuine ambition which makes Henry V great overthrows Percy, in whom it rises too high. Exaggerated virtue brings Angelo to ruin; and when in those near him the excess of punishment proves harmful and cannot hinder sin, then mercy, the most Godlike gift that man possesses, is also exhibited in its excess as the producer of sin.'

Shakespeare, says Gervinus, taught that one *may do too much good*. 'He teaches,' says Gervinus, 'that morality, like politics, is a matter so complicated with relations, conditions of life, and motives, that it is impossible to bring it to final principles.

'In Shakespeare's opinion (and here also he is one with Bacon and Aristotle) there is no positive law of religion or morals which could form a rule of moral action in precepts ever binding and suitable for all cases.'

Gervinus most clearly expresses Shakespeare's whole moral theory by saying that Shakespeare does not write for those classes for whom definite religious principles and laws are suitable (that is to say, for nine hundred and ninety-nine people out of every thousand), but for the cultivated, who have made their own a healthy rule of life and such an instinctive feeling as, united with conscience, reason and will, can direct them to worthy aims of life. But even for these fortunate ones, this teaching may be dangerous if it is taken incompletely. It must be taken whole. 'There are classes,' says Gervinus, 'whose morality is best provided for by the positive letter of religion and law; but for such as these Shakespeare's writings are in themselves inaccessible; they are only readable and comprehensible to the cultivated, of whom it can be required that they should appropriate to themselves the healthy measure of life, and that self-reliance in which the guiding and inherent powers of conscience and reason, united with the will, are, when consciously apprehended, worthy aims of life . . . But even for the cultivated also, Shakespeare's doctrine may not always be without danger . . . The condition on which his doctrine is entirely harmless is this, that it should be fully and completely received and without any expurging and separating. Then it is not only without danger, but it is also more unmistakable and more infallible, and therefore more worthy of our confidence, than any system of morality can be.'

And in order to accept it all, one should understand that according to his teaching it is insane and harmful for an individual to rise against or 'disregard the bonds of religion and the state'. For Shakespeare would abhor a free and independent personality who, strong in spirit, should oppose any law in politics or morals and should disregard the union of the state and religion, 'which has kept society together for centuries'. 'For in his opinion the practical wisdom of man should have no higher aim than to carry into society the utmost possible nature and freedom, but for that very reason, and that he might maintain sacred and inviolable the natural laws of society, he would respect existing forms, yet at the same time penetrate into their rational substance with sound criticism, not forgetting nature in civilization, nor, equally, civilization in nature.' Property, the family, the state, are sacred. But the aspiration to recognize the equality of man is insane. 'Its realization would bring the greatest harm to humanity.'

'No man has fought more strongly against rank and class prejudices than Shakespeare, but how could his liberal principles have been pleased with the doctrines of those who would have done away with the prejudices of the rich and cultivated only to replace them by the interests and prejudices of the poor and uncultivated? How would this man, who draws us so eloquently to the course of honour, have approved, if in annulling rank, degrees of merit, distinction, we extinguish every impulse to greatness, and by the removal of all degrees, "shake the ladder to all high designs"? If indeed no surreptitious honour and false power were longer to oppress mankind, how would the poet have acknowledged the most fearful force of all, the power of barbarity? In consequence of these modern doctrines of equality he would have apprehended that everything would resolve itself into power; or if this were not the final lot which awaited mankind from these aspirations after equality, if love between nationalities, and endless peace, were not that "nothing" of impossibility, as Alonso expresses it in the *Tempest*, but could be an actual fruit of these efforts after equality, then the poet would have believed that with this time the old age and decrepitude of the world had arrived, in which it were worthless for the active to live.'

Such is Shakespeare's view of life as explained by his greatest exponent and admirer. Another of the recent laudators of Shakespeare, Brandes, adds the following:

'No one, of course, can preserve his life quite pure from injustice, from deception, and from doing harm to others, but injustice and deception are not always vices and even the harm done to other people is not always a vice: it is often only a necessity, a legitimate weapon, a right. At bottom, Shakespeare had always held that there were no such things as unconditional duties and absolute prohibitions. He had never, for example, questioned Hamlet's right to kill the King, scarcely even his right to run his sword through Polonius. Nevertheless he had hitherto been unable to conquer a feeling of indignation and disgust when he saw around him nothing but breaches of the simplest moral laws. Now, on the other hand, the dim divinations of his earlier years crystallized in his mind into a coherent body of thought: no commandment is unconditional; it is not in the observance or non-observance of an external fiat that the merits of an action, to say nothing of a character, consists: everything depends upon the volitional substance into which the individual, as a responsible agent, transmits the formal imperative at the moment of decision.'*

In other words Shakespeare now sees clearly that the morality of the aim is the only true, the only possible one; so that,

* *William Shakespeare*, by Georges Brandes, translated by William Archer and Miss Morison, London, 1898, p. 921. [L. T.]

according to Brandes, Shakespeare's fundamental principle, for which he is extolled, is that *the end justifies the means*. Action at all costs, the absence of all ideals, moderation in everything, the maintenance of established forms of life, and the maxim that the end justifies the means.

If one adds to this a chauvinistic English patriotism, expressed in all his historical plays: a patriotism according to which the English throne is something sacred, the English always defeat the French, slaughtering thousands and losing only scores, Jeanne d'Arc is a witch, Hector and all the Trojans – from whom the English are descended – are heroes, while the Greeks are cowards and traitors, and so forth: this is the view of life of the wisest teacher of life according to his greatest admirer. And anyone who reads attentively the works of Shakespeare cannot but acknowledge that the attribution of this view of life to Shakespeare by those who praise him is perfectly correct.

The value of every poetical work depends on three qualities:

1. The content of the work: the more important the content, that is to say the more important it is for the life of man, the greater is the work.

2. The external beauty achieved by the technical methods proper to the particular kind of art. Thus in dramatic art the technical method will be: that the characters should have a true individuality of their own, a natural and at the same time a touching plot, a correct presentation on the stage of the manifestation and development of feelings, and a sense of proportion in all that is presented.

3. Sincerity, that is to say that the author should himself vividly feel what he expresses. Without this condition there can be no work of art, as the essence of art consists in the infection of the contemplator of a work by the author's feeling. If the author has not felt what he is expressing, the recipient cannot become infected by the author's feeling, he does not experience any feeling, and the production cannot be classed as a work of art.

The content of Shakespeare's plays, as is seen by the explanations of his greatest admirers, is the lowest, most vulgar view of life which regards the external elevation of the great ones of the earth as a genuine superiority; despises the crowd, that is to say, the working classes; and repudiates not only religious, but even any humanitarian, efforts directed towards the alteration of the existing order of society.

The second condition is also absent in Shakespeare except in his handling of scenes in which a movement of feelings is expressed. There is in his works a lack of naturalness in the situations, the characters lack individuality of speech, and a sense of proportion is also wanting, without which such works cannot be artistic.

The third and chief condition – sincerity – is totally absent in all Shakespeare's works. One sees in all of them an intentional artificiality; it is obvious that he is not in earnest but is playing with words.

VII

The works of Shakespeare do not meet the demands of every art, and, besides that, their tendency is very low and immoral. What then is the meaning of the immense fame these works have enjoyed for more than a hundred years?

To reply to this question seems the more difficult, because if the works of Shakespeare had any kind of excellence the achievement which has produced the exaggerated praise lavished upon them would be at least to some extent intelligible. But here two extremes meet: works which are beneath criticism, insignificant, empty and immoral – meet insensate, universal laudation, that proclaims these works to be above everything that has ever been produced by man.

How is this to be explained?

Many times during my life I have had occasion to discuss Shakespeare with his admirers, not only with people little sensitive to poetry but also with those who felt poetic beauty keenly, such as Turgenev, Fet,* and others, and each time I have

* A Russian poet of much delicacy of feeling, for many years a great friend of Tolstoy. [A. M.]

encountered one and the same attitude towards my disagreement with the laudation of Shakespeare.

I was not answered when I pointed out Shakespeare's defects; they only pitied me for my want of comprehension and urged on me the necessity of acknowledging the extraordinary supernatural grandeur of Shakespeare. They did not explain to me in what the beauties of Shakespeare consist, but were merely indefinitely and exaggeratedly enthusiastic about the whole of Shakespeare, extolling some favourite passages: the undoing of Lear's button, Falstaff's lying, Lady Macbeth's spot which would not wash out, Hamlet's address to the ghost of his father, the 'forty thousand brothers', 'none does offend, none, I say none', and so forth.

'Open Shakespeare,' I used to say to these admirers of his, 'where you will or as may chance, and you will see that you will never find ten consecutive lines that are comprehensible, natural, characteristic of the person who utters them, and productive of an artistic impression.' (Anyone may make this experiment.) And the laudators of Shakespeare opened pages in Shakespeare's dramas by chance, or at their own choice, and without paying any attention to the reasons I adduced as to why the ten lines selected did not meet the most elementary demands of aesthetics or good sense, praised the very things that appeared to me absurd, unintelligible and inartistic.

So that in general, in response to my endeavours to obtain from the worshippers of Shakespeare an explanation of his greatness, I encountered precisely the attitude I have usually met with, and still meet with, from the defenders of any dogmas accepted not on the basis of reason but on mere credulity. And it was just this attitude of the laudators of Shakespeare – an attitude which may be met with in all the indefinite, misty articles about him, and in conversations – that gave me the key to an understanding of the cause of Shakespeare's fame. There is only one explanation of this astonishing phenomenon: it is one of those epidemic suggestions to which people always have been, and are, liable. Such irrational suggestion has always existed, and still exists in all spheres of life. The medieval Crusades, which influenced not only adults but children, are glaring examples of such suggestion, considerable in scope and deceptiveness, and there have been many other epidemic suggestions astonishing in their senselessness, such as the belief in witches, in the utility of torture for the discovery of truth, the search for the elixir of life, for the philosopher's stone, and the passion for tulips valued at several thousand guilders a bulb, which overran Holland. There always have been and always are such irrational suggestions in all spheres of human life – religious, philosophic, economic, scientific, artistic, and in literature generally, and people only see clearly the insanity of such suggestions after they are freed from them. But as long as they are under their influence these suggestions appear to them such indubitable truths that they do not consider it necessary or possible to reason about them. Since the development of the printing-press these epidemics have become particularly striking.

Since the development of the press it has come about that as soon as something obtains a special significance from accidental circumstances, the organs of the press immediately announce this significance. And as soon as the press has put forward the importance of the matter, the public directs yet more attention to it. The hypnotization of the public incites the press to regard the thing more attentively and in greater detail. The interest of the public is still further increased, and the organs of the press, competing one with another, respond to the public demand.

The public becomes yet more interested, and the press attributes yet more importance to the matter; so that this importance, growing ever greater and greater like a snowball, obtains a quite unnatural appreciation, and this appreciation, exaggerated even to absurdity, maintains itself as long as the outlook on life of the leaders of the press and of the public remains the same. There are in our day innumerable examples of such a misunderstanding of the importance of the most insignificant occurrences, occasioned by the mutual reaction of press and public. A striking example of this was the excitement which seized the whole world over the Dreyfus affair. A suspicion arose that some captain on the French staff had been guilty of treason. Whether because this captain was a Jew, or from some special internal party disagreements in French society, this event, which resembled others that continually occur without arousing anyone's attention and without interesting the whole world or even the French military, was given a somewhat prominent position by the press. The public paid attention to it. The organs of the press, vying with one another, began to describe, to analyse, to discuss the event, the public became yet more interested, the press responded to the demands of the public and the snowball began to grow and grow, and grew before our eyes to such an extent that there was not a family which had not its disputes about *l'affaire*. So that Caran d'Ache's caricature, which depicted first a peaceful family that had decided not to discuss the Dreyfus affair any more, and then the same family represented as angry furies fighting one another, quite correctly depicted the relation of the whole reading world to the Dreyfus question. Men of other nationalities who could not have any real interest in the question whether a French officer had or had not been a traitor – men moreover who could not know how the affair was going – all divided for or against Dreyfus, some asserting his guilt with assurance, others denying it with equal certainty.

It was only after some years that people began to awaken from the 'suggestion' and to understand that they could not possibly know whether he was guilty or innocent, and that each one of them had a thousand matters nearer and more interesting to him than the Dreyfus affair. Such infatuations occur in all spheres, but they are specially noticeable in the sphere of literature, for the press naturally occupies itself most of all with the affairs of the press, and these are particularly powerful in our day when the press has obtained such an unnatural development. It continually happens that people suddenly begin to devote exaggerated praise to some very insignificant works, and then, if these works do not correspond to the prevailing view of life, suddenly become perfectly indifferent to them and forget both the works themselves and their own previous attitude towards them.

So within my recollection, in the 1840s, there occurred in the artistic sphere the exaltation and laudation of Eugène Sue and

George Sand; in the social sphere, of Fourier; in the philosophic sphere, of Comte and Hegel; and in the scientific sphere, of Darwin.

Sue is quite forgotten, George Sand is being forgotten and replaced by the writings of Zola and the Decadents – Baudelaire, Verlaine, Maeterlinck and others. Fourier, with his phalansteries, is quite forgotten, and has been replaced by Karl Marx. Hegel, who justified the existing order, and Comte, who denied the necessity of religious activity in humanity, and Darwin, with his law of struggle for existence, still maintain their places, but are beginning to be neglected and replaced by the teachings of Nietzsche, which though perfectly absurd, unthought-out, obscure, and bad in their content, correspond better to the present-day outlook on life. Thus it sometimes happens that artistic, philosophic and literary crazes in general, arise, fall rapidly, and are forgotten.

But it also happens that such crazes, having arisen in consequence of special causes accidentally favouring their establishment, correspond so well to the view of life diffused in society and especially in literary circles, that they maintain their place for a very long time. Even in Roman times it was remarked that books have their fate, and often a very strange one: failure in spite of high qualities, and enormous undeserved success in spite of insignificance. And a proverb was made: *Pro captu lectoris habent sua fata libelli*, that is, that the fate of books depends on the understanding of those who read them. Such was the correspondence of Shakespeare's work to the view of life of the people among whom his fame arose. And this fame has been maintained, and is still maintained, because the works of Shakespeare continue to correspond to the view of life of those who maintain this fame.

Until the end of the eighteenth century Shakespeare not only had no particular fame in England, but was less esteemed than his contemporaries: Ben Jonson, Fletcher, Beaumont and others. His fame began in Germany, and from there passed to England. This happened for the following reason:

Art, especially dramatic art which demands for its realization extensive preparations, expenditure and labour, was always religious, that is to say, its object was to evoke in man a clearer conception of that relation of man to God attained at the time by the advanced members of the society in which the art was produced.

So it should be by the nature of the case, and so it always had been among all nations: among the Egyptians, Hindus, Chinese and Greeks – from the earliest time that we have knowledge of the life of man. And it has always happened that with the coarsening of religious forms art diverged more and more from this original aim (which had caused it to be recognized as an important matter – almost an act of worship), and instead of religious aims it adopted worldly aims for the satisfaction of the demands of the crowd, or of the great ones of the earth, that is to say, aims of recreation and amusement.

This deflection of art from its true and high vocation occurred everywhere, and it occurred in Christendom.

The first manifestation of Christian art was in the worship of God in the temples: the performance of Mass and, in general, of the liturgy. When in course of time the forms of this art of divine worship became insufficient, the Mysteries were produced, depicting those events regarded as most important in the Christian religious view of life. Afterwards, when in the thirteenth and fourteenth centuries the centre of gravity of Christian teaching was more and more transferred from the worship of Jesus as God, to the explanation of his teaching and its fulfilment, the form of the Mysteries, which depicted external Christian events, became insufficient and new forms were demanded; and as an expression of this tendency appeared the Moralities, dramatic representations in which the characters personified the Christian virtues and the opposite vices.

But allegories by their very nature, as art of a lower order, could not replace the former religious drama, and no new form of dramatic art corresponding to the conception of Christianity as a teaching of life had yet been found. And dramatic art, lacking a religious basis, began in all Christian countries more and more to deviate from its purpose, and instead of a service of God became a service of the crowd (I mean by 'crowd' not merely the common people, but the majority of immoral or non-moral people indifferent to the higher problems of human life). This deviation was helped on by the fact that just at that time the Greek thinkers, poets and dramatists, with whom the Christian world had not hitherto been acquainted, were rediscovered and favourably accepted. And therefore, not having yet had time to work out for themselves a clear and satisfactory form of dramatic art suitable to the new conception entertained of Christianity as a teaching of life, and at the same time recognizing the previous Mysteries and Moralities as insufficient, the writers of the fifteenth and sixteenth centuries, in their search for a new form, began to imitate the newly discovered Greek models, which were attractive by their elegance and novelty. And as it was chiefly the great ones of the earth who could avail themselves of the drama – the kings, princes and courtiers – the least religious people, not merely quite indifferent to questions of religion but for the most part thoroughly depraved – it followed that to satisfy the demands of its public the drama of the fifteenth, sixteenth and seventeenth centuries was chiefly a spectacle intended for depraved kings and the upper classes. Such was the drama of Spain, England, Italy and France.

The plays of that time, chiefly composed in all these countries according to ancient Greek models, from poems, legends and biographies, naturally reflected the national characters. In Italy comedies with amusing scenes and characters were chiefly elaborated. In Spain the worldly drama flourished, with complicated plots and ancient historical heroes. The peculiarity of English drama was the coarse effect produced by murders, executions and battles on the stage, and popular comic interludes. Neither the Italian, nor the Spanish, nor the English drama had European fame, and each of them enjoyed success only in its own country. General fame, thanks to the elegance of its language and the talent of its writers, was enjoyed only by the French drama, which was distinguished by strict adherence to the Greek models, and especially to the law of the three Unities.

So matters continued till the end of the eighteenth century, but at the end of that century this is what happened: in

Germany, which lacked even mediocre dramatists (though there had been a weak and little known writer, Hans Sachs), all educated people, including Frederick the Great, bowed down before the French pseudo-classical drama. And yet at that very time there appeared in Germany a circle of educated and talented writers and poets who, feeling the falsity and coldness of the French drama, sought a newer and freer dramatic form. The members of this group, like all the upper classes of the Christian world at that time, were under the charm and influence of the Greek classics and, being utterly indifferent to religious questions, thought that if the Greek drama depicting the calamities, sufferings and struggles of its heroes supplied the best model for the drama, then such representation of the sufferings and struggles of heroes would also be a sufficient subject for drama in the Christian world, if only one rejected the narrow demands of pseudo-classicism. These men, not understanding that the sufferings and strife of their heroes had a religious significance for the Greeks, imagined that it was only necessary to reject the inconvenient law of the three Unities, and the representation of various incidents in the lives of historic personages, and of strong human passions in general, would afford a sufficient basis for the drama without its containing any religious element corresponding to the beliefs of their own time. Just such a drama existed at that time among the kindred English people, and the Germans, becoming acquainted with it, decided that just such should be the drama of the new period.

The masterly development of the scenes which constitutes Shakespeare's speciality caused them to select Shakespeare's dramas from among all other English plays, which were not in the least inferior, but often superior, to Shakespeare's.

At the head of the circle stood Goethe, who was then the dictator of public opinion on aesthetic questions. And he it was who – partly from a wish to destroy the fascination of the false French art, partly from a wish to give freer scope to his own dramatic activity, but chiefly because his view of life agreed with Shakespeare's – acclaimed Shakespeare a great poet. When that falsehood had been proclaimed on Goethe's authority, all those aesthetic critics who did not understand art threw themselves upon it like crows upon carrion, and began to search Shakespeare for non-existent beauties and to extol them. These men, German aesthetic critics – for the most part utterly devoid of aesthetic feeling, ignorant of that simple direct artistic impression which for men with a feeling for art clearly distinguishes artistic impression from all other, but believing the authority that had proclaimed Shakespeare as a great poet – began to belaud the whole of Shakespeare indiscriminately, selecting passages especially which struck them by their effects or expressed thoughts corresponding to their own view of life, imagining that such effects and such thoughts constitute the essence of what is called art.

These men acted as blind men would if they tried by touch to select diamonds out of a heap of stones they fingered. As the blind man, long sorting out the many little stones, could finally come to no other conclusion than that all the stones were precious and the smoothest were especially precious, so the aesthetic critics, deprived of artistic feeling, could come to no other result about Shakespeare. To make their praise of the whole of Shakespeare more convincing they composed an aesthetic theory, according to which a definite religious view of life is not at all necessary for the creation of works of art in general or for the drama in particular; that for the inner content of a play it is quite enough to depict passions and human characters; that not only is no religious illumination of the matter presented required, but that art ought to be objective, that is to say, it should depict occurrences quite independently of any valuation of what is good or bad. And as this theory was educed from Shakespeare, it naturally happened that the works of Shakespeare corresponded to this theory and were therefore the height of perfection.

And these were the people chiefly responsible for Shakespeare's fame.

Chiefly in consequence of their writings, that interaction of writers and the public came about which found expression, and still finds expression, in the insensate laudation of Shakespeare without any rational basis. These aesthetic critics wrote profound treatises about Shakespeare (11,000 volumes have been written about him, and a whole science of Shakespearology has been formulated); the public became more and more interested, and the learned critics explained more and more, that is to say, they added to the confusion and laudation.

So that the first cause of Shakespeare's fame was that the Germans wanted something freer and more alive to oppose to the French drama of which they were tired, and which was really dull and cold. The second cause was that the young German writers required a model for their own dramas. The third and chief cause was the activity of the learned and zealous aesthetic German critics who lacked aesthetic feeling and formulated the theory of objective art, that is to say, deliberately repudiated the religious essence of the drama.

'But,' I shall be asked, 'what do you mean by the words "religious essence of the drama"? Is not what you demand for the drama religious instruction, didactics: what is called a tendency – which is incompatible with true art?' By 'the religious essence of art,' I reply, I mean not an external inculcation of any religious truth in artistic guise, and not an allegorical representation of those truths, but the expression of a definite view of life corresponding to the highest religious understanding of a given period: an outlook which, serving as the impelling motive for the composition of the drama, permeates the whole work though the author be unconscious of it. So it has always been with true art, and so it is with every true artist in general and with dramatists especially. Hence, as happened when the drama was a serious thing, and as should be according to the essence of the matter, he alone can write a drama who has something to say to men – something highly important for them – about man's relation to God, to the universe, to all that is infinite and unending.

But when, thanks to the German theories about objective art, an idea had been established that, for drama, this is not wanted at all, then a writer like Shakespeare – who in his own soul had not formed religious convictions corresponding to his period, and who had even no convictions at all, but piled up in his plays all possible events, horrors, fooleries, discussions and effects – could evidently be accepted as the greatest of dramatic geniuses.

But all these are external reasons: the fundamental inner cause of Shakespeare's fame was, and is, that his plays fitted *pro captu lectoris*, that is to say, responded to the irreligious and immoral attitude of the upper classes of our world.

VIII

A series of accidents brought it about that Goethe at the beginning of the last century, being the dictator of philosophic thought and aesthetic laws, praised Shakespeare; the aesthetic critics caught up that praise and began to write their long foggy erudite articles, and the great European public began to be enchanted by Shakespeare. The critics, responding to this public interest, laboriously vied with one another in writing more and more articles about Shakespeare, and readers and spectators were still further confirmed in their enthusiasm, and Shakespeare's fame kept growing and growing like a snowball, until in our time it has attained a degree of insane laudation that obviously rests on no other basis than suggestion.

'There is no one even approximately equal to Shakespeare either among ancient or modern writers.' 'Poetic truth is the most brilliant gem in the crown of Shakespeare's service.' 'Shakespeare is the greatest moralist of all times.' 'Shakespeare displays such diversity and such objectivity as place him beyond the limits of time and nationality.' 'Shakespeare is the greatest genius that has hitherto existed.' 'For the creation of tragedies, comedies, historical plays, idylls, idyllic comedies, aesthetic idylls, for representation itself, as also for incidental verses, he is the only man. He not only wields unlimited power over our laughter and our tears, over all phases of passion, humour, thought and observation, but he commands an unlimited realm of imagination, full of fancy of a terrifying and amazing character, and he possesses penetration in the world of invention and of reality, and over all this there reigns one and the same truthfulness to character and to nature, and the same spirit of humanity.'

'To Shakespeare the epithet of great applies naturally; and if one adds that independently of his greatness he has also become the reformer of all literature, and moreover has expressed in his works not only the phenomena of the life of his time, but also from thoughts and views that in his day existed only in germ has prophetically foreseen the direction which the social spirit would take in the future (of which we see an amazing example in Hamlet) – one may say without hesitation that Shakespeare was not only a great, but the greatest of all poets that ever existed, and that in the sphere of poetic creation the only rival that equals him is life itself, which in his productions he depicted with such perfection.'

The obvious exaggeration of this appraisement is a most convincing proof that it is not the outcome of sane thought, but of suggestion. The more insignificant, the lower, the emptier, a phenomenon is, once it becomes the object of suggestion, the more supernatural and exaggerated is the importance attributed to it. The Pope is not only holy, but most holy, and so forth. So Shakespeare is not only a good writer, but the greatest genius, the eternal teacher of mankind.

Suggestion is always a deceit, and every deceit is an evil. And really the suggestion that Shakespeare's works are great works of genius, presenting the climax both of aesthetic and ethical perfection, has caused and is causing great injury to men.

This injury is twofold: first, the fall of the drama and the substitution of an empty immoral amusement for that important organ of progress, and secondly, the direct degradation of men by presenting them with false models for imitation.

The life of humanity only approaches perfection by the elucidation of religious consciousness (the only principle securely uniting men one with another). The elucidation of the religious consciousness of man is accomplished through all sides of man's spiritual activity. One side of that activity is art. One part of art, and almost the most important, is the drama.

And therefore the drama, to deserve the importance attributed to it, should serve the elucidation of religious consciousness. Such the drama always was, and such it was in the Christian world. But with the appearance of Protestantism in its broadest sense – that is to say, the appearance of a new understanding of Christianity as a teaching for life – dramatic art did not find a form corresponding to this new understanding of religion, and the men of the Renaissance period were carried away by the imitation of classical art. This was most natural, but the attraction should have passed and art should have found, as it is now beginning to find, a new form corresponding to the altered understanding of Christianity.

But the finding of this new form was hindered by the teaching, which arose among German writers at the end of the eighteenth and beginning of the nineteenth centuries, of the so-called objectivity of art – that is to say, the indifference of art to good or evil – together with an exaggerated praise of Shakespeare's dramas, which partly corresponded to the aesthetic theory of the Germans and partly served as material for it. Had there not been this exaggerated praise of Shakespeare's dramas, accepted as the most perfect models of drama, people of the eighteenth and nineteenth centuries, and of our own, would have had to understand that the drama, to have a right to exist and be regarded as a serious matter, ought to serve, as always was and cannot but be the case, the elucidation of religious consciousness. And having understood this they would have sought a new form of drama corresponding to their religious perception.

But when it was decided that Shakespeare's drama is the summit of perfection, and that people ought to write as he did without any religious or even any moral content – all the dramatists, imitating him, began to compose plays lacking content, like the plays of Goethe, Schiller, Hugo and, among us Russians, Pushkin and the historical plays of Ostrovski, Alexey Tolstoy, and the innumerable other more or less well-known dramatic works which fill all the theatres and are continually composed by anyone to whom the thought and desire to write plays occurs.

Only thanks to such a mean, petty, understanding of the importance of the drama does there appear among us that endless series of dramatic works presenting the actions, situations, characters and moods of people, not only devoid of any spiritual content but even lacking any human sense. And let not the reader suppose that I exclude from this estimate of contemporary drama the pieces I myself have incidentally written for the theatre. I recognize them, just like all the rest, to be lacking in that religious content which should form the basis of the future drama.

So that the drama, the most important sphere of art, has become in our time merely an empty and immoral amusement for the empty and immoral crowd. What is worst of all is that to the art of the drama, which has fallen as low as it is possible to fall, people continue to attribute an elevated significance unnatural to it.

Dramatists, actors, theatrical managers, the press – the latter most seriously publishing reports of theatres, operas, and so forth – all feel assured that they are doing something very useful and important.

The drama in our time is like a great man fallen to the lowest stage of degradation, who yet continues to pride himself on his past, of which nothing now remains. And the public of our time is like those who pitilessly get amusement out of this once great man, now descended to the lowest depths.

Such is one harmful effect of the epidemic suggestion of the greatness of Shakespeare. Another harmful effect of that laudation is the setting up of a false model for men's imitation.

If people now wrote of Shakespeare that, for his time, he was a great writer, managed verse well enough, was a clever actor and a good stage-manager, even if their valuation were inexact and somewhat exaggerated, provided it was moderate, people of the younger generations might remain free from the Shakespearian influence. But no young man can now remain free from this harmful influence, for instead of the religious and moral teachers of mankind being held up to him as models of moral perfection, as soon as he enters on life he is confronted first of all by Shakespeare, who learned men have decided (and transmitted from generation to generation as an irrefragable truth) is the greatest of poets and the greatest of life's teachers.

On reading or hearing Shakespeare the question for a young man is no longer whether Shakespeare is good or bad, but only to discover wherein lies that extraordinary aesthetic and ethical beauty of which he has received the suggestion from learned men whom he respects, but which he neither sees nor feels. And perverting his aesthetic and ethical feeling, he tries to force himself to agree with the prevailing opinion. He no longer trusts himself, but trusts to what learned people whom he respects have said (I myself have experienced all this). Reading the critical analyses of the plays and the extracts from books with explanatory commentaries, it begins to seem to him that he feels something like an artistic impression, and the longer this continues the more is his aesthetic and ethical feeling perverted. He already ceases to discriminate independently and clearly between what is truly artistic, and the artificial imitation of art.

But above all, having assimilated that immoral view of life which permeates all Shakespeare's works, he loses the capacity to distinguish between good and evil. And the error of extolling an insignificant, inartistic and not only non-moral but plainly immoral writer, accomplishes its pernicious work.

That is why I think that the sooner people emancipate themselves from this false worship of Shakespeare the better it will be: first because people when they are freed from this falsehood will come to understand that a drama which has no religious basis is not only not an important or good thing, as is now supposed, but is most trivial and contemptible; and having understood this they will have to search for and work out a new form of modern drama – a drama which will serve for the elucidation and confirmation in man of the highest degree of religious consciousness; and secondly because people, when themselves set free from this hypnotic state, will understand that the insignificant and immoral works of Shakespeare and his imitators, aiming only at distracting and amusing the spectators, cannot possibly serve to teach the meaning of life, but that, as long as there is no real religious drama, guidance for life must be looked for from other sources.

[Translated by Aylmer Maude.]

FROM *THE LAW OF LOVE AND THE LAW OF VIOLENCE* [1908]

CHAPTER 18

The Creator himself pre-ordained that the criterion of all human behaviour was not profit but justice, and on the strength of this all efforts to define levels of profit are always useless. Not one person has ever known, or can know, what the final results of a certain action, or series of actions, will be, either for himself or for others. But each one of us can know which action is just and which is not. And likewise, we can all know that the consequences of justice will, at the end of the day, be as good for ourselves as for others, although it is beyond our power to say beforehand what this good will be and of what it will consist. – John Ruskin

And ye shall know the truth, and the truth shall make you free. – John 8: 32

Man thinks therefore he is. It is clear that he must think rationally. A rationally thinking person thinks first of all about the purpose for which he must live; he thinks about his soul and about God. Just look at what worldly people think about; of anything you like except that. They think about dancing, about music and singing and similar entertainments; they think about buildings, about wealth, about power; they envy kings and the rich. But they never think about what it means to be a man. – Pascal

All you suffering men of the Christian world, both rulers and rich and poor and oppressed, need only free yourselves from the deception of false Christianity and government (concealing what Christ revealed to you and what is demanded by your reason and your heart) and it will become clear to you that it is in yourselves and only in yourselves that you will find the cause of all the bodily suffering (want), and spiritual suffering (awareness of injustice, envy and annoyance) that torments you – the oppressed and poor. And that it is also in yourselves, the rich and powerful, that you will find the cause of those fears, pangs of conscience and awareness of the sinfulness of your lives, all of which disturbs you, in varying degrees according to your moral sensitivity.

Understand, all of you, that you were born neither to be slaves, nor to be masters; that you are free men, but that you only become free and rational when you fulfil the supreme law of life. This law has been revealed to you, and you need only discard those lies which conceal it from you to be able to see clearly of what this law consists and in what your happiness consists. This law consists in love, and well-being is only found in the fulfilment of this law. Realize it and you will become truly free and acquire everything that you now vainly seek through those complicated means to which you are attracted by confused and corrupted men, who believe in nothing.

'Come unto me, all ye that labour and are heavy laden, and I will give you rest. Take my yoke upon you, and learn of me; for I am meek and lowly in heart: and ye shall find rest unto your souls. For my yoke is easy, and my burden is light' (Matthew 11: 28–30). You will be saved and delivered from the evil you endure and receive the true well-being you so clumsily strive after, not through personal desire, nor envy, nor through adherence to a party programme; nor through hatred, indignation or the pursuit of fame, nor even through a sense of justice, and above all not through troubling yourselves about the organization of other people's lives. However strange it may seem, it is only through an activity within your own soul, involving no external aim and no consideration of what might come of it.

Understand that the assumption that a man may organize

the lives of others is a crude superstition that people have only accepted because of its antiquity. And understand that those who are preoccupied with organizing the lives of others, be they monarchs, presidents and ministers, or spies and executioners, or members and leaders of a party, or dictators, understand that these people manifest nothing worthy – as people seem to think – but, to the contrary, are pitiable, deeply misled people, preoccupied with a task that is not only vain and stupid, but is one of the most horrible things man can choose to do.

People are already recognizing the pitiful degradation of a spy, or executioner, and are starting to feel the same about the police force, police agents, and even to some extent about the army; but they have not yet begun to feel this about judges, senators, ministers, political leaders and revolutionaries. And yet the work of the senator, the minister, the monarch and the leaders of political parties is just as base, vile and alien to human nature and, perhaps, even worse than the task of the executioner or spy, since it is just the same, but covered in hypocrisy.

Understand then, all of you, especially you young ones, that to dedicate your lives, or even to occupy yourselves with the forcible construction of other people's lives, according to your own ideas, is not just a primitive superstition, but a vile, criminal affair, destructive to the soul. Realize that the desire of an enlightened soul for the welfare of others is in no way satisfied by vainly organizing their lives through violence, but that it is only achieved through one's own inner work – the only thing where man has complete freedom and control. Only this task, increasing the love within oneself, can enhance the satisfaction of this desire. You must understand that no activity aimed at the organization of other people's lives through coercion can enhance people's welfare, but is always a more or less consciously hypocritical deceit used to cover up men's basest desires: vanity, pride and self-interest, under the guise of personal dedication to mankind.

Understand this, especially you young ones, the generation of the future, and cease, as the majority of us are doing at the moment, to search for illusory happiness in creating people's welfare by participating in the administration of the State, or judiciary, or by instructing others and, in order to do so, by entering institutions (namely schools and universities) where you are involved in vanity, self-importance and pride, and thus perverted. Cease participating in the various organizations whose aim is supposedly to further the welfare of the masses, and seek only that one thing that is always necessary and within the reach of us all, and which gives the greatest well-being to ourselves, and is the most likely thing to enhance the welfare of our neighbours. Seek this one thing within yourselves: an increase of love through eradicating all the mistakes, sins and passions which hinder its manifestation and you will further the well-being of the people in the most effective way. Understand that for the people of today the fulfilment of the supreme law of love now known to us (which excludes violence) is as unavoidable as is the law of migration and nest-building for birds, and the law of feeding on grass for herbivorous animals, and on meat for carnivorous ones; and that every transgression of this law is detrimental to us.

Just understand this and dedicate your life to this joyous work; only begin to do this and you will instantly realize that it is this, and only this, which can lead to that improvement of life for all, for which you strive so vainly and along such mistaken paths. Realize that man's welfare lies only in unity and that unity cannot be attained through violent means. Unity will only be achieved when, without thinking about unity, each person thinks only of fulfilling the law of life. And it is only the SUPREME law of life, one and the same for us all, that unites people.

The supreme law of life revealed by Christ is now clear to man and unity will only be achieved through following it, until there appears a new law that is even closer and dearer to the hearts of man.

CHAPTER 19

Some people seek well-being, or happiness, in power, others seek it in science or in sensuality. Those who are truly close to bliss realize that it cannot exist in something that only a few, rather than everyone, can possess. They realize that the genuine well-being of man is such that all people can possess it at once, without division and without jealousy; it is such that no one can lose it unless he wants to. – Pascal

We have one, and only one, infallible guide: the eternal spirit that penetrates each and every one of us in unity and fills us with the ambition to attain that which we ought; it is the same spirit that urges the tree to grow towards the sun, the flower to drop its seeds in autumn, and which urges us to strive after God, thereby uniting ourselves.

We are not attracted to genuine belief by the well-being the believer is promised, but by something that manifests itself as the only recourse to deliverance from all misfortune and death.

Salvation does not lie in the rituals and profession of faith, but in a lucid understanding of the meaning of one's life.*

This is all I wanted to say.

I wanted to say that we have now reached a situation in which we can no longer remain, and that whether we like it or not, we must enter a new path of existence and, in order for us to do that, we do not need to invent either a new faith, or new scientific theories, that might explain the meaning of life and guide it. And, above all, we do not need any particular kind of activity, except to free ourselves from the superstitions, of false Christianity and political structures alike.

* The last three epigraphs are culled by Tolstoy from his own writings. [J. P.]

Simply let everyone understand that he has neither the right nor the possibility of organizing other people's lives and that the task of each man is only to observe his own life in accordance with the supreme religious law revealed to him, and this in itself will obviate that tortuous, bestial order of life existing amongst the Christian nations which is so contrary to the requirements of our souls, and growing worse and worse.

Whoever you may be: tsar, judge, landowner, craftsman or beggar, think about it and take pity, take pity on your soul . . . For however obscured and stupefied you may be by your sovereignty, power or wealth, however exhausted and numbed you may be by your needs and grudges, like all of us you possess, or rather you manifest, that spirit of God that exists in us all and which now says to you, clearly and comprehensibly: why and for what purpose do you torment yourselves and all the others with whom you come into contact in this world? Just realize who you are, how insignificant, on the one hand, is that which you mistakenly call yourself, identifying it as your body; and how immensely great is that which is really you: your spiritual being. Just realize this and begin to spend each moment of your life living not for external ideals, but in fulfilling the true purpose of your life, which has been revealed to you through the wisdom of the whole world, the teachings of Christ, and your own personal awareness. Begin to live by seeing the purpose and well-being of your life in the daily progress of your soul's liberation from the illusions of the flesh, and in the increasing perfection of love (which amounts to one and the same thing). Just begin to do this and from the first day, the first hour, you will experience a new and joyous sensation of the awareness of complete freedom and well-being flowing ever increasingly into your soul. And what will strike you most of all is how those very external circumstances which troubled you so much, but which were nevertheless so far from your desires, cease (whether they leave you in the same external situation, or whether they lead you out of it) to be a hindrance, and become greater and greater joys of your life.

And if you are unhappy – and I know that you are unhappy – remember that what has been suggested here was not invented by me, but is the fruit of the spiritual works of all the best and loftiest minds and hearts of mankind, and is the only means of deliverance from your unhappiness, providing the greatest well-being man can attain in this life.

This is what I wanted to say to my fellow-men before I die.

[Translated by Jane Kentish]

ADDRESS TO THE SWEDISH PEACE CONGRESS IN 1909

DEAR BROTHERS:

We have met here to fight against war. War, the thing for the sake of which all the nations of the earth – millions and millions of people – place at the uncontrolled disposal of a few men or sometimes only one man, not merely milliards of roubles, talers, francs or yen (representing a very large share of their labour), but also their very lives. And now we, a score of private people gathered from the various ends of the earth, possessed of no special privileges and above all having no power over anyone, intend to fight – and as we wish to fight we wish also to conquer – this immense power not of one government but of all the governments, which have at their disposal these milliards of money and millions of soldiers and who are well aware that the exceptional position of those who form the governments rests on the army alone: the army which has a meaning and purpose only if there is a war, the very war against which we wish to fight and which we wish to abolish.

For us to struggle, the forces being so unequal, must appear insane. But if we consider our opponents' means of strife and our own, it is not our intention to fight that will seem absurd but that the thing we mean to fight against can still exist. They have milliards of money and millions of obedient soldiers; we have only one thing, but that is the most powerful thing in the world – Truth.

Therefore, insignificant as our forces may appear in comparison with those of our opponents, our victory is as sure as the victory of the light of the rising sun over the darkness of night.

Our victory is certain, but on one condition only – that

when uttering the truth we utter it all, without compromise, concession or modification. The truth is so simple, so clear, so evident, to all reasonable men, that it is only necessary to speak it out completely in its full significance for it to be irresistible.

The truth in its full meaning lies in what was said thousands of years ago (in the law accepted among us as the Law of God) in four words: *Thou Shalt Not Kill*. The truth is that man may not and should not in any circumstances or under any pretext kill his fellow-man.

That truth is so evident, so binding and so generally acknowledged, that it is only necessary to put it clearly before men for the evil called war to become quite impossible.

And so I think that if we who are assembled here at this Peace Congress should, instead of clearly and definitely voicing this truth, address ourselves to the governments with various proposals for lessening the evils of war or gradually diminishing its frequency, we should be like men who having in their hand the key to a door, should try to break through walls they know to be too strong for them. Before us are millions of armed men, ever more and more efficiently armed and trained for more and more rapid slaughter. We know that these millions of people have no wish to kill their fellows and for the most part do not even know why they are forced to do that repulsive work, and that they are weary of their position of subjection and compulsion; we know that the murders committed from time to time by these men are committed by order of the governments; and we know that the existence of the governments depends on the armies. Can we, then, who desire the abolition of war, find nothing more conducive to our aim than to propose to the governments – which exist only by the aid of armies and consequently by war – measures which would destroy war? Are we to propose to the governments that they should destroy themselves?

The governments will listen willingly to any speeches of that kind, knowing that such discussions will neither destroy war nor undermine their own power, but will only conceal yet more effectually what must be concealed if wars and armies and themselves in control of armies are to continue to exist.

'But,' I shall be told, 'this is anarchism; people never have lived without governments and States, and therefore governments and States and military forces defending them are necessary for the existence of the nations.'

But leaving aside the question of whether the life of Christian and other nations is possible without armies and wars to defend their governments and States, or even supposing it to be necessary for their welfare that they should slavishly submit to institutions called governments (consisting of people they do not personally know), and that it is necessary to yield up the produce of their labour to these institutions and fulfil all their demands – including the murder of their neighbours – granting all that, there yet remains in our world an unsolved difficulty.

This difficulty lies in the impossibility of making the Christian faith (which those who form the governments profess with particular emphasis) accord with armies composed of Christians trained to slay. However much you may pervert the Christian teaching, however much you may hide its main principles, its fundamental teaching is the love of God and one's neighbour; of God – that is of the highest perfection of virtue, and of one's neighbour – that is of men without distinction. And therefore it would seem inevitable that we must repudiate one of the two, either Christianity with its love of God and one's neighbour, or the State with its armies and wars.

Perhaps Christianity may be obsolete, and when choosing between the two – Christianity and love or the State and murder – the people of our time will conclude that the existence of the State and murder is so much more important than Christianity, that we must forgo Christianity and retain only what is more important: the State and murder.

That may be so – at least people may think and feel so. But in that case they should say so! They should openly admit that people in our time have ceased to believe in what is said by the Law of God they profess: have ceased to believe in what is written indelibly on the heart of each man, and must now believe only in what is ordered by various people who by the accident of birth have happened to become emperors and kings, or by various intrigues and elections have become presidents or members of senates and parliaments – even if those orders include murders. That is what they ought to say!

But it is impossible to say it; and yet one of these two things has to be said. If it is admitted that Christianity forbids murders, both armies and governments become impossible. If it is admitted that the government acknowledges the lawfulness of murder and denies Christianity, no one will wish to obey a government that exists merely by its power to kill. And besides, if murder is allowed in war it must be still more allowable when a people seeks its rights in a revolution. And therefore the governments, being unable to say either the one thing or the other, are anxious only to hide from their subjects the necessity of solving the dilemma.

And for us who are assembled here to counteract the evil of war, if we really desire to attain our end, only one thing is necessary: namely to put that dilemma quite clearly and definitely both to those who form the governments and to the masses of the people who compose the army. To do that we must not only clearly and openly repeat the truth we all know and cannot help knowing – that man should not slay his fellow-man – but we must also make it clear that no considerations can destroy the demand made by that truth on people of the Christian world.

Therefore I propose to our Meeting to draw up and publish an appeal to all men, and especially to the Christian nations, in which we clearly and definitely express what everybody knows but hardly anyone says: namely that war is not – as most people now assume – a good and laudable affair, but that like all murder, it is a vile and criminal business not only for those who voluntarily choose a military career but for those who submit to it from avarice or fear of punishment.

With regard to those who voluntarily choose a military career, I would propose to state clearly and definitely in that appeal that notwithstanding all the pomp, glitter and general approval with which it is surrounded, it is a criminal and shameful activity; and that the higher the position a man holds in the military profession the more criminal and shameful is his occupation. In the same way with regard to men of the people who are drawn into military service by bribes or by threats of punishments, I propose to speak clearly and definitely of the gross mistake they make – contrary to their faith, morality and common sense – when they consent to enter the army; contrary to their faith, because by entering the ranks of murderers they infringe the Law of God which they acknowledge; contrary to morality, because for pay or from fear of punishment they agree to do what in their souls they know to be wrong; and contrary to common sense, because if they enter the army and war breaks out they risk having to suffer consequences as bad or worse than those they are threatened with if they refuse. Above all they act contrary to common sense in that they join that caste of people which deprives them of freedom and compels them to become soldiers.

With reference to both classes I propose in this appeal to express clearly the thought that for men of true enlightenment, who are therefore free from the superstition of military glory (and their number is growing every day), the military profession and calling, notwithstanding all the efforts to hide its real meaning, is as shameful a business as an executioner's and even more so. For the executioner only holds himself in readiness to kill those who have been adjudged harmful and criminal, while a soldier promises to kill all whom he is told to kill, even though they be those dearest to him or the best of men.

Humanity in general, and our Christian humanity in particular, has reached a stage of such acute contradiction between its moral demands and the existing social order, that a change has become inevitable, and a change not in society's moral demands which are immutable, but in the social order which can be altered. The demand for a different social order, evoked by that inner contradiction which is so clearly illustrated by our preparations for murder, becomes more and more insistent every year and every day. The tension which demands that alteration has reached such a degree that, just as sometimes only a slight shock is required to change a liquid into a solid body, so perhaps only a slight effort or even a single word may be needed to change the cruel and irrational life of our time – with its divisions, armaments and armies – into a reasonable life in keeping with the consciousness of contemporary humanity. Every such effort, every such word, may be the shock which will instantly solidify the super-cooled liquid. Why should not our gathering be that shock? In Andersen's fairy tale, when the King went in triumphant procession through the streets of the town and all the people were delighted with his beautiful new clothes, a word from a child who said what everybody knew but had not said changed everything. He said: 'he has nothing on!' and the spell was broken and the King became ashamed and all those who had been assuring themselves that they saw him wearing beautiful new clothes perceived that he was naked! We must say the same. We must say what everybody knows but does not venture to say. We must say that by whatever name men may call murder – murder always remains murder and a criminal and shameful thing. And it is only necessary to say that clearly, definitely and loudly, as we can say it here, and men will cease to see what they thought they saw and will see what is really before their eyes. They will cease to see the service of their country, the heroism of war, military glory and patriotism, and will see what exists: the naked, criminal business of murder! And if people see that, the same thing will happen as in the fairy tale: those who do the criminal thing will feel ashamed, and those who assure themselves that they do not see the criminality of murder will perceive it and cease to be murderers.

But how will nations defend themselves against their enemies, how will they maintain internal order, and how can nations live without an army?

What form the life of men will take if they repudiate murder, we do not and cannot know; but one thing is certain: that it is more natural for men to be guided by the reason and conscience with which they are endowed, than to submit slavishly to people who arrange wholesale murders; and that therefore the form of social order assumed by the lives of those who are guided in their actions not by violence based on threats of murder but by reason and conscience, will in any case be no worse than that under which they now live.

That is all I want to say. I shall be very sorry if it offends or grieves anyone or evokes any ill-feeling. But for me, a man eighty years old, expecting to die at any moment, it would be shameful and criminal not to speak out the whole truth as I understand it – the truth which, as I firmly believe, is alone capable of relieving mankind from the incalculable ills produced by war.

[Translated by Aylmer Maude]

FROM *TOLSTOY'S LETTERS* [1895–1910]

415. TO A. L. TOLSTOY

[Tolstoy's fourth son, Andrey (1877–1916), was not yet eighteen when the following letter was written. He never completed his secondary education, spent most of his time with gipsies, and led a profligate life. The plans for marriage mentioned in the letter came to nothing. In 1899 he married Countess Olga Dieterichs, Chertkov's sister-in-law, but the marriage did not last. He later married the former wife of the governor of Tula. Andrey joined the army as a volunteer in 1896, fought in the Russo-Japanese War, and was a member of the 'Black Hundred' organization, a right-wing, anti-Semitic group which indulged in terrorist acts. Maude records that Andrey 'grieved his father in various ways'. He later held various administrative posts in Tambov and Petersburg, and died during the First World War at the age of thirty-eight.]

Yasnaya Polyana, 16(?) October 1895

Andryusha,

Although I promised not to approach you any more, but to wait until you approached me for advice (and I'm still waiting for this), I'm writing to you all the same – firstly, because your situation torments me too much and I think about it incessantly; secondly, because there is a misapprehension about your understanding of the words I said to you, and it must be corrected so that neither you nor others will be misled; and thirdly, because I hope that a letter will be easier for you to read and understand properly than any words. I earnestly beg you to read attentively and think carefully about what I write.

The misapprehension which I'm talking about consists of your taking my words that in my opinion it's exactly the same whether one marries a princess or a peasant girl (I even consider a peasant girl better than a princess) to mean my agreement to your marriage to Akulina Makarova* in the state in which you now are. I not only cannot agree to this, but would consider my agreement or even my indifference to such an action on your part the greatest of sins against yourself, against the girl, and, most important, against God. I told you then that it's always possible and even necessary to marry if a young man feels that he can't live purely without a wife, or if he's so much in love that he loses his peace of mind and the ability to do anything, but that marriage and acquaintance with Bibikov and the Bergers† and drinking vodka with them and the peasants and playing the accordion have nothing in common with marriage. On the contrary, such a frame of mind and such a way of passing the time and, most important, the continual stupefying of oneself with vodka show that a man certainly can't marry while he's in such a state. In order to go shopping, to go out hunting, or to write a letter, a man must be in a sober, clear-headed state; but in order to marry, to do the most important thing in life which is only done once, one must be all the more clear-headed, and get rid of everything which might cloud one's judgement or distract one's attention. But you, on the contrary, ever since you wanted to get married, have continually done your best to stupefy yourself by every means – tobacco, vodka, the accordion, every kind of distraction which prevents you from remaining alone and at peace with your thoughts for a single minute. Thus this state of yours shows that you not only haven't thought out the significance of this action which you wish

* A peasant girl from the village of Yasnaya Polyana. [All footnotes in this chapter, except those marked 'J. P.', are by R. F. C.]

† V. A. Bibikov, the son of Tolstoy's old neighbour and acquaintance A. N. Bibikov; the Berger brothers – one of them later became manager of Andrey's estate of Taptykovo.

to perform, but on the contrary you don't want to think about it, you want to force yourself to forget its significance, and it also shows that it's not a question of marriage, but of an unnatural state of excitement which you are in and which you must try by all means to overcome, because such artificial excitement won't stop with marriage but will grow and grow and lead you to ruin. Therefore, I not only can't agree to your marriage now, but, on the contrary, I would consider it the most decisive step to ruin, after which a return to a good life would hardly be possible. Your marriage now in all probability would mean that – in a week's time or perhaps even earlier – you would find yourself not only with an unloved wife, but with a hated, repulsive wife round your neck (as always happens as a result of purely sensual intimacy), and in the hands of your wife's coarse and greedy parents who won't let you out of their clutches with the fortune you will have. Because of the habit you have adopted of drowning all unpleasantness in vodka, with the help of those same relatives with whom you drink even now, drunkenness will take complete control of you, and it's terrible to think of the unhappy situation which you will surely be in in two or three or at the most five years, i.e. in those years when you should begin to live a family life, if it's so necessary for you to marry.

And so I repeat to you what I said when I said that it's all the same whether one marries a princess or a peasant girl, namely that before thinking about any marriage at all you must calm down and get back to a normal state in which you can associate with those who are close to you, can think calmly, can refrain from offending those closest to you and, most important, can work, can do some job or other and live like that not for a week or a month but at least for a year or two. To do this, the main thing necessary is for you to stop drinking vodka, and *in order to stop drinking it – to stop associating with people who drink it*. God has given man an immortal soul and for the guidance of this soul – reason. And now man has thought up a means to stifle his reason so that his soul is left without guidance. Vodka does this, and for that reason it is not only a dreadful sin, but a dreadful deception, because a soul without guidance always leads man into a situation where he suffers terribly. You are already beginning to suffer, and I'm sure that you suffer, and suffer greatly, because you are torturing your mother (I know you have a good heart and love her) and you are suffering from the awareness of your fall which you want to conceal from yourself. Don't try to conceal it but admit it to yourself, repent before God and with His help begin a new life, and set yourself as the main aim in it your own improvement, your moral self-perfection. To attain this goal, I advise four things: (1) most important, abstinence from everything which clouds the reason, especially any alcohol; (2) association with people higher than yourself in education, intelligence, social position, even fortune, and not with those lower than yourself; (3) an outward change in the conditions of your life – go away somewhere from those conditions in which you have lived badly, and don't remain in them; and (4) abstain from amusements and distractions and don't fear boredom to begin with. This is so that you can find a job to do, start doing it, and get to like it. The devil ensnares us by wiles and we need wiles to struggle against him. These four rules are such wiles; they destroy his intrigues. However, if you want to live well, you will discover for yourself what you need. Where is a will is a way. If you could only understand who you are. If only you could understand that you are a son of God whom God in His love sent into the world so that you could do work that is pleasing to Him there, and that for this purpose He gave you reason and love which will certainly give you happiness, if only you develop them and don't stifle them.

Yours affectionately, L. Tolstoy

417. TO M. L. TOLSTOY

[Mikhail Lvovich Tolstoy (1879–1944) – Tolstoy's youngest son to survive childhood. He volunteered for army service in the late 1890s and was a source of considerable anxiety to his father, especially before his marriage in 1901. After Tolstoy's death he emigrated to France where he lived until 1935. He eventually moved to Morocco and died there in 1944.]

Yasnaya Polyana, 27–30 October 1895

Misha,

The long letter I wrote to you is too serious, lengthy and generalized, i.e. it might seem uninteresting to you now, and so I'm not sending it to you,* but I want to say what is most important and, I think, necessary to you, and necessary at this very time.

Your situation is bad because you are living without any religious or moral principles; you don't believe in Orthodox-aristocratic or bourgeois rules of social propriety – and quite rightly so, because these rules won't last long in our time – but you don't have any other ones. And what is worst of all is that other religious and moral principles which are natural and proper to people of our time – principles by which all the best people in the world live – are hidden from you by the very fact that they are right in front of you, so that you don't see them, as one doesn't see an object which is close to one's eyes. It seems to you that everything I profess and preach is something which, though not bad, is ill-defined, vague and inapplicable. I don't think you've even glanced once at any of my books except the novels, but nevertheless I profess and preach what I profess and preach only because I consider it the most precise, clear, applicable and necessary guide for the behaviour of just such young people as yourself.

So you live without any guiding principle, except the instinct for good, under the influence of your lusts which have been inflated to terrible proportions by your luxurious and idle life. But one can't live this way, because the instinct for good is always stifled by lusts, and this type of life inevitably leads to dreadful sufferings and to the ruin of what is most precious in man – his soul, his reason. This type of life leads to ruin because, if life's happiness lies in the satisfaction of one's lusts, then as they are satisfied, one's pleasure decreases and decreases, and one must arouse newer and stronger lusts in order to obtain the

* A letter of 16–19 October which is not translated here, as it covers similar ground in an even more ponderous manner. Mikhail Tolstoy was sixteen at the time and like his brother Andrey had found a girl in the village of Yasnaya Polyana whom he thought he loved and wanted to marry.

same pleasure. And this increase in one's lusts always inevitably leads to the two strongest ones: women and vodka. And there lies true ruin. You will probably think a bit and say that you don't lust after women, but that you are in love. I don't know which is better: sin with a woman or being in love, as you think of it. Both are bad. If being in love is to be pure and lofty, it's necessary for both lovers to be on an equally high level of spiritual development; apart from that, being in love has a beneficial influence when, in order to attain reciprocity from the object of one's love, great efforts and achievements are needed on the part of the one who is in love, and not when, as in your case, nothing except the accordion and honey cakes is needed to attain reciprocity and, to place yourself on an equal level with the object of your love, you don't have to raise yourself to her, but to lower yourself; such being in love is nothing else but hidden lust, magnified by the charm of the primitive life of the people.

The consequences of your present relationship with a peasant girl can only be these: at the worst, that you will marry without a church wedding before reaching full maturity, i.e. before the age of 21–25, and after living that way for a while and becoming coarse in mind and conscience with the aid of what is always at your service, especially in that way of life – vodka – you will separate from her, and realizing that you have thereby committed a crime, you will seek forgetfulness of this crime in similar relationships with other girls, and again in vodka. This is the worst and most probable consequence – one which will complete the ruin of your soul and body.

Less bad, is that before the age of 25, i.e. before full maturity, you will marry a peasant girl in the proper way, with a church wedding, and as a consequence of your immaturity and lack of firmness, you will not only fail to raise her to a higher moral level but, on the contrary, will yourself fall to the level of coarseness and immorality in which she has lived and will continue to live. Recognizing your fall, you will drink or debauch yourself so as to forget, or else abandon her altogether. That is the second outcome. The third outcome, less bad again, is that you will spend the best, most energetic and most important years of your life for the development of character and habits – years in which the main progress is made in moral development and in which the foundations of one's whole life are laid – you will spend these years in an enervating, stupefying, immobilizing state of being in love (which in essence is only lust disguised by the imagination) and will then wake up, having realized that you have irretrievably lost the best years of your life, weakened your best powers through acquiring the fatal habit of stupefying yourself, and lost irretrievably the possibility of future family happiness. This is the best outcome. But even this is terrible, and it is awful for me to foresee this for you. What you are probably dreaming about vaguely, without forming a clear picture of how it will come about, namely that you will marry the object of your love and will live a good life, is as improbable as winning with one ticket in a million. For this to happen it's necessary, firstly, that you should marry no earlier than the age of 21, consequently no sooner than in 5 years' time, or even 8 or 10 years; to take the average, let's say in 7 years; secondly, that in these 7 years you should stop learning to play the accordion and to dance, and should inure yourself to every form of abstinence and hard work and, in addition, should not only not sink lower in mental and moral development, but should raise and consolidate yourself so as to raise your wife in this respect too; thirdly, that you and she should live for these 7 years chastely, without ceasing to work on yourselves.

However hard this may be, and however remote from your present course in life, it is possible, and if you want to try to accomplish it, I shall only rejoice and assist you with all my strength. Only you need to begin by doing just the exact opposite of what you are doing now: to restrain yourself in everything, to work on yourself constantly, making yourself work hard either for other people or for your own perfection, and not for your own pleasure as you do now.

The need to get married is only legitimate in a man who is fully mature, and then a meeting with a woman may cause you to fall in love, i.e. to feel an exclusive love for that woman; then this feeling is natural, although even then you mustn't stimulate this feeling as you are doing, but struggle against it. At your age this is just simply over-indulgence, caused by your luxurious, idle and unprincipled life, and by the wish to imitate. Therefore what is most important, what is necessary for you now, is for you to come to your senses, to take a look at yourself and at the lives of other people, and ask yourself: what are you living for?* And what do you want of yourself?

To say to yourself what the animal in you prompts – that you want as much satisfaction and pleasure as possible for yourself – and that this is the goal and the meaning of your life, is simply impossible for a person who hasn't yet entirely stupefied himself, who hasn't become a complete swine; it's impossible because in our rich way of life (this is our advantage) we quickly come to the end of these pleasures and see what they are leading us to – sweetmeats, rides, bicycles, theatres, etc.; they all become tiresome and one thing remains: a woman's love, in no matter what form, and vodka. Both one and the other fundamentally ruin a man's soul. You will say: why is man given this desire for a woman's love, stronger than any other, if he ought not to desire it? It is given to us, as you know, for the continuation of the species and certainly not for pleasure. Pleasure only accompanies this feeling when it isn't made the goal of life. Pleasure comes as a reward only to the man who doesn't seek it or make it the goal of his life. When a man makes it his goal in life, the absolute opposite always happens, he destroys life: you get debauchery, illness, onanism, or that stupefying state of being in love which you have succumbed to and its inevitable consequence: the crippling of body and soul and the incapacity for any type of enjoyment. Vodka, tobacco and other means of stupefaction such as the accordion invariably accompany this frame of mind because, by befogging the reason, they hide from a man the falseness of his goal. This goal is false, firstly, because its attainment destroys our lives and souls and bodies and, secondly, because this goal is a short distance away and can be attained. So, you marry the object of

* A lengthy section of the letter was deleted at this point, on Tolstoy's instructions, when his manuscript version was being copied out.

your love – and then what? – particularly since the object of your love grows old and inevitable disenchantment sets in.

And so the question, why are you living and what do you want of yourself, must certainly not be answered: for pleasure; but one must inevitably establish another goal in life, one which, firstly, will not ruin the life and soul and body given to you and, secondly, can always be attained but never fully attained, so that you can always strive towards it while you are living, and constantly get nearer to it. There is only one such goal towards which every man is involuntarily drawn, and which is natural, not only to you at 16 but to me at 67, and satisfies me as equally as it can satisfy you, and its attainment cannot be impeded by anything. I don't want to say it, I would like you yourself to name this goal – you will surely guess that the only important and joyful thing in which no one can ever hinder us and which can never be entirely finished so that there should be nothing more to do – is one thing only: one's own spiritual and moral perfection. As a blindfolded man is guided on his path by being pushed by people from all sides where he shouldn't go, and is only left with one direction to go in, so all our lusts which end in disenchantment and unhappiness push us all from all sides and leave open to us only the one path of moral perfection – moral, not physical and not mental – because there may be conditions in which I can't be strong and agile (if I'm a cripple), there may be conditions in which I can't develop mentally (if I live in a backwater, if I'm mentally slow), but moral perfection is always and everywhere possible for everyone, and the joy which comes from making progress is enormous, as you will find out if only you try it. And not only does striving and making progress bring about spiritual joy in life, but in such a life it usually happens that worldly joys also come just when one isn't seeking them, when one doesn't set them as a goal – it usually happens that both worldly and higher joys come of their own accord to such a man.

Therefore, this is what I advise you to do: first of all, come to your senses, take a look at yourself – this means, once you have seen the falseness of your life, having serious doubts about yourself, acknowledging the one goal of life which is natural to man and trying to live for this goal. Try it for yourself and then you will find out whether it's true. And if you begin to do this, don't give in to the one most common temptation which most frequently scares off beginners. This temptation consists in the fact that having once begun the inner work of perfecting himself, a person of our circle finds himself in such senseless conditions, so far removed from moral perfection, and with such bad and false habits, that he has so much work to do that he gives up, and wants to abandon it all and do nothing. A moral life must be one in which a person doesn't take advantage of the labours of other people, in which he doesn't make the poor work for his own whims, in which he himself must work for others: but we live by devouring the labours of thousands of people and giving them nothing. What are we to do? We must change everything, temptation says, and when the time comes I'll do so, but at present I must live like everyone else. There lies the deception. It's just like a man stopping ploughing because the field he has to plough is too large. A man only needs to begin work to see that the further the work progresses, the more joyful it is. So it is with our lives too. If my goal is perfection, how can I stop working now because there is too much to do? Do whatever comes to hand first: decrease your demands for work for yourself and increase your work for others: carry and clean what you can carry and clean yourself, travel on foot instead of riding, do a service for another person, rather than for yourself. And the further this work progresses, the more joyful it will be. You must do what you can now, and not despise small things. To put it off means to deceive yourself. This is one thing I advise you, if you are to try to live not for animal pleasure, but for moral perfection. Another very important thing which I also advise you is to remember that reason is the instrument given us in order to know the good, and therefore in order that we may perfect ourselves and see the ideal of good towards which we should strive, we should try to protect our reason with all our strength, not to destroy its growth, but to increase its content by absorbing in our reason all that has been accomplished by the reason of people who have lived before us, i.e. to associate with the most reasonable people, both living and dead, through the ideas expressed in their writings. If we don't yet have an inclination to do this, then at least don't let us do that terrible thing which is now being done more and more by all of us – i.e. don't stupefy ourselves, don't kill our reason with strong food which is unnatural to man, and with stupefying drinks and smoking.

Reason is the highest spiritual force in man, it's a small particle of God in us and therefore every attempt to stifle it is a most terrible sin, which doesn't pass without consequence.

One more piece of advice, and a very important one, is that if you begin such a life and try to live for moral perfection and then for some reason you weaken, or get distracted, and return again to those bad habits which you've already adopted – don't despair and don't give it up as a bad job, but realize that such falls and turnings back are natural to any progress, and that the only person who doesn't fall is the one who doesn't strive towards anything, but only lives an animal life. Fall a thousand times and get up a thousand times and if you don't despair, you will make constant progress and, as I've already said, apart from the very great spiritual joy of life, all the worldly joys of life which you wanted before will also be added unto you and will be increased an hundred-fold, as Christ promised.

Goodbye. May God help you. He who is in you and in me and outside us. This letter is directed both at Andryusha and at Mitya.* It would be a great joy to me if it helped either of you to free yourselves from the temptations which are drowning you, and at least to see the true road, in order to get on to it.

L. Tolstoy

* Andrey Tolstoy and Dmitry Dyakov [an early friend of Tolstoy from Kazan, where Tolstoy attended the university. They remained friends throughout Tolstoy's life. J. P.].

468. TO P. I. BIRYUKOV

[Pavel Ivanovich Biryukov (1860–1931) wrote a Life of Tolstoy, *published in 1911, that was based on extensive interviews with Tolstoy. He was a major disciple of Tolstoy and an advocate for social justice, especially among the persecuted Dukhabors. J. P.]*

Moscow, 10 April–5 May 1901

I got your letter today, my dear Posha, and am very glad that you and Pasha* were sympathetically inclined towards my idea, that this was your idea, and . . .

I wrote these lines almost a month ago and since then I haven't been near my desk – I've been constantly ill with rheumatism and a fever. Now I'm better. Since then I've also had a good letter from Pasha† and another one from Bodyansky,‡ and now I'll try to answer everything, and most of all for my own benefit, the educational problems which have always faced, and still face me. At the basis of everything must stand what has been discarded in our schools – a religious understanding of life – and not so much in the shape of teaching, but as a guiding principle of all educational activity. The religious understanding of life, which, to my way of thinking, can and should become the foundation of life for people of our time could be expressed very briefly as follows: the meaning of our lives consists in fulfilling the will of that infinite principle of which we recognize ourselves to be a part; and this will lies in the union of all living things, above all of people – in their brotherhood, in their service to each other. From a different angle, this religious understanding of life can be expressed like this: the business of

* Biryukov's wife.

† A letter in which she expressed her agreement with Tolstoy's ideas about the education of children.

‡ A. M. Bodyansky, a Tolstoyan imprisoned several times and then living in England. His letter is unknown.

life is union with all living things – above all the brotherhood of men, their service to each other.

And this is so because we are alive only to the extent to which we recognize ourselves to be a part of the infinite; and the law of the infinite is this union.

In any case, the manifestation of this religious understanding in life – the union of everything attained by love – is above all the brotherhood of man: it is the practical, central law of life, and it should be made the basis of education, and therefore it is good and advisable to develop in children all that leads towards union, and to suppress all that leads towards its opposite. Children are always – and the younger they are, the more so – in a state which doctors call the first stage of hypnosis. And children learn and are educated thanks only to this state of theirs. (Their capacity for suggestion puts them at the complete mercy of their elders, and therefore one can't be too attentive about how and what we suggest to them.) So then, people always learn and are educated only through suggestion, which operates in two ways: consciously and unconsciously. Everything that we teach children to do, from prayers and fables to dances and music, is all conscious suggestion; everything that children imitate independently of our desires, especially in our lives, in our actions, is unconscious suggestion. Conscious suggestion is teaching and instruction – unconscious suggestion is example, education in its narrow sense, or, as I shall call it, enlightenment. In our society all efforts are directed at the first type, while the second, involuntarily and as a consequence of the fact that our lives are bad, is neglected. The people who are responsible for education either hide their lives and the lives of adults in general from children, by placing them in abnormal conditions (military schools, institutes, boarding schools, etc.) – this is a most common thing – or transfer what should take place unconsciously into the sphere of the conscious: they prescribe moral rules for life, to which it is necessary to add: *fais ce que je dis, mais ne fais pas ce que je fais.** It is because of this that in our society instruction has

* 'Do what I say, not what I do.' [J. P.]

gone so disproportionately far, while genuine education or enlightenment has not only lagged behind, but is absent altogether. If it does exist anywhere, it is only in poor, working families. However, of the two types of influence on children, unconscious and conscious, incomparably the more important both for individuals and for society as a whole is the first, i.e. unconscious moral enlightenment.

A family of a rentier, a landowner, a civil servant, even an artist or a writer, lives a bourgeois life; they don't get drunk or lead a dissolute life, don't quarrel or offend people, and they want to give their children a moral education. But this is just as impossible as it is to teach children a new language without speaking this language and without showing them books written in this language. Children will listen to rules about morality, about respect for people, but unconsciously they will not only imitate, but will assimilate as a rule the fact that some people's job is to clean shoes and clothing, carry water and slops, and cook meals, while the job of other people is to dirty clothing and rooms, and to eat meals, etc. If one is seriously to understand the religious basis of life – the brotherhood of man – then one can't help seeing that people who live on money taken from others and who force these others to serve them in return for that money are living an immoral life, and no sermons of theirs will save their children from this unconscious, immoral suggestion, which will either remain with them all their lives, perverting all their judgements about the phenomena of life, or will be destroyed by them with great effort and hard work, after many sufferings and mistakes. I'm not saying this for your sake because, as far as I know, you are free of this evil, and in this respect your life can only exercise a moral suggestion on children. The fact that you are far from doing everything yourselves and use the services of other people for money cannot have a harmful effect on the children, if they see that you are not striving to shift the work which is necessary for your daily life from your shoulders to others, but just the opposite.

Therefore education, unconscious suggestion, is the most important thing. For it to be good and moral, what is needed – strange to say – is for the whole life of the person responsible for education to be good. What do you call a good life? people will ask. The degrees of goodness are infinite, but there is one common and important feature of a good life: striving towards perfection in love. If this is there in the people responsible for education, and if the children are infected by it, then their education will not be bad.

For children's education to be successful, it is necessary for those who educate them to educate themselves continually and to help each other to accomplish more and more of what they are striving towards. The methods of doing this, apart from the main inner method – the work of each man on his own soul (for me, with the help of solitude and prayer) – can be very many. One must search for them, think about them, apply them and discuss them. I think that criticism, which is used by the Perfectionists,* is a good method. I also think it is good to get together on certain days and inform each other of methods for struggling against our own weaknesses, and our own formulas for perfection, or those derived from books. It is good, I think, to seek out the most unfortunate people, who are repulsive physically or morally, and try to serve them. It is good, I think, to try to make friends with our enemies who hate us. I write this at random *au courant de la plume*,† but I think that this is a whole and most important province of the science of educating oneself in order to influence children. If only we recognized the importance of this aspect of education, we would cultivate it ourselves.

These are hints about one side of the business – education. Now about instruction. This is what I think about instruction: science and scholarship is nothing other than the transmission of what the most intelligent people have thought. Intelligent people have always thought along three different lines, or ways of thought; they have thought (1) philosophically, religiously, about the meaning of their lives – religion and philosophy, (2) experimentally, drawing conclusions from observations

* The Perfectionists, an American fundamentalist sect dating from 1831 which abolished private property among its members.

† 'As the pen runs.' [J. P.]

organized in a certain way – the natural sciences: mechanics, physics, chemistry and physiology, and (3) mathematically, drawing conclusions from propositions of their own thinking – mathematics and the mathematical sciences.

All these three varieties of sciences are genuine sciences. It is impossible to pretend to a knowledge of them, and there can be no half-knowledge – you know it or you don't. All these three varieties of sciences are cosmopolitan; they not only don't separate people, but they unite them. They are all accessible to all people and satisfy the criterion of the brotherhood of man.

But the theological sciences, the legal and especially the historical sciences, Russian and French, are not sciences, or else they are harmful sciences, and should be excluded. But apart from the fact that there exist three branches of science, there also exist three means of transmission of their knowledge (please don't think that I'm reducing everything to threes: I'd like there to be four or ten, but they've come out in threes).

The first means of transmission – the most common – is words. But words are in different languages, and so another science has appeared – languages – again conforming to the criterion of the brotherhood of man (maybe the teaching of Esperanto is needed as well, if there is time and the pupils want it). The second means is the plastic arts, drawing or modelling, the science of how to transmit what you know to another for the eye to see. And the third means – music and singing – is the science of how to transmit one's mood or feeling.

In addition to these 6 branches of teaching, a 7th should be introduced: the teaching of a trade, and again this conforms to the criterion of brotherhood, i.e. the sort of thing everybody needs – metal-working, house-painting, carpentry, sewing . . .

And so teaching can be broken down into 7 subjects.

The inclination of each pupil will decide what amount of time to devote to each, apart from the work required to supply one's daily needs.

I imagine it this way: the teachers arrange the hours for themselves, but the pupils are free to come or not. However strange this may seem to us who have so distorted instruction, full freedom of teaching, i.e. so that a boy or girl can come of their own accord to study when they want to, is a *conditio sine qua non* of every fruitful type of teaching, just as a *conditio sine qua non* of nourishment is that the person taking nourishment should want to eat. The only difference is that in material matters the harm of giving up one's freedom shows up at once – there will be immediate vomiting or indigestion; but in spiritual matters, the harmful consequences won't show up so quickly, perhaps years later. Only given full freedom can one take the best pupils as far as they can go and not hold them back for the sake of the weak ones; and these best students are the most necessary ones. Only given freedom can one find out what specialization a pupil has a bent for; only freedom doesn't destroy the educational influence. Otherwise, I shall be telling the pupil that he mustn't use violence in life, while I perpetrate the most oppressive intellectual violence on him. I know this is difficult, but what can you do when you realize that every retreat from freedom is ruinous for the very cause of instruction. But it isn't so difficult once you firmly decide not to act foolishly. I think one should do it this way. A. gives lessons in mathematics from 2–3 p.m., i.e. teaching what the pupils want to know in this field. B. does the same with drawing, etc., from 3–5 p.m. You will say: what about the youngest children? The youngest, if they are properly behaved, always ask for and love a regular routine, i.e. they submit to the hypnosis of imitation: yesterday there was a lesson after dinner, so today they want a lesson after dinner . . .

In general, I imagine the division of time and subjects roughly like this. There are 16 waking hours altogether. I suggest spending half of them, with breaks for rest and games (the younger the pupils, the longer the breaks), on education in its narrowest sense – enlightenment – i.e. on work for oneself, one's family and others: cleaning, carrying things, cooking, chopping wood, etc.

The other half I would give to studying. I would let the pupil choose from the 7 subjects the ones he is attracted to.

All this, as you see, is written out carelessly. I'll work it up again, God willing, but I'm sending it to you anyway as an answer. My greetings to Zoya Grigoryevna* and Ivan Mikhaylovich† whose letter I received, and I advise him not to pay any attention to what the newspapers write. They are both good workers. I send loving greetings to you and your family and all our friends.

In a practical sense and in answer to what A. M. Bodyansky suggests,‡ I would like to add that I wouldn't advise undertaking anything new like moving to another place, or any theoretical predetermination of what the school should be; I would advise you not to invite either teachers and assistants, or pupils, but to take advantage of the conditions which already exist, developing what is there, or rather, leaving it to the future to develop.

I'll add something more about drawing and music, which, especially music . . . [gap in text] . . . the letter of young Gay§ who wrote to his father that he was being taught to play the piano, partly prompted my wish to write to you and contributed to it. Teaching the piano is a clear sign of falsely organized education. As in drawing, so in music, children should be taught by making use of the most readily accessible means (in drawing – chalk, charcoal, pencil; in music – the ability to transmit what they see or hear with their own throats). That's the beginning. If later on – which is a great pity – exceptional children should prove to have special gifts, then they can learn to paint with oils or to play expensive instruments.

I know there are good new manuals for teaching the elementary grammar of drawing and music.

As for the teaching of languages – the more, the better – I think this is what your children, in my opinion, ought to be taught: French and German without a doubt, English and Esperanto if possible.

* Zoya Grigoryevna Ruban-Shchurovskaya, Gay's niece. [Nikolay Nikolayevich Gay was the son of a writer and friend of Tolstoy. J.P.]

† I. M. Tregubov, who had sent Tolstoy some reviews of his article: 'My peace I give you . . .'

‡ A. M. Bodyansky evidently was planning to start a school on Tolstoyan lines in England.

§ The two sons of N. N. Gay junior were living with the Biryukovs in England.

And one should teach them by giving them a book they are familiar with in Russian, trying to make them understand its general sense, drawing attention in passing to the most necessary words, the roots of words and grammatical forms. Moreover, one should teach foreign languages first and foremost, and not one's own.

Please don't judge this letter of mine harshly, but accept it as an attempt to sketch out 'a programme of a programme'.

I've been unwell all winter and am now in a far from normal state: my arms and legs hurt from rheumatism, my liver is bad, and I'm generally weak physically, but I'm beginning to live better and better, and this life is so good that death not only won't upset it, but will only make it better.

Yours,
Lev Tolstoy*

471. TO V. G. CHERTKOV

[Vladimir Grigoryevich Chertkov (1854–1936) was Tolstoy's chief disciple and supporter. He was a bitter opponent of Countess Sofya Tolstoy and he did everything he could to wrest control of Tolstoy's publishing rights to his later work from her. Tolstoy admired him and sought his friendship and advice throughout his later years. J. P.]

Yasnaya Polyana, 28(?) June 1901

I'm much better today. I looked through *Fruits of Philosophy*.† It's impossible to write about it and argue against it, just as it's impossible to argue against a man trying to prove that copulation with dead bodies is pleasant and harmless. A man who doesn't feel what elephants feel, that copulation generally is an act humiliating both to oneself and one's partner, and therefore

* For the sake of consistency in this letter, the translation uses the words 'education' for *vospitaniye*, 'instruction' for *obrazovaniye*, 'teaching' for *prepodovaniye* and 'enlightenment' for *prosveshcheniye*.

† Chertkov, occupied with a pamphlet about Tolstoy's views on sex, had sent him a recent English tract defending contraception.

repulsive, an act in which a man pays involuntary tribute to his animal nature and which is only redeemed by the fact that it fulfils the purpose for which the need for this repulsive and humiliating act, irresistible at certain times, is implanted in his nature – such a man, despite his ability to argue, is on the level of an animal, and it is impossible to explain and prove this to him. I don't mention the falseness of Malthusianism which makes objective (and false) considerations the basis of an act of morality which is always subjective. Nor do I mention the fact that between the killing and destruction of the foetus and this act* there is no qualitative difference.

Forgive me: it's shameful and offensive to talk seriously about it. We should be talking and thinking about what perversion or blunting of moral feeling could bring people to it. And we should be treating them, not arguing with them. Really, an illiterate, drunken Russian peasant who believes in 'Friday' and who would be horrified at such behaviour, and who always regards the act of copulation as a sin, is immeasurably higher than people who write beautifully and have the audacity to cite philosophy in support of their barbarity. [Last paragraph deleted J. P.]

507. TO JAMES LEY

[James William Thomas Ley (1879–1943), English journalist and author of several books and articles on Dickens. He founded the Bristol and Clifton Dickens Society in 1902, and was one of the founders of the journal The Dickensian. *He wrote to Tolstoy in 1904 to ask his opinion about Dickens.]*

[Original in English] Yasnaya Polyana,
21 January/3 February 1904

Dear Sir,

I think that Charles Dickens is the greatest novel writer of the nineteenth century, and that his works, impressed with the

* I.e. contraception.

true Christian spirit, have done and will continue to do a great deal of good to mankind.

Yours truly,
Leo Tolstoy

508. TO V. G. CHERTKOV

Yasnaya Polyana, 19 February 1904

My dear Vladimir Grigoryevich,

I would have been very glad to reply to your questions, but in the field of thought to which these questions refer it is impossible, or at least I am unable, to reply; I can only follow the trend of my own thought. Perhaps what has been occupying me recently in this field of thought might serve as a partial answer to your questions. I'll try and set out, at least in a rough and ready way, these thoughts which are very dear to me.

I think, to begin again from the beginning (and this is why I disliked the publication of my thoughts about consciousness),* that all that any man knows for certain about his own life and that of the world is that he is awakened to the life of this world by the consciousness of his own separate material existence, and it seems to him that there is himself and his body which he can control by his own thoughts, and the whole world round about – from a tiny insect to Sirius – which he can't control. On this level of consciousness (the lowest), a man doesn't usually think that he didn't exist before and has been awakened by consciousness, but it seems to him that there is himself – his physical being – and outside him the whole world. The enormous majority of people start life, live and die with this consciousness.

But apart from the consciousness of his separateness as a material being, a man, if he thinks about it, asks himself the question: what constitutes his real being, his body or that which controls his body and can change it (even to the extent of being

* Excerpts from Tolstoy's diaries on the subject of consciousness had been published in *The Free Word* in 1903. Chertkov wrote to him in February 1904 to question him further, and Tolstoy's reply is one of several attempts by him to clarify his thoughts on the subject.

able to destroy the consciousness in it), and inevitably, if he thinks in a strictly scientific way, he's bound to admit that what constitutes the essence of his life is his spiritual being which receives impressions not only of the external world but also of his own body. A man is only aware of his body because there is a spiritual being which is conscious of itself in his body (Berkeley's idealism). And this consciousness of self as a spiritual being, separated from other beings by boundaries represented by matter and movement, is the second stage of consciousness, higher than the first. But just as the first stage of consciousness contained in itself an inner contradiction consisting of the fact that a material being feels and is aware of things, i.e. does something not natural to matter and incapable of being deduced from it, so does the second stage of consciousness present the same insoluble contradiction, consisting of the fact that a spiritual being, i.e. something outside space and time, is confined to limits and forms a part of something. And so a thinking man inevitably comes to the third stage of consciousness consisting of the fact that in human life a separate material being is conscious of itself (the first stage), not a separate spiritual being, but an infinite, eternally living, unified being which manifests itself in an infinite number of forms (beings), one of which is me, in the midst of forms or beings which are contiguous with me and limit me. Such, I think, is the third and highest stage of consciousness, the one which is revealed in true Brahmanism, in Buddhism and in Christianity. According to this view of the world, there is no me, but only the eternal, infinite power of God working in the world through me and through my consciousness. Life consists in the growth of consciousness: in the transition from the first to the second and third stage, and in the strengthening, purification and vitalization of consciousness at this highest stage. In this strengthening, purification and vitalization of consciousness, to which there is no end, is the meaning of life and the good of life and all moral teaching.

God willing, I'll try to set this out better sometime, but it was very important for me to say it and has greatly added to the good of my spirit . . . [ten lines omitted]

545. TO EUGEN REICHEL

[Eugen Reichel (1853–1916), German author of a book Literature about Shakespeare *(1887) challenging the authorship of Shakespeare's plays and sonnets and Francis Bacon's authorship of* Novum Organum. *Reichel had read Tolstoy's attack on Shakespeare's plays,* Shakespeare and the Drama, *and sent a copy of his book to Tolstoy with the suggestion that he might support his theory in print. Tolstoy's reply disappointed him and he wrote a second letter in an injured tone.]*

Yasnaya Polyana, 2/15 March 1907

Dear Sir,

I have read your book with great interest. Your arguments that *Novum Organum* was not written by Bacon and also that the dramas attributed to Shakespeare were not written by him are very convincing, but I am not sufficiently competent in this matter *ein entscheidenden Urtheil zu fällen.** One thing I know for certain is that not only the majority of dramas attributed to Shakespeare, but all of them, not excluding *Hamlet* and others, not only don't deserve the praise with which critics are accustomed to judge them, but are in an artistic sense *unter aller Kritik.*† So it is only in a recognition of the merits of those few dramas which you single out from all the rest that I don't agree with you.

Your criticism of those much-vaunted dramas, *Lear*, *Macbeth* and others, is so well founded and just that one ought to be surprised how people who have read your book can continue to enthuse over the apparent beauties of Shakespeare if one didn't bear in mind the nature of the crowd, whereby it always follows in its opinions the opinion of the majority, quite irrespective of its own judgement. We are not surprised that people who have been hypnotized look at white and say, as they have been prompted to, that they can see black; why then should we

* 'To give a definitive opinion.' [J. P.]

† 'Beneath contempt.' [J. P.]

be surprised that when they try to apprehend a work of art, for an understanding of which they have no judgement of their own, they stubbornly say what the majority of voices has prompted them to say. I wrote – a long time ago now – my article on Shakespeare with the certainty that I wouldn't convince anyone, but I only wanted to state that I wasn't the victim of general hypnosis. And therefore I think that neither your excellent book nor mine nor many articles, whether the proofs of Theodor Eichhoff* which were recently sent to me or other articles on the same theme in English newspapers which I have also recently received, will convince the public at large.

Having looked carefully into the process of establishing public opinion given the present circulation of the press whereby, thanks to the papers, people read and pass judgement on the most important matters when they themselves have no idea about these matters and because of their education don't even have the right to pass judgement on them, while daily newspapermen just as little qualified to pass judgement on these matters write and publish their judgements about them – given this sort of press circulation one should be surprised, not at the false judgements rooted in the masses, but only at the fact that correct judgements about these matters are sometimes encountered, if only very rarely. This particularly concerns the evaluation of works of poetry.

Any person can pass judgement on tasty dishes, pleasant smells or pleasant sensations generally (although there are people devoid of the faculty of sensing a smell and seeing all colours), but to pass judgements on works of art one needs an artistic sense which is very unevenly distributed. The merit of works of art is determined by the publishing and reading multitude. But the multitude always contains more people both stupid and unreceptive to art, and so public opinion about art is always very crude and false. It has always been like this and

* Theodor Eichhoff, author of several Shakespeare studies. He also questioned the authenticity of some of Shakespeare's work, but believed that seven plays and sixteen sonnets were definitely his, while the others (including *Macbeth* and *King Lear*) were not. Eichhoff had sent Tolstoy the proofs of his study of *Hamlet* in January 1907.

is particularly so in our time when the influence of the press more and more unites people who are unreceptive both to thought and art. And so in art nowadays – in literature, music and painting – the result has been staggering examples of success and praise for works which have nothing artistic about them, still less any common sense. I don't want to name names, but if you look at those barbaric manifestations of the mental illness which in our time is called art, you yourself will be able to name names and works.

And therefore I not only don't expect that the false reputation of Shakespeare and the ancients (I don't want to name them in order not to irritate people) can be destroyed, but I expect and can see the establishment of just the same sort of reputation for new Shakespeares, based only on the stupidity and unreceptiveness of the people of the press and the public at large. I also expect that this decline in the general level of reasonableness will become greater and greater, not only in art but in all other spheres too; in science and in politics and especially in philosophy (nobody knows Kant any longer, they know Nietzsche), and will end in a general collapse, the fall of the civilization in which we live, a fall of the same kind as that of the Egyptian, Babylonian, Greek and Roman civilizations.

Psychiatrists know that when a man begins to talk a lot, to talk non-stop about everything on earth without thinking, and only rushing to say as many words as possible in the shortest time – they know that this is a bad and sure sign of incipient or already advanced mental illness. But when in addition to this the patient is fully convinced that he knows everything better than anyone else and that he can and must teach everyone his wisdom, the signs of mental illness are indisputable. Our so-called civilized world is in this dangerous and sorry position – and I think it is already close to the destruction to which earlier civilizations were subjected. The distortion of ideas of the people of our time, expressed not only in the overrating of Shakespeare but in their whole attitude to politics and science and philosophy and art, is the principal and most significant indication of this.

Lev Tolstoy

557. TO BERNARD SHAW

[George Bernard Shaw (1856–1950) had sent his play Man and Superman *(including an appendix,* The Revolutionist's Handbook and Pocket Companion by John Tanner, M.I.R.C. (Member of the Idle Rich Class)*) to Tolstoy in December 1906. Tolstoy's first reading of it in January 1907 made a bad impression on him, but on re-reading it in August 1908 and making notes, Tolstoy decided to write the following letter to Shaw with a criticism of his play.*

In September 1909 Tolstoy remarked to Aylmer Maude during Maude's last visit to Yasnaya Polyana that he had been reading Shaw's plays and liked them, but thought Shaw suffered from the defect of wanting to be original. Maude told him the plot of* The Shewing-up of Blanco Posnet *(as yet unpublished) and as Tolstoy was interested, Maude asked Shaw to send the play to Tolstoy. Later that year, Tolstoy reportedly said that there were very few good writers left 'except, perhaps, Shaw'. (See Letter 585 for Tolstoy's reaction to Shaw's only letter to him, accompanying* Blanco Posnet.*) There are several plays by Shaw in Tolstoy's private library at Yasnaya Polyana, with numerous marginal comments and markings.*

Shaw's comments on Tolstoy and his works include the following: on What is Art? *(letter to Henry Arthur Jones, May 1898) – 'It is beyond all comparison the best treatise on art that has been done by a literary man (I bar Wagner) in these times.' On Tolstoyism (letter to R. Ellis Roberts in February 1900) – 'Even if we embrace it, we cannot live for ever afterwards on one another's charity. We may simplify our lives and become vegetarians; but even the minimum of material life will involve the industrial problems of its production and distribution, and will defy Anarchism . . . Anarchism in industry, as far as it is practicable, produces exactly the civilization that we*

* His friend, translator and authorized biographer. Maude (1858–1938) met Tolstoy in 1888 and thereafter visited him often. They were in regular correspondence. [J. P.]

have today, and ... the first thing a Tolstoyan community would have to do would be to get rid of it.'

Shaw once included Tolstoy in a list of five men in 'the Grand School – the people who are building up the intellectual consciousness of the race' (the others being Nietzsche, Wagner, Schopenhauer and Ibsen).]

Yasnaya Polyana, 17 August 1908

Dear Mr Shaw,

Please excuse me for not having thanked you before this for the book you sent through Mr Maude.

Now on re-reading it and paying special attention to the passages you indicated, I particularly appreciate Don Juan's speeches in the Interlude* (although I think that the subject would have gained greatly from a more serious approach to it, rather than its being a casual insertion in a comedy) and *The Revolutionist's Handbook*.†

In the first I could without any effort agree fully with Don Juan's words that a hero is 'he who seeks in contemplation to discover the inner will of the world ... [and] in action to do that will by the so-discovered means'‡ – the very thing which is expressed in my language by the words: 'to recognize the will of God in oneself and to fulfil it'.

In the second I particularly liked your attitude to civilization and progress, and the very true thought that however long both may continue, they cannot improve the state of mankind unless people themselves change.

The difference in our views only amounts to this that in your opinion the improvement of mankind will be accomplished when ordinary people become supermen or new supermen are born, while in my opinion it will come about when people divest true religions, including Christianity, of all the excrescences which deform them and when all people, uniting in that one understanding of life which lies at the base of all

* In English in the original.
† In English in the original.
‡ In English in the original.

religions, establish a reasonable attitude of their own towards the world's infinite first principle, and follow the guidance for life which stems from it.

The practical advantage which my way of freeing people from evil has over yours is that one can easily imagine that very large masses of even poorly educated or quite uneducated people will be able to accept true religion and follow it, whereas to evolve supermen from the people who now exist or to give birth to new ones would need the sort of exceptional conditions which are as little capable of being attained as the improvement of mankind through progress and civilization.

Dear Mr Shaw,* life is a great and serious matter, and all of us generally, in this short interval of time granted to us, must try to find our appointed task and fulfil it as well as possible. This applies to all people, and especially to you with your great talents, your original powers of thought and your penetration into the essence of any question.

And so in the confident hope of not offending you, I will tell you what seem to me to be the defects of your book.

Its first defect is that you are not sufficiently serious. One should not speak jokingly about such a subject as the purpose of human life or the causes of its perversion and of the evil that fills the life of all of us mankind. I would prefer the speeches of Don Juan to be not the speeches of an apparition, but the speeches of Shaw, and similarly that *The Revolutionist's Handbook* should be attributed not to the non-existent Tanner but to the living Bernard Shaw, responsible for his own words.

A second reproach is that the questions you deal with are of such enormous importance that, for people with such a deep understanding of the evils of our life and such a brilliant aptitude for exposition as yourself, to make them only the object of satire may often harm rather than help the solution of these important problems.

I see in your book a desire to surprise and astonish the reader by your great erudition, talent and intelligence. And yet all this is not only not necessary for the solution of the problems you

* In English in the original.

deal with, but very often distracts the reader's attention from the essence of the subject, attracting it by the brilliance of the exposition.

In any case I think that this book of yours expresses your views not in their full and clear development, but only in their embryonic state. I think that these views as they develop more and more will arrive at the one truth which we all seek and which we are all gradually approaching.

I hope you will forgive me if you find anything unpleasant in what I have said to you. I said what I did only because I recognize in you very great gifts, and have for you personally the most friendly feelings, with which I remain,

Lev Tolstoy

567. TO S. A. TOLSTAYA

[Sofya Andreyevna Tolstoy (née Behrs) (1844–1919) was Tolstoy's wife, and the daughter of a court physician. She married Tolstoy in 1862 when she was eighteen and he was thirty-four. She and Tolstoy had a long and fruitful marriage that ended in fighting and his abandonment of her shortly before his death in 1910. J. P.]

Yasnaya Polyana, 13 May 1909

[Draft letter. Not sent]

This letter will be given to you when I'm no longer here. I write to you from beyond the grave in order to tell you what I wanted to tell you so many times and for so many years for your own good, but was unable to tell you while I was alive. I know that if I had been better and kinder I would have been able to tell you during my lifetime in such a way that you would have listened to me, but I was unable to. Forgive me for this and forgive me for everything in which I was to blame throughout the whole time of our life together and especially the early time. I have nothing to forgive you for; you were what your mother made you; a kind and faithful wife and a good mother. But just because you were what your mother made you and stayed like that and didn't want to change, didn't want to work on yourself, to progress towards goodness and truth, but on the contrary clung with such obstinacy to all that was most evil and the opposite of all that was dear to me, you did a lot of evil to other people and sank lower and lower yourself and reached the pathetic condition you are now in.

585. TO BERNARD SHAW

[Original in English]

Yasnaya Polyana, 9 May 1910

My dear Mr Bernard Shaw,

I have received your play and your witty letter.* I have read your play with pleasure. I am in full sympathy with its subject.

Your remark that the preaching of righteousness has generally little influence on people and that young men regard as laudable that which is contrary to righteousness is quite correct. It does not however follow that such preaching is unnecessary. The reason of the failure is that those who preach do not fulfil what they preach, i.e. hypocrisy.

I also cannot agree with what you call your theology. You enter into controversy with that which no thinking person of our time believes or can believe: with a God-creator. And yet you seem to recognize a God who has got definite aims comprehensible to you. 'To my mind,' you write, 'unless we conceive God engaged in a continual struggle to surpass himself as striving at every birth to make a better man than before, we are conceiving nothing better than an omnipotent snob.'

* George Bernard Shaw had sent Tolstoy his play *The Shewing-up of Blanco Posnet*, together with a letter in which he quoted Blake's poem 'The Tyger', saying that God had created evil beings as well as good ones, and had made mistakes in creation. He ended by saying, 'Supposing the world were only one of God's jokes, would you work any the less to make it a good joke instead of a bad one?', to which Tolstoy took objection because of its flippancy. Tolstoy's letter was written in Russian, translated into English by Chertkov, and returned to Tolstoy to sign and forward. Chertkov's translation is retained here with very minor changes.

Concerning the rest of what you say about God and about evil, I will repeat the words I said, as you write, about your *Man and Superman*, namely that the problem about God and evil is too important to be spoken of in jest. And therefore I tell you frankly that I received a very painful impression from the concluding words of your letter: 'Suppose the world were only one of God's jokes, would you work any the less to make it a good joke instead of a bad one?'

Yours sincerely,
Leo Tolstoy

586. TO COUNTESS S. A. TOLSTAYA

Yasnaya Polyana, 14 July 1910

1. I shan't give my present diary to anyone; I'll keep it myself.
2. I'll take back the old diaries from Chertkov and will keep them myself, probably in a bank.*

If you are troubled by the thought that my diaries, or those passages in which I wrote, under the impression of the moment, about our disagreements and conflicts – that those passages might be used by future biographers ill-disposed towards you, then, not to mention the fact that such expressions of temporary feelings both in my diaries and in yours can in no way give a correct idea of our true relations, I am glad of the opportunity, if you are afraid of this, to express in my diary, or simply in this letter, my attitude towards you and my appreciation of your life.

* Sofya Andreyevna had given Tolstoy's diaries for 1847–1900 to the Rumyantsev Museum in Moscow, and the originals of the diaries for the past ten years were in a Moscow bank in the possession of A. B. Goldenweiser. However, Chertkov had copies of these diaries and Sofya Andreyevna wanted them safely out of his hands. After writing this letter Sasha [Tolstoy's beloved daughter, Alexandra Lvovna Tolstoy (1884–1979) J. P.] was sent to Chertkov to collect the copies and bring them back for her mother. They were then to be put in a Tula bank under the care of Mikhail Sukhotin. After getting her way, Sofya Andreyevna, who had been highly distraught, temporarily calmed down.

My attitude towards you and my appreciation of you are as follows: just as I loved you when you were young, so I have never ceased to love you and still love you despite the various causes of coolness between us. The causes of this coolness were (I don't mention the cessation of conjugal relations – such a cessation could only remove deceptive expressions of what is not true love) – the causes were, firstly, my greater and greater alienation from the interests of worldly life and my revulsion towards them, whereas you didn't wish to and weren't able to part with them, not having in your soul those principles that led me to my convictions, which was very natural and for which I don't reproach you. That's the first thing. Secondly (forgive me if what I shall say is disagreeable to you, but what is now happening between us is so important that we shouldn't be afraid to express and to hear the whole truth) – secondly, your character over these last years has become more and more irritable, despotic and uncontrollable. The manifestations of these traits of character couldn't help but cool, not my feeling itself, but the expression of it. That's the second thing. Thirdly, the chief cause was that fateful one for which neither you nor I are to blame – namely our completely contrary understanding of the meaning and purpose of life. Everything about our understanding of life was completely contrary: our way of life, our attitude to people and our means of livelihood – property – which I considered a sin and you – a necessary condition of life. In our way of life, so as not to part from you, I submitted to conditions of life which were painful for me, but you took this as a concession to your views, and the misunderstanding between us grew greater and greater. There were other causes of coolness as well, for which we were both to blame, but I won't mention them because they are not to the point. The point is that despite all our past misunderstandings, I have never ceased to love you and appreciate you.

My appreciation of your life with me is as follows: I, a dissolute and profoundly depraved man sexually, and no longer in the prime of youth, married you, a pure, good and intelligent girl of 18, and despite my filthy and depraved past, you have lived with me and loved me for nearly 50 years, living a difficult and laborious life, bearing children, nursing them, bringing them up, looking after them and after me, without yielding to the temptations which might so easily have overtaken any woman in your position, strong, healthy and beautiful. But you have lived in such a way that I have nothing to reproach you with. As for the fact that you didn't follow me in my exceptional spiritual journey, I cannot and do not reproach you, because the spiritual life of every man is a secret between that man and God, and other people shouldn't demand anything of him. And if I did demand anything of you, I was wrong and was to blame for it.

This is a true description of my attitude to you and my appreciation of you. As for what may turn up in the diaries, I only know that nothing harsh or contrary to what I write now will be found there.

So this is the third point, namely what may, but oughtn't to trouble you about the diaries.

Fourthly, if my relations with Chertkov at this time are painful for you, I'm prepared not to see him, although I must say that this would be not so much unpleasant for me as for him, knowing how painful it would be for him. But if you wish, I'll do so.

Now, fifthly, if you don't accept these conditions of mine for a good and peaceful life, I shall take back my promise not to leave you. I shall go away. I'll certainly not go to Chertkov. I shall even make it an absolute condition that he shouldn't come to live near me, but I'll certainly go away, because it's impossible to go on living as we are doing now.

I could continue to live like this if I could endure your sufferings calmly, but I can't. Yesterday you went away, agitated and suffering. I wanted to go to sleep, but I began not so much to think of you as to feel you, and I couldn't sleep, but listened till one o'clock, then two – and I woke up again and listened and then I saw you in a dream, or almost a dream. Try to think calmly, dearest, try to listen to your heart, try to feel, and you will decide everything in the right way. As for myself, I must say that I have decided everything for my part in such a way that *I cannot, cannot* decide otherwise. Stop torturing yourself, darling – not others, but yourself – because you are suffering a hundred times worse than anyone. That's all.

Lev Tolstoy

593. TO MOHANDAS GANDHI

[Mohandas Gandhi (1869–1948) was a major spiritual leader, who worked for Indian independence from Britain. He was a pioneer of the idea of civil disobedience. He had many things in common with Tolstoy, whom he admired, including a penchant for vegetarianism and a passionate belief in peace and non-violence as an appropriate response to violence. J. P.]

Kochety, 7 September 1910

I got your journal *Indian Opinion*, and was glad to learn all that was written there about those who practise non-resistance.* I also wanted to tell you the thoughts that reading it aroused in me.

The longer I live, and especially now when I feel keenly the nearness of death, I want to tell others what I feel so particularly keenly about, and what in my opinion is of enormous importance, namely what is called non-resistance, but what is essentially nothing other than the teaching of love undistorted by false interpretations. The fact that love, i.e. the striving of human souls towards unity and the activity resulting from such striving, is the highest and only law of human life is felt and known by every person in the depth of his soul (as we see most clearly of all with children) – known by him until he is ensnared by the false teachings of the world. This law has been proclaimed by all the world's sages, Indian, Chinese, Jewish, Greek and Roman. I think it has been expressed most clearly of all by Christ who even said frankly that on this alone hang all the

* This letter was published in Gandhi's Transvaal newspaper *Indian Opinion* on 26 November 1910 (English translation by Chertkov).

Law and the prophets. Furthermore, foreseeing the distortion to which this law is subject or may be subject, he pointed frankly to the danger of its distortion which comes naturally to people who live by worldly interests, namely the danger of allowing themselves to defend these interests by force, i.e. as he said, returning blow for blow, taking back by force objects which have been appropriated, etc., etc. He knows, as every reasonable person is bound to know, that the use of violence is incompatible with love as the basic law of life, that once violence is tolerated in any cases whatsoever, the inadequacy of the law of love is recognized and therefore the law itself is repudiated. The whole of Christian civilization, so brilliant on the surface, grew up on this obvious, strange, sometimes conscious but for the most part unconscious misunderstanding and contradiction.

Essentially speaking, once resistance was tolerated, side by side with love, there no longer was or could be love as a law of life, and there was no law of love except violence, i.e. the power of the stronger. For nineteen centuries Christian mankind has lived in this way. True, people at all times have been guided by violence alone in organizing their lives. The difference between the lives of Christian peoples and all others is merely the fact that in the Christian world, the law of love was expressed so clearly and definitely, as it hasn't been expressed in any other religious teaching, and that people in the Christian world solemnly accepted this law but at the same time allowed themselves to use violence and built their lives on violence. And so the whole life of Christian peoples is an outright contradiction between what they profess and what they build their lives on; a contradiction between love, recognized as the law of life, and violence recognized even as a necessity in various forms such as the power of rulers, courts and armies – recognized and extolled. This contradiction kept growing with the advancement of the peoples of the Christian world and has recently reached the ultimate degree. The question now obviously amounts to one of two things – either we recognize that we don't recognize any religious and moral teaching and are guided in the organization of our lives only by the power of the strong, or that all our taxes collected by force, our judicial and police institutions and above all our armies must be abolished.

This spring, at a scripture examination at one of the women's institutes in Moscow, the scripture teacher, and then a bishop who was present, asked the girls about the commandments and particularly the sixth one. When the correct answer was given about the commandment, the bishop usually asked a further question: is killing always and in all cases forbidden by the scriptures, and the unfortunate girls, corrupted by their mentors, had to answer and did answer – not always; that killing is permitted in war and in executing criminals. However, when one of these unfortunate girls (what I am telling you is not fiction but a fact, reported to me by an eyewitness), after giving her answer, was asked the usual question: is killing always sinful? She blushed nervously and gave the firm answer that it always was, and she answered all the bishop's usual sophisms with the firm conviction that killing was always forbidden, that killing was forbidden even in the Old Testament and that not only was killing forbidden by Christ but also any evil against one's brother. And despite all his grandeur and art of eloquence, the bishop fell silent and the girl went away victorious.

Yes, we may talk in our papers about the successes of aviation, about complicated diplomatic relations, about various clubs, discoveries, alliances of every kind, or so-called works of art, and still pass over in silence what this girl said; but we oughtn't to do so, because every person in the Christian world feels it – feels it more or less vaguely, but still feels it. Socialism, communism, anarchism, the Salvation Army, the growth of crime, unemployment among the population, the growth of the insane luxury of the rich and the destitution of the poor, the terrible growth in the number of suicides – all these things are signs of this internal contradiction which ought to and must be solved – and, of course, solved in the sense of recognizing the law of love and renouncing all violence. And so your work in the Transvaal, at the other end of the world as it seems to us, is the most central and most important of all tasks now being done in the world, and not only Christian peoples, but peoples of the whole world will inevitably take part in it. I think you will be pleased to know that this work is also rapidly developing in Russia in the form of refusals to do military service, of which there are more and more every year. However insignificant may be the number of your people who practise non-resistance and of our people in Russia who refuse military service, both can boldly say that God is with them. And God is more powerful than men.

In recognizing Christianity, even in the distorted form in which it is professed among Christian peoples, and in recognizing at the same time the necessity for armies and arms to kill in wars on the most enormous scale, there is such an obvious and crying contradiction that sooner or later, probably very soon, it will be exposed and will put an end either to the acceptance of the Christian religion which is necessary to maintain power, or to the existence of an army and any violence supported by it, which is no less necessary to maintain power. This contradiction is felt by all governments, your British as well as our Russian, and from a natural feeling of self-preservation is prosecuted more vigorously than any other anti-government activity, as we see in Russia and as is seen from the articles in your journals. Governments know where their main danger lies, and in this question are keeping a careful eye not only on their own interests, but on the question: to be or not to be.

With the utmost respect,
Leo Tolstoy*

* Signed in English in the original.

607. TO S. L. TOLSTOY and T. L. SUKHOTINA

[Sergey Lvovich Tolstoy (b. 1863) was one of Tolstoy's sons. T. L. Sukhotina (b. 1864) was a daughter, Tanya. J. P.]

Astapovo, 1 November 1910*

My dear children, Seryozha and Tanya,†

I hope and trust that you won't reproach me for not having asked you to come. To have asked you and not Mama would have caused her great distress, as well as your other brothers. You will both understand that Chertkov, whom I did ask to come, occupies a special position in relation to me. He has devoted his whole life to the service of the cause which I have also served for the last 40 years of my life. It's not so much that this cause is dear to me as that I recognize its importance – rightly or wrongly – for all people, including yourselves. I thank you for your kind relations towards me. I don't know whether I'm saying goodbye or not, but I felt the need to express what I have expressed. I also wanted to add some advice to you, Seryozha, that you should think about your own life, who you are, what you are, what is the meaning of a man's life and how every reasonable man should live it. The views you have acquired about Darwinism, evolution and the struggle for existence won't explain to you the meaning of your life and won't give you guidance in your actions, and a life without an explanation of its meaning and importance, and without the unfailing guidance that stems from it, is a pitiful existence.

* At approximately 8 a.m. on 31 October Tolstoy boarded a train in Kozelsk with the three people accompanying him, intending to go south to the Caucasus: they purchased tickets to Rostov-on-Don. However, towards evening, between 4 p.m. and 5 p.m., Tolstoy began to shiver, and proved to have a high temperature. They decided to leave the train at the next station, which was Astapovo, about 140 miles south-east of Tula. The station master offered them space in his home at the station and Tolstoy was installed there. The next day he sent this telegram to Chertkov and also asked Sasha to send for him. Chertkov arrived at Astapovo at 9 a.m. on 2 November with Sergeyenko.

† This last letter to Tolstoy's children was dictated to Sasha, as he was now too weak to write himself.

Think about it. I say it, probably on the eve of my death, because I love you.

Goodbye; try to calm your mother, for whom I have the most genuine feeling of compassion and love.

Your loving father,
L. Tolstoy

608. TO AYLMER MAUDE

[Original in English]

Astapovo, 3 November 1910

On my way to the place where I wished to be alone I was taken ill . . .*

[Translated by R. F. Christian]

* Tolstoy's last letter, dictated to Chertkov and written in English, but unfinished owing to Tolstoy's extreme fatigue. It is a reply to a letter he received from Maude before his departure from Yasnaya, asking about Tolstoy's health, promising to send his new biography of Tolstoy, and asking what to do with fifty pounds remaining from the Dukhobor fund.

Tolstoy lost consciousness at about 5 a.m. on 7 November and died an hour later.

FROM *TOLSTOY'S DIARIES* [1900–1910]

*Today is 27 October [1900], Kochety**

Thought:

(1) Life is continual creation, i.e. the formation of new, higher forms. When this formation comes to a stop in our view or even goes backwards, i.e. when existing forms are destroyed, this only means a new form is taking shape, invisible to us. We see what is outside us, but we don't see what is within us, we only feel it (if we haven't lost our consciousness, and don't take what is visible and external to be the whole of our life). A caterpillar sees itself shrivel up, but doesn't see the butterfly which flies out of it.

(2) Memory destroys time: it unites things that seem to have taken place separately.

(3) I've just been for a walk and thought: there is a religion, a philosophy, a science, a poetry, an art of the great majority of the people; a religion, although covered over with superstitions, a belief in God as the origin of things, in the indestructibility of life; an unconscious philosophy: of fatalism, of the material nature and the reasonableness of all that exists; a poetry of fairy tales, of true happenings in life, of legends; and an art of the beauty of animals, of the products of labour, of carved shutters and weather-vanes, of songs and dances. And there is a religion of true Christianity: philosophy from Socrates to Amiel; poetry: Tyutchev, Maupassant; art (I can't find any examples from painting) – Chopin in certain works, Haydn. And there is also a religion, a philosophy, a poetry, an art of

* Kochety was the country home of Tolstoy's daughter, Tanya. [J. P.]

the cultured masses: religion – the Evangelicals, the Salvation Army; philosophy – Hegel, Darwin, Spencer; poetry – Shakespeare, Dante, Ibsen; art – Raphael, the Decadents, Bach, Beethoven, Wagner. [. . .]

(10) Thought that if I'm to serve people by my writing, the one thing I'm entitled and obliged to do is to expose the lies of the rich, and reveal to the poor the delusion practised on them.

Today is 29 December [1900], Moscow Grief always has its spiritual reward and enormous profit. Grief calls – God has visited you and remembered you . . . Tanya gave birth to a stillborn baby, and is very good and sensible. Sonya is at Yasnaya. Ilya is here. He's astonishingly childish. [. . .]

Must note down the following:

(1) Read about some amazing machines which are a substitute for human toil and suffering. But it's just like inventing a complete apparatus, by means of which one can flog and kill without toil and effort. It's simpler not to flog and not to kill. It's the same with machines which make beer, wine, velvet, mirrors, etc. The whole complexity of our urban life lies in the fact that people think up and accustom themselves to harmful requirements, and then use all their mental energies to satisfy them or reduce the harm caused by satisfying them: all medicine, hygiene, artificial lighting, and all our harmful urban life. *Before speaking about the goodness of satisfying one's requirements, one ought to decide what requirements constitute goodness*. That's very important.

(2) Read Nietzsche's *Zarathustra*, and his sister's note about how he wrote it, and am absolutely convinced that he was completely mad when he wrote it, and mad not in a metaphorical sense, but in the straightforward and most exact sense: incoherence, jumping from one idea to another, comparisons with no indication of what is being compared, beginnings of ideas with no endings, leaping from one idea to another for contrast or consonance, and all against the background of the *pointe* of his madness, his *idée fixe*, that by denying all the higher principles of human life and thought he is proving his own superhuman genius. What will society be like if

such a madman, and an evil madman, is acknowledged as a teacher? [. . .]

(5) It's amusing, the opinion people have that non-resistance to evil by force or paying back good for evil are very good rules for individuals, but can't be applied to the state. As though the state isn't a combination of people, but something separate from people. Oxygen has such and such properties. But they are only the properties of the atoms and molecules of oxygen. But oxygen in big compounds acquires quite different, opposite properties. This opinion alone that states have properties which are the opposite of human ones is the most obvious proof of the obsolete nature of the state as a form of government.

(6) People talk about the equality of men and women. There is complete equality in an immaterial sense, but not in a sexual one. In a sexual (animal) sense, the difference is enormous: the male is always ready for any female, because sexual intercourse doesn't disturb his activity: deer, wolves, hares, drones. There are always a lot of males running after one female. But the female isn't always ready. But when she is ready, she gives herself up entirely, and is fit for nothing else when she is producing offspring. There are many conclusions to be drawn from this.

10 October [1901, Gaspra]

Noted during this time:

(1) It's difficult to live for God by oneself in the midst of people who don't even understand the idea, and live only for themselves. How glad one is in such a situation to have the help of people of the same belief. [. . .]

(10) One of the most common and serious mistakes people make in their judgements is that they consider to be good the things that they like. [. . .]

(13) Life is a serious business! Oh, if only one could always remember that, especially in moments of decision! [. . .]

(16) Entrepreneurs (capitalists) rob the people in that they are intermediaries between the workers and the suppliers of the instruments and means of labour, and merchants likewise rob the people in that they are intermediaries between consumers and vendors. Similarly state robbery is organized under the

pretext of mediation between wrongdoers and the wrongly done by. But the most terrible deceit of all is the deceit of the intermediaries between God and men.

13 December [1902, Yasnaya Polyana]

(1) Critics are wrong to think that the intelligentsia as a movement can guide the popular masses (Milyukov). It would be still more wrong for a writer to think that he can consciously guide the masses by his works. [. . .]

(2) If in answer to the question: 'Can you play the violin?' you reply: 'I don't know, I haven't tried yet', we would understand at once that it was a joke. But when in answer to the question: 'Can you write books?' we reply: 'Perhaps I can, I haven't tried', we not only do not take this for a joke, but we continually see people acting on the basis of such reasoning. This only goes to prove that anyone can pass judgement on the ugliness of meaningless sounds made by an untrained violinist (absurd people will be found who will find even such music beautiful), but that refined sensibility and intellectual maturity are needed to distinguish between a collection of words and phrases and a true literary work of art.

(3) The whole first half of the nineteenth century is full of attempts to destroy despotic state regimes by revolutionary violence. All attempts ended in reaction, and the power of the ruling classes only increased. Obviously revolution cannot now overcome the power of the state. There is only one thing left: a change of outlook on life by the people, whereby they would cease to minister to the violent acts of governments. Only religion, and actually the Christian religion, can produce such a change. But this religion is so perverted that it might as well not exist. And what is worst of all is that its place is occupied. And so not just the main, but the sole means in our time of serving mankind is by destroying perverted Christianity and establishing the true Christian religion. That is the very thing that everyone considers most insignificant; and not only does nobody do it, but the smartest, quasi-intellectual people are busy doing just the opposite: making perverted Christianity even more confused and obscure.

January 1903 [Yasnaya Polyana]
At present I suffer the torments of hell itself. I remember vividly the horrors, the sins, of my earlier life, and these recollections do not just fade; they circulate as poison in my blood. I hear that people often feel sorry about the fact that, after death, all sense of individual consciousness dies as well. I'm delighted that it does not! It would anguish me if I could recall after death all the evil I'd done in my earlier life, all that remains painful to my conscience. What a good thing that death obliterates these recollections, that what survives is consciousness alone.

[Translation by Jay Parini]

24 November [1903, Yasnaya Polyana]
Normally people (myself included) who recognize the spiritual life as the basis of life deny the reality, the necessity, the importance of studying the physical life, which evidently cannot lead to any conclusive results. In just the same way, those who only recognize the physical life completely deny the spiritual life and all deductions based on it – deny, as they say, metaphysics. But it is now absolutely clear to me that both are wrong, and both forms of knowledge – the materialistic and the metaphysical – have their own great importance, if only one doesn't wish to make inappropriate deductions from the one or the other. From materialistic knowledge based on the observation of external phenomena one can deduce scientific data, i.e. generalizations about phenomena, but one should not deduce any guiding principles for people's lives, as the materialists – Darwinists for example – have often tried to do. From metaphysical knowledge based on inner consciousness one can and should deduce the laws of human life – how should we live? why are we living? – the very thing that all religious teachings do; but one should not deduce, as many people have tried to do, the laws of phenomena and generalizations about them.

Each of these two kinds of knowledge has its own purpose and its own field of activity.

7 May [1904], Yasnaya Polyana The day before yesterday I met a beggar in the street, in rags. I got talking to him: he was an ex-pupil of the Pedagogical Institute. A Nietzschean *sans le savoir* [without knowing it]. And what a convinced one. 'Service to God and one's neighbours, the suppression of one's passions is narrow-mindedness, the violation of the laws of nature. One must follow one's passions, they give us strength and greatness.' It's astonishing how Nietzsche's teaching, egoism, is a necessary consequence of the whole aggregate of quasi-scientific, artistic and, above all, quasi-philosophical and popularizing activity. We are not surprised and we don't doubt that, if seeds fall on well-cultivated land and if moreover there is warmth and moisture and nothing tramples down the crops, certain plants will grow. Likewise it is possible to determine accurately what the spiritual consequences of certain intellectual, artistic and scientific influences will be.

20 January [1905], Yasnaya Polyana Haven't written my diary for a long time. [. . .]

(2) Music is the stenography of the feelings. What I mean is: the quick or slow succession of sounds, their pitch, their volume – all this, in speech, embellishes words and their meaning, indicating those shades of feelings which are associated with our parts of speech. Music without speech takes these expressions of feelings and shades of feelings and combines them, and we get a play of feelings without the things that gave rise to them. For this reason music has such a particularly strong effect, and for this reason the combination of music with words is an adulteration of the music, a retrogression, a writing out in letters of stenographic signs.

18 January [1906], Yasnaya Polyana Still unwell. I'm working a little on the *Cycle of Reading*.

Thought today about what I, an old man, should do. I haven't much strength, and it's getting noticeably weaker. Several times in my life I've considered myself close to death. And – how foolishly! – I would forget, or try to forget it – forget what? That I would die, and that in any case – whether in five, ten, twenty or thirty years – death is still very close. And now, because of my years, I naturally consider myself close to death, and there's no point in trying to forget it, and I can't forget it. But what should I, an old feeble person do? I asked myself. And it seemed that there was nothing to do, that I had no strength for anything. But today I realized so clearly the clear and joyful answer. What should I do? It's already been revealed – I must die. This is my task now, as it always has been. And I must perform this task as well as possible: die, and die well. The task is before you, a noble and inevitable task, and you are searching for one. This made me very glad. I'm beginning to get used to regarding death and dying not as the end of my task, but as the task itself.

2 April [1906], Yasnaya Polyana Easter. All the time recently (two weeks) I've felt poorly. I've hardly written anything. Weakness and physical depression. But it's a strange thing. In those rare moments of clarity of thought which came to me, my thoughts worked more clearly and profoundly than in periods of constant mental activity. It's bound to occur to one that the revelation of life goes on all the time at a steady pace. If it seems to me that life is standing still within me, it isn't standing still but going on underground, and later on reveals itself all the more forcibly the longer it has been held in check. Whether this is true will be seen from what I've noted down and am now entering in my diary for these two weeks. Note:

(1) It has become absolutely clear recently that an agricultural way of life is not merely one of various ways of life, just as a book – the Bible – is not one of various books, but *is* life, life itself, the only human life which alone makes possible the manifestation of all the highest human qualities. The chief mistake in the organization of human societies and one which eliminates the possibility of any reasonable organization of life is that people want to organize society without agricultural life, or with the sort of organization in which agricultural life is only one form, and the most insignificant form, of life.

16 April [1906], Yasnaya Polyana Five days have passed and I'm in quite a different mood today. I can't overcome my dissatisfaction with those close to me. I feel melancholy and want to cry. Everything seems depressing. Just now after dinner and a lesson with the children – only two came – I sat alone and thought that only now was I fully and completely entrusting myself to the will of God. Come what may. There was no point in wanting to perform any task – writing a scripture for children or whatever it may be; I had to surrender myself entirely to Him, retaining only my love for Him, privately and publicly . . . and suddenly Sonya came in and we started talking about the wood, about people stealing, and about the children selling things at half price, and I couldn't suppress my anger. As if it wasn't all the same to me. Lord, help me. Help me. I'm sorry for myself and feel disgusted with myself.

31 January [1908], Yasnaya Polyana I've been reading Shaw. His triviality amazes me. Not only does he not have a single thought of his own rising above the triviality of the urban masses, but he doesn't understand a single great thought of the thinkers of the past. The only special thing about him is that he can express the most banal trivialities in a very elegantly distorted, new manner, as though he were saying something new and original. His main characteristic is his terrifying self-assurance, only equalled by his complete philosophical ignorance.

10 March [1908], Yasnaya Polyana This is how I live: I get up, my head is clear, good thoughts occur to me as I sit on the pot and I note them down. I get dressed and I empty the contents of the pot with an effort but with pleasure. I go for a walk. On my walk I wait for the post from force of habit, although I don't need it. I often guess to myself how many steps it will take to get to such and such a place, and I count them, dividing each one into four, six and eight breaths: one and *a* and *a* and *a*; and two and *a* and *a* and *a* . . . Sometimes, from force of habit, I'm disposed to guess that if there are as many steps as I suppose, all will be well. But now I ask myself: what is 'well'? and I know that everything is very well as it is, and there's no need to try and guess. Then when I meet someone I try to remember – though for the most part I forget that I wanted to remember – that he and I are one. It's particularly difficult to remember during a conversation. Then my dog Belka barks and prevents me from thinking, and I get angry and reproach myself for getting angry. I reproach myself for getting angry with a stick I stumble over. Yes, I forget to say that as I wash and dress I remember the poverty of the village and feel bad about the luxury of my clothes, but cleanliness is a habit. When I get back from my walk I start on the letters. Begging letters irritate me. I remember that they are all my brothers and sisters, but always too late. Praise is irksome. I am only glad when there are expressions of unity. I read the newspaper *Rus*. I'm horrified at the executions, and to my shame, my eyes look out for T. and L. N., but when I find them it's rather unpleasant.* I drink coffee. Always too much – I can't restrain myself – and settle down to my letters.

17 August [1908], Yasnaya Polyana (For a work of fiction.)

(1) The child of a wealthy, atheistic, liberal-scientific bourgeois family devotes himself to religion. Fifteen years later he is a revolutionary and an anarchist.

(2) The gentle, sincere son of a priest does well at school and theological college, and is married and ordained. The daughter of a neighbour in his parish gives his mother, a vain intellectual woman, a book to read. He reads Tolstoy and questions begin to arise.

(3) A young boy, the sixth son of a blind beggar, arouses the sympathy of the wife of a leading liberal atheist. He is taken from home and sent to school, shows brilliant ability and gets a science degree. He goes abroad, meets some of his comrades, is shocked, thinks everything out again, renounces science and sees the one truth and salvation in belief in God.

(4) One of his comrades had started up in business and made a million, and now lives on the labours of his workers, while playing the liberal.

* 'T. and L. N.' refers to Tolstoy himself, as Tolstoy or Leo Nikoleyvich. [J. P.]

(5) The son of an aristocratic family introduces clients to a procuress; then philanthropy; then the renunciation of everything.

(6) One son of a ruined half-aristocrat, a vain man, makes a career through marriage; another son, a reserved man, makes a career as a hangman. The second used to pander to the first, now he gives himself airs.

(7) A similar sort of aristocratic writer, the son of a bourgeois, lives by journalism, feels the vileness of it and can't go on.

9 July [1908, Yasnaya Polyana] I'm thinking of writing her a letter. I've no unkind feelings, thank God. Only one thing is more and more agonizing to me: the injustice of this insane luxury amid the unwarranted poverty and need amid which I live. Everything is becoming worse and worse, more and more depressing. I can't forget it and I can't fail to see it.

They're all writing my biography – and it's the same with all biographies – there won't be anything about my attitude to the seventh commandment. There won't be any of that terrible filth of masturbation and worse, from thirteen or fourteen to fifteen or sixteen (I don't remember when my debauchery in brothels began). And it will be the same up to the time of my liaison with the peasant woman Aksinya – she's still alive. Then my marriage in which again, although I have never once been unfaithful to my wife, I experienced a loathsome, criminal desire for her. Nothing of this appears or will appear in the biographies. And this is very important – very important as the vice of which I at least am most conscious, and which more than any others is forcing me to come to my senses.

10 January [1909], Yasnaya Polyana Yesterday I almost wrote with enthusiasm, but badly. It's not worth making the effort. I've no enthusiasm at all today, and yesterday's writing seems weak, or simply bad. The day before yesterday I had a conversation with Andrey, a very edifying one for me. It began with the fact that the brothers, all of them, are short of money.

I: How is that?

He: Well everything has got more expensive, and we live in a particular milieu.

I: You should live better, more abstemiously.
He: May I object?
I: Go on.
He: You say that people should live as follows: not eat meat, refuse military service. But what is one to think about the millions who live like everybody else?
I: Don't think about them at all, think about yourself.

And it became clear to me that there is no other guiding principle for him in life except what *everybody else* does. It became clear that that is all that matters, that with minute exceptions everybody lives like that, and can't help living like that, because they have no other guiding principle. And therefore to reproach them and advise them differently is useless and harmful to oneself, since it causes ill feelings. For thousands of years mankind has progressed by the century, and you want to see this progress by the year. It progresses because people of advanced views change the environment little by little, pointing the way to an eternally remote state of perfection, pointing the way there (Christ, Buddha, yes, and Kant and Emerson and others), and little by little the environment changes. And these people do like everybody else again, only in a different way than before.

Intellectuals are people who do the same as 'everybody else' – as other intellectuals.

I've done nothing today and have no wish to. I'm writing this in the evening, at 6 o'clock. I woke up, and two things became especially and absolutely clear to me: (1) that I am a very worthless man. I say this absolutely sincerely, and (2) that it would be good for me to die, and that I would like to do so.

I'm very bad-tempered today. Perhaps I go on living in order to become just a little less vile. Very likely that is the reason. And I will try. Help me, Lord.

20 April [1909, Yasnaya Polyana] I've just been out on to the balcony and was besieged by petitioners, and I couldn't sustain my good feelings towards everyone. Some astonishing words yesterday from Sergey: 'I feel and know,' he said, 'that I now have such powers of reasoning that I can discuss and resolve everything correctly . . . It would be good if I could apply these powers of reasoning to my own life,' he added, with astonishing naiveté. The whole family – but especially the men – have a self-assurance that knows no limits. But I think it is greater in him than in all the others. Hence his incorrigible narrow-mindedness.

20 June [1909, Yasnaya Polyana] [. . .] Yes, yesterday I read Engels on Marx . . . Today I woke up from a dream about a clear, simple refutation of materialism comprehensible to all. When I was awake it wasn't so clear as when I was asleep, but something remained – namely that materialists must grant the absurdity of a creator in order to explain how matter took shape in such a way that out of it were formed individual creatures, first of all 'I', and with such properties as feelings and reason.

But for the non-materialist it is clear that everything that I call the material world is the product of my own spiritual 'I'. The chief mystery for him is my own and other creatures' separate identity.

21 July [1909, Yasnaya Polyana] In the evening Sofya Andreyevna was weak and irritable. I couldn't get to sleep till 2 or later. I woke up feeling weak. Somebody had woken me up. Sofya Andreyevna hadn't slept all night. I went to see her. It was something quite mad. Dusan had poisoned her, etc. A letter from Stakhovich which I ought to have told her about because the thought I was hiding something from her made her condition still worse. I'm tired and I can't do any more and I feel quite ill. I feel the impossibility, the absolute impossibility of a reasonable and loving relationship. At present I only want to withdraw and take no part in anything. I can't do anything else, and I've already thought seriously of running away as it is. Well then, show your Christianity. *C'est le moment ou jamais* [It's now or never]. But I terribly want to go away. My presence here is hardly of use to anybody. A sorry victim, and harmful to everyone. Help me, my God, teach me. The only thing I want is to do not my will, but Thine. I write this and ask myself – is it true? Am I not putting on an act for myself? Help, help, help.

22 July [1909, Yasnaya Polyana] Yesterday I didn't eat or sleep at all, as usual. Was very depressed. I'm still depressed, but feel good at heart. Yes, love them that do us evil, you say. Well, try it. I do try, but badly. I'm thinking more and more about going away and disposing of my property.

23 July [1909, Yasnaya Polyana] Decided to give up the land. Talked yesterday to Ivan Vasilevich. How difficult to be rid of this nasty, sinful property. Help, help, help.

9, 10 November [1909, Yasnaya Polyana] In the evening I read Gorky. A knowledge of the lowest strata of the people, and wonderful language, i.e. the idiom of the people. But a completely arbitrary and quite unjustified psychology – i.e. the attribution of feelings and thoughts to his characters – which gets more and more heroic, and then an exclusively immoral milieu. And on top of that a slavish respect for science.

16 January [1910, Yasnaya Polyana] Woke up in good spirits and decided to go to the court in Tula. Read my letters and answered a few. Then set off. First came the trial of some peasants: lawyers, judges, soldiers, witnesses. All very new to me. Then came the trial of a political prisoner. The charge was that he had read and, at cost to himself, disseminated ideas for a more just and sane organization of life than the one which now exists. Felt very sorry for him. People gathered to look at me, but not many, thank goodness. The oath upset me. I could hardly refrain from saying it was a mockery of Christ.

3 April [1910, Yasnaya Polyana] [. . .] This morning I meant to write about my funeral and what should be read at it. I'm sorry I didn't write anything down. I feel death approaching nearer and nearer. There's no doubt that my life, and probably that of all people, becomes more spiritual with the years. The same happens to the life of mankind as a whole. In this lies the essence and meaning of all and every life, and so the meaning of my life lies only in this spiritualization of it. If you are aware of this and act accordingly, you know you are doing the task assigned to you: you become more spiritual yourself, and by your life contribute at least to some extent to the general spiritualization – to becoming better.

1 May [1910, Yasnaya Polyana] Alive. Note:
(1) One of the main causes of suicides in the European world is the false teaching of the Christian Church about heaven and hell. People don't believe in heaven and hell, but all the same the idea that life should be either heaven or hell is so firmly fixed in their heads that it doesn't permit of a rational understanding of life as it is – namely neither heaven nor hell, but struggle, unceasing struggle, unceasing because life consists only of struggle; only not a Darwinian struggle of creatures and individuals against other creatures and individuals, but a struggle of spiritual forces against their bodily restrictions. Life is the struggle of the soul against the body. If life is understood in this way, suicide is impossible, unnecessary and senseless. The good is only to be found in life. I seek the good; how then can I leave this life in order to attain the good? I seek mushrooms. Mushrooms are only to be found in the forest. How then can I leave the forest in order to find mushrooms?

29 September [1910], Yasnaya Polyana
What terrible mental poison modern literature is, especially for young folk from the people. First of all they stuff their minds with the obscure, self-assured, empty chatter of writers who are writing for the modern reader. The chief peculiarity and harmfulness of such chatter is that it all consists of allusions to, and quotations from the most various of writers, the most modern as well as the most ancient. Phrases are quoted from Plato, Hegel and Darwin, about whom the writers themselves haven't the least conception, and alongside them are phrases from people like Gorky, Andreyev, Artsybashev and others, about whom it isn't worth while having any conception. Secondly, this chatter is harmful because, by filling their heads in this way, it leaves no room or leisure for them to get to know the old writers who have stood the test of time not only for decades, but for hundreds and thousands of years.

29 October [1910] Optina Monastery Everything is the same; worse even. If only I don't sin. And don't bear malice. I don't at present.

[Translated by R. F. Christian]

PENGUIN CLASSICS

A DEAD MAN'S MEMOIR (A THEATRICAL NOVEL)
MIKHAIL BULGAKOV

'I confess quite frankly that what I produced was some kind of gibberish'

Sergei Maksudov has failed as a novelist and made a farce of a suicide attempt, but only after a surprise break as a playwright on the Moscow stage does his turmoil truly begin. Thrown uncomprehending into theatre life, he soon sees his beloved play dragged into chaos by inflated egos, jealous critics, literary double-dealers, communist censors and insanely bad acting. Full of affectionately drawn characters, *A Dead Man's Memoir* is a brilliant, absurdist tale of the exhilaration and black desperation wrought on one man by his turbulent love affair with the theatre. Based on his own experiences at the famous Moscow Art Theatre of the 1920s and 30s, it reaches its comic height in a merciless lampooning of Stanislavsky's fashionable stage techniques.

Andrew Bromfield's powerful new translation is accompanied by an introduction by Keith Gessen, which discusses the autobiographical basis of these fictionalized memoirs and Bulgakov's artistic integrity in the face of Soviet repression. This edition also contains notes and a chronology.

Translated with notes by Andrew Bromfield

With a new introduction by Keith Gessen

THE COSSACKS AND OTHER STORIES
LEO TOLSTOY

'You will see war ... in its authentic expression – as blood, suffering and death'

In 1851, at the age of twenty-two, Tolstoy travelled to the Caucasus and joined the army there as a cadet. The four years that followed were among the most significant in his life, and deeply influenced the stories collected here. Begun in 1852 but unfinished for a decade, 'The Cossacks' describes the experiences of Olenin, a young cultured Russian who comes to despise civilization after spending time with the wild Cossack people. 'Sevastopol Sketches', based on Tolstoy's own experiences of the siege of Sevastopol in 1854–55, is a compelling description and consideration of the nature of war. In 'Hadji Murat', written towards the end of his life, Tolstoy returns to the Caucasus of his youth and portrays the life of a great leader, torn apart and destroyed by a conflict of loyalties: it is amongst the greatest of his shorter works.

The translations in this volume convey the beauty and power of the original pieces, while the introduction reflects on Tolstoy's own wartime experiences. This edition also includes notes and maps.

Translated with notes by David McDuff and Paul Foote
With an introduction by Paul Foote

PENGUIN CLASSICS

WAR AND PEACE
LEO TOLSTOY

'Yes! It's all vanity, it's all an illusion, everything except that infinite sky'

At a glittering society party in St Petersburg in 1805, conversations are dominated by the prospect of war. Terror swiftly engulfs the country as Napoleon's army marches on Russia, and the lives of three young people are changed forever. The stories of quixotic Pierre, cynical Andrey and impetuous Natasha interweave with a huge cast, from aristocrats and peasants, to soldiers and Napoleon himself. In *War and Peace* (1863–9), Tolstoy entwines grand themes – conflict and love, birth and death, free will and fate – with unforgettable scenes of nineteenth-century Russia, to create a magnificent epic of human life in all its imperfection and grandeur.

Anthony Briggs's superb translation combines stirring, accessible prose with fidelity to Tolstoy's original, while Orlando Figes's afterword discusses the novel's vast scope and depiction of Russian identity. This edition also includes appendices, notes, a list of prominent characters and maps.

'A book that you don't just read, you live' Simon Schama

'A masterpiece … This new translation is excellent' Antony Beevor

Translated with an introduction and notes by Anthony Briggs
With an afterword by Orlando Figes

THE LADY WITH THE LITTLE DOG AND OTHER STORIES, 1896–1904
ANTON CHEKHOV

'We must remember that nothing in this world is accidental, everything has its final purpose'

In the final years of his life, Chekhov had reached the height of his powers as a dramatist, and also produced some of the stories that rank among his masterpieces. The poignant 'The Lady with the Little Dog' and 'About Love' examine the nature of love outside of marriage – its romantic idealism and the fear of disillusionment. And in stories such as 'Peasants', 'The House with the Mezzanine' and 'My Life' Chekhov paints a vivid picture of the conditions of the poor and of their powerlessness in the face of exploitation and hardship. With the works collected here, Chekhov moved away from the realism of his earlier tales – developing a broader range of characters and subject matter, while forging the spare minimalist style that would inspire such modern short-story writers as Hemingway and Faulkner.

This is the third of three volumes of Chekhov's short stories in Penguin Classics. This edition also includes a publishing history and notes for each story, a chronology and further reading.

Translated with notes by Ronald Wilks

With an introduction by Paul Debreczeny

THE STORY OF PENGUIN CLASSICS

Before 1946 … 'Classics' are mainly the domain of academics and students; readable editions for everyone else are almost unheard of. This all changes when a little-known classicist, E. V. Rieu, presents Penguin founder Allen Lane with the translation of Homer's *Odyssey* that he has been working on in his spare time.

1946 Penguin Classics debuts with *The Odyssey*, which promptly sells three million copies. Suddenly, classics are no longer for the privileged few.

1950s Rieu, now series editor, turns to professional writers for the best modern, readable translations, including Dorothy L. Sayers's *Inferno* and Robert Graves's unexpurgated *Twelve Caesars*.

1960s The Classics are given the distinctive black covers that have remained a constant throughout the life of the series. Rieu retires in 1964, hailing the Penguin Classics list as 'the greatest educative force of the twentieth century.'

1970s A new generation of translators swells the Penguin Classics ranks, introducing readers of English to classics of world literature from more than twenty languages. The list grows to encompass more history, philosophy, science, religion and politics.

1980s The Penguin American Library launches with titles such as *Uncle Tom's Cabin*, and joins forces with Penguin Classics to provide the most comprehensive library of world literature available from any paperback publisher.

1990s The launch of Penguin Audiobooks brings the classics to a listening audience for the first time, and in 1999 the worldwide launch of the Penguin Classics website extends their reach to the global online community.

The 21st Century Penguin Classics are completely redesigned for the first time in nearly twenty years. This world-famous series now consists of more than 1300 titles, making the widest range of the best books ever written available to millions – and constantly redefining what makes a 'classic'.

The Odyssey continues …